UNCONTAINED

UNCONTAINED

DIGITAL DISCONNECTION
AND THE EXPERIENCE OF TIME

Robert Hassan

 **Grattan Street Press**

Published by Grattan Street Press, 2019

Grattan Street Press is the imprint of the teaching press based in the School of Culture and Communication at the University of Melbourne, Parkville, Australia.

Cover image copyright © Cameron Venti, 2019

Grattan Street Press
School of Culture and Communication
John Medley Building,
Parkville, VIC 3010
www.grattanstreetpress.com

Printed in Australia

ISBN 9780 6482 09614

A catalogue record for this book is available from the National Library of Australia.

For JD, MH and CC

Intellectual effort, when conducted without books or notes, gives an entirely different sensation than when carried out under normal conditions. One's involuntary memory acts much more forcefully, the memory of which Proust speaks and which he considered to be the sole source of literary creation. After a certain amount of time, things surface in our consciousness, details we hadn't the slightest idea were even 'stored' anywhere in our brain. What is more, those memories that come from our subconscious are more deeply rooted, more intimately bound up one with another, more personal.

Józef Czapski, *Memories of Starobielsk*

CONTENTS

Prologue   1

Chapter 1: Zero-Sum Time   13

Chapter 2: Digital Life   47

Chapter 3: Anticipate   67

Chapter 4: Waiting   89

Chapter 5: To See   128

Chapter 6: Dissolves in Water   158

Chapter 7: Things Around You   184

Chapter 8: Time For Work   206

Chapter 9: The *Züing* of the Mouldmaster®   237

Reading Notes   271

About the Author   280

Author Acknowledgements   281

Grattan Street Press Personnel   282

Grattan Street Press Acknowledgements   283

About Grattan Street Press   284

Index   285

PROLOGUE

A YEAR OR SO ago, my teenage daughter Camille had a mild obsession with the 2007 film *Into the Wild*. Based upon Jon Krakauer's 1996 book of the same name, it recounts the real-life story of Christopher McCandless, a young American who dropped out of university, abandoned a life of middle-class comfort, gave away what money he had to Oxfam, changed his name to Alexander Supertramp, and began to hitchhike, walk and kayak his way across North America. For two years he lived how he could, relying in no small part on the generosity of strangers for food and shelter and, occasionally, work. Something had changed in McCandless's mind. Stresses at home, his family's expectation for him to be successful, and the pressure to strive for material wealth had become too much for him. It was a transformation that was related to a deep yearning for what had been the opposite of his reality up until that point – a connection to nature. In trips he made alone in his battered yellow Datsun, McCandless travelled into the southern California desert outside his hometown of El Segundo and there he discovered nature's authentic beauty and its magnificent austerity. He believed that, when uncontaminated by technology, the wilderness was his home, and where he had found his true self.

Camille talked about the film so much that I decided that I had to watch it with her if our conversations on this ongoing subject were not to be all one way. We watched it one Saturday night on Netflix, doing what we try to do, though not always successfully, which is to watch television – even if only for an hour – as a family, instead of all heading off after dinner to our separate rooms, succumbing to the lure of the laptop or the phone and its virtual world of apps. Kate, my wife, watched half-distractedly and was in and out of the room every twenty minutes to ask for plot updates. Theo, my son, was going out to a twenty-first birthday party, and only came in to watch whilst polishing his shoes or recharging his phone. 'I've already seen it,' he said, which was his stock phrase for almost anything we watch.

But I could see what Camille meant when she had waxed about the essential otherworldliness of the film; it seemed to depict not only another time (yet it was only the 1990s) but also another world. Both seemed alien, disconnected, far away. I'd become a little obsessed, too.

Things ended badly for McCandless. In his travels through the warmer latitudes of the United States, where he hangs out with hippies, or strikes up a touching relationship with a retired soldier, McCandless tells anybody who will listen of his ultimate desire to go to what he imagines to be the pristine wilderness of northern Alaska, and to live off the land there. He finally arrives in Alaska but is completely unprepared for survival, without warm clothes or boots that can keep out frostbite. By chance, he finds an abandoned bus in a totally remote area, and decides to make it his home. It has a wood burning stove inside and so he can make it warm, and he begins to settle and make do with his meagre supplies. McCandless is happy for a while in his isolation. He reads and writes and thinks and connects with his beautiful surroundings, far from the polluting aviation industries of El Segundo, far from the university he could not stand, and far from the materialist culture that he'd now completely rejected. But things begin to get tough as his food stocks dwindle.

Eventually, McCandless becomes desperate and tries to return to 'civilisation'. But he finds that the stream he had crossed some months earlier is now a wide and torrential river with currents that are too strong to navigate. He has no choice but to go back to the bus, or be lost in the yawning space of forest and tundra. Almost starving, he eats any roots or berries he can find nearby. Soon, he realises he has eaten something poisonous and, when checking this particular plant in a botany book, he is convinced he is going to die. He was right. One of his last diary entries reads: 'Extremely weak. Fault of pot[ato] seed. Much trouble just to stand up. Starving. Great jeopardy.'

I went to bed that night with thoughts of McCandless and his possible mental states eddying around in my head. Was his death a cautionary tale about how we are no longer creatures of the wild? Cities and technology are now our natural habitat, aren't they? The lesson surely is that, for the untrained and average city-dweller, going into the wild is going into big trouble? Who in their right mind would trade a warm bed, good food and people for an abandoned bus in the frozen wilderness? But again, why the fascination for the story? And why the nagging feeling that, even in the disastrous and pointless death that befell McCandless, he did something heroic? I was beginning to think that he had revived something in himself, something that is ancient and latent in all of us. He lived for a time in another way, closer to nature, closer to who we really are but are denied due to the social and technological systems we have created.

I woke up the next day still thinking about it. And so, over breakfast, I did what we increasingly do to resolve a thought or question or issue: I Googled it. McCandless, the book and the movie were all over the web. Thousands, if not millions, of people, I discovered, obsess over every aspect of his misadventure and discuss whether or not it acts as a parable for modern life. Across the internet, entire websites, blogs, YouTube videos, high school essays, student cheat-sheets, Prezis, and a substantial Wikipedia entry debate and relate McCandless's wanderings in Alaska. There's even a Goodreads page where meaningful quotes from Krakauer's book are picked out by readers and 'liked' and commented on by thousands more. Part of the first quote on the website gives the flavour of what its many readers select:

> The joy of life comes from our encounters with new experiences, and hence there is no greater joy than to have an endlessly changing horizon, for each day to have a new and different sun. If you want to get more out of life, you must lose your inclination for monotonous security and adopt a helter-skelter style of life that will at first appear to you to be crazy. But once you become accustomed to such a life you will see its full meaning and its incredible beauty.

Krakauer here is channelling McCandless. But I think that they both are channelling something buried in many of us. I've become more and more convinced of this in recent years, especially in respect of our digital life, the aspect of life that's increasingly taking over our hours and days.

I teach media and communications, and so the internet, mobile phones, email and apps for multiple functions are an indispensable part of my life. It's the same for many other people in many other walks of life. But like them, I find that our use of digital technology can, and often does, become too much. Too much information, too many devices, too many times when we are compelled to use them for work, education, or just to stay in touch with family and friends. Serious information overload has happened quickly, so quickly, in fact, that the process has blindsided policy-makers and users alike. For example, it was only in 2006 that Facebook became something no longer confined to students at Harvard. But just a decade later, and with the data of 2.3 billion users on its secret servers, Facebook would be blamed for just about everything: from purposely trying to habituate (addict) users to social media, to playing fast and loose with its own privacy regulations, to selling our most intimate and personal data to third parties without our knowledge.

The more serious scrutiny of Facebook by governments and by the media around 2017 was only one part of a wider questioning by ordinary people about digital life more broadly – and digital life is now very broad indeed. People increasingly ask: where is the control here? Do we simply trust our fate to Apple or Amazon? What about our kids who, if we are to believe some of the moral-panic-inducing news stories that circulate through the very same media under question, are becoming scrolling morons, or narcissistic Instagrammers, or deeply insecure and depressed individuals? And what about me? Can't *I* get a break from phones and laptops and notifications and 150 emails a day, a break from trying to 'relax' at night by watching YouTube or Netflix, a break from hopping constantly between both, then eventually going to bed and exhaustedly checking emails or Messenger in the dark, yet again, before forcing myself to turn off the sleep-depriving blue light for a few hours before it all begins anew as soon as I wake up?

Digital detox has become a thing recently, a mooted antithesis to digital poisoning. The Oxford Dictionary defines it as:

> A period of time during which a person refrains from using electronic devices such as smartphones or computers, regarded as an opportunity to reduce stress or focus on social interaction in the physical world.

This is quite bland but also quite good and it covers a good deal of my own understandings of it. It's also seen as a kind of wellness issue, suggesting the body and mind can benefit from a break from the ubiquitous screen. Digital detox has an interesting political subtext, too: a pushback to the Silicon Valley billionaires, to the computer-driven workplace and school, and to the people with power who think of digital only in terms of advertising data, or worker efficiency, or unproblematic student learning. Google it for yourself and you will find news articles, academic research and individual opinion telling you that either it is impossible to detox now because it's too late, or it's an urgent moral imperative for everyone, and that we need to detox now before it's too late. With a few more clicks, you can find lots of practical strategies for being tied less to the digital grindstone, and even support groups that will help you in this. And in government or HR-looking websites, you can find reasonable and bullet-pointed baby steps, such as downloading an app that will disable your phone for a preset time. You can even find sites that advocate the nuclear option of returning to a pre-digital time and eschewing all electronic devices altogether.

The latter is not an option for most of us. But it does provide an outer limit that we can work back from to a place that is more feasible, so that we may feel a bit more in control, such that we and the world become a little better for it. Irishman Mark Boyle is a man a bit like Christopher McCandless. He does not use money, he advocates for a barter economy and for a 'rewilding' of the environment. Boyle is at this outer limit of digital detox. In 2018, he wrote an article, using pencil and paper and posting it the old way to an editor at the *Guardian* newspaper, to tell of his experiment of a year without technology. Boyle advocates a turn towards a sustainable ecology to nourish nature's needs. A part of this, he says, is to 'curb our addictions to more stuff, more growth, more dehumanising, distracting technologies' and to give ourselves the time, individually and collectively, to reflect and to understand nature's and society's needs.

This perspective may be difficult for most of us to adopt, but Boyle does add something important to the 'wellness' aspect of digital detox that many of us automatically (and vaguely) associate with it. It's more focused. But it's also something more subjective than a hazily imagined amelioration of stress, or to be more in touch with people, or with nature. Boyle alludes to it in his reference to 'distraction'. And it's about what it actually means to be distracted, to be not focused, or to be not able to have a time where you are not preoccupied with everything that digital life makes you preoccupied with.

This is more the baby step approach as opposed to the Boylean overthrow of the system. Yet, even the taking of baby steps needs a reason: a motivation or a sense that digital detox might yield some answers to a particular question. In all my previous research on digital detox, I found that the overriding motivation for people who pursue it is to gain something: a sense of calm, an appreciation of our physical surroundings, an appreciation of face-to-face time with our friends and family. And of course, there's the motivation that we might have more time for ourselves. This is doubtless all true. But none of it really makes sense unless we have a prior idea of what it is we are *losing* in our digital life of information overload. Having more time must surely be a good thing. But what is it really that we are gaining? Is it simply more hours in the day? To do what?

As I said, I teach media, but I also have an abiding interest in the nature of time. It was this concern, and the knowledge acquired through several years of study and writing about time, that really motivated interest in my own digital detox experiment. I wanted to ask: what happens to my time when it's not stolen or squandered online? When I talk about my time (and your time) it's important to realise that this is not the abstract time of the clock or the calendar of days and weeks. Rather, it is the individuated and subjective time that I (and you) experience as the objective clock ticks inexorably on, with no regard to me (or you). These are two different forms of time. Subjective time is what Marcel Proust called 'elastic' time, a time that is within us and which can contract or expand depending upon our particular experience of it. The objective time of the clock, by contrast, is a machine time, an invented time that is out there in the world, and that from childhood, we are trained to synchronise with — at the expense of our own subjective time.

How do we identify and understand and somehow regain the time that is in us? As a university teacher, I am fortunate to have access to research time. And fortunately, this is time that can accrue and be accessed quickly, if properly justified to my employers. My idea was to spend a period of time on a container ship. This turned out to be a five-week voyage aboard the CMA CGM *Rossini* from Melbourne, navigating around much of Australia, then north through the Java Sea to Singapore. This was time spent disconnected, and time spent essentially alone, to see what happened to my experience of hours and days without any technological communication — and barely any contact with people.

My cabin wasn't McCandless's bus. It was big, air-conditioned, had two beds, a hot shower and an incredible view that, to quote Jon Krakauer, offered an 'endlessly changing horizon' where every day I saw a 'new and different sun'. However, my trip was not 'into the wild'. It was not even close. But it was a less radical way to a place that poor Christopher McCandless tried to get to: a place of isolation and reflection. At the very least, it was a place that was different from the digital reality that suffocates important aspects of time and life; a place that offered the possibility of more self-knowledge than I had ever known before; a place that revealed memories, realizations and attitudes that I didn't know existed within me. What I found was a place that we can all find and, more importantly, we can find it without having to detox for five weeks. The voyage to Singapore was meant to be a proof of concept. It proved that if we recognise subjective time for what it is, then it's possible, using practical and incremental steps, to curate and manage our digital lives in ways that express more who we really are – or wish to become.

McCandless had his books to guide him. He took a practical book on plants. He also took along *Walden* by Henry Thoreau, *Education of a Wandering Man* by Louis L'Amour and *The Call of the Wild* by Jack London. All were chosen, presumably, to sustain his morale as he wandered and searched and discovered. And they sustained him and made him happy for a time. I took what might be called the practical metaphysical approach and sustained my own morale with books about time. These were practical, in that they offered ways to think about the nature and experience of time; they were also metaphysical, in that they acted as signposts and helped me to understand another subjective reality whilst onboard. Marcel Proust was the most sustaining, not least because his writing is so long and involving and sucks you into his memory world. Proust's engagement with memory as a form of exploration became my guide as a way to both invoke distant memories of my own, and to explore them more deeply than I had ever done before.

What I gained in those five weeks was more time for myself, of course. But the important aspect of this was understanding the nature and quality of this time. I found that my time had little to do with the clock or the calendar or the accelerated time of digital life. What I found was that my time – and by extension, the time of all of us – lies sublimated beneath the time of the clock and the time of digital life. I found this time relatively quickly onboard the container ship, and this showed me that our own subjective time can be accessed and experienced and understood more authentically – if we know how to look for it within us.

The fact that you have got this far in this little prologue means that you also feel that there must be more to life than living through the pervasive filter of digital technology. Getting here means that you might also feel that although we cannot uninvent the computer or the smartphone, we can at least be smarter in our use of them – or their use of us.

What follows is my story of finding my own time by taking the digital out of my life for five weeks. This is a relatively short time, but it was nonetheless a life-changing experience, one I simply felt compelled to document somehow and somewhere. So I've written this book from a mass of notes I took on my 'field work'. I use that term deliberately. Digital detox was as much an academic venture as it was a philosophical and personal one. Using Proust as my cue for what he terms *mémoire involontaire*, I have interspersed the narrative with what might in my case be called *mémoire volontaire* – memories that I have discovered within me after purposively searching for them. This was Proustian in that the initial memory was triggered involuntarily from some aspect of my surroundings onboard the *Rossini*. However, by consciously searching around inside that memory, a process that was to me like opening a kind of lace curtain and stepping through it voluntarily into another dimension, another room of the memory, into a new memory of remembered detail, or aspect of the memory's context: a phrase from someone, a colour, an accent, a new figure appearing whom I'd forgotten about, a look in someone's eye, and so on. Through concentration, I found that I could exhaust this new memory room and pull back the curtain and step into another, and sometimes another, in an act of recall and discovery I'd never experienced before.

A technical note is that grammatical tense moves around in this book. This is both deliberate, as the book concerns itself with the plasticity and elasticity of time, and natural as it deals with the rhythms of thought and memory when they are unconstrained by clock and calendar and network. As Theodor Adorno put it in his *Minima Moralia*, 'The task of art today is to insert chaos into order.' In this spirit, I urge you to go with the flow.

More formally, this was also a social science experiment. It was an auto-ethnography that sought to document and analyse what turned out to be a temporal transformation in the life of an individual – me.

The story begins with a short introductory chapter on how we might think of the effect of digital technology upon subjective time. It is followed by a general contextualization into technological time as *affect*: that is to say how it shapes us as individuals, as members of groups, and as elements in a living culture. The next chapter focuses this affect perspective upon the digital context. I discuss the idea that our digital life, notwithstanding the general upbeat ideology in our media and politics about freedom and choice, is, in fact, homogenising ways of being and seeing in our post-modernity. The discussions in these initial chapters are the writing-up of my gradual realisations about our digital world that, in essence, were what drove me to seek a way out of digital life's constrictions and suffocating sameness, where the overriding metaphor for me had become the mouse on the wheel – running faster and faster and going nowhere. Moreover, Christopher McCandless's story reminded me (and the daily distractions of digital life mean that we always need to be reminded somehow) that it's up to us to look for alternatives to what we are offered. The rest of the book is about how my need for an alternative was expressed in seeking and understanding a different relationship with time. I found it on the *Rossini*, and amazingly it has stayed with me.

It is hardly necessary for me to state that my family were wonderful and generous about my idea. They all supported it wholeheartedly in the very short time that we had to discuss it together. I often go on trips for work, as does Kate, but we are always able to keep in touch through phone calls, Skype or texts. This was different. They would have no idea what I was doing or if I was constantly seasick and homesick, or bored, or had been washed overboard, or taken by pirates. I didn't have any idea myself until I went, and so for them to encourage me, I am still grateful.

1

ZERO-SUM TIME

D
O YOU CHECK yourself sometimes and realise that someone is talking to you face-to-face but you are looking at your smartphone, perhaps running your thumb or index finger expectantly over one of its smooth and warm and familiar edges, and hoping that it will buzz or ring?

Perhaps you keep your laptop on sleep mode instead of shutting it down so you can access the internet about a minute faster that way, but stress just a little when the battery icon dips under 30 per cent. What about when the battery icon goes into the red zone and there's no charger nearby?

And then there're the memes! And two dogs pulling a rubber tyre from a swimming pool that suddenly seem so much more interesting than the daily news or your job, as you unobtrusively flick back to your work browser in less than a second when your boss appears? If it's not memes or YouTube videos it's in-content ads – those adidas trainers that you don't need but whose link you click anyway have led you unconsciously from the shopping basket to the checkout and then to PayPal, and now they're yours.

Can you believe what you just did at the supermarket counter, speaking on your phone throughout the whole transaction, oblivious to the sales assistant's presence as if they did not exist as a person at all? And was that you sitting in class behind your laptop lid and messaging your classmate just four feet away on the front row, as oblivious to the teacher as you were to the sales assistant?

And did you happen to catch the reflection of your disembodied self in the train window , speaking hands-free and at normal volume to a virtual presence with everyone else around doing the same?

Apparently a majority – over 70 per cent – of mobile phone users even sleep with their devices. Many use them after they've switched off the lights and are tucked up in bed, and any part-ner who happens to be alongside will quite probably be texting or browsing, too. And if they wake in the middle of the night from a troubling dream, their reaction may not be to reflect on the dream and try to resolve it. It is very likely they will reach for their phone on their bedside table or under their pillow, and activate its friendly glow to see if any comfort may be found in the form of a post, a notification or, even better, a text from someone they know, which can reassure them that they are not alone in the universe. Even if the whole night has been one of blissful and undisturbed sleep, the first and almost unconscious physical movement of the new day is often to reach out for the reassuring touch of the digital bedfellow.

Many people between the ages of eighteen and thirty-five say they would hand over their car keys instead of their sim card if they were forced to choose between going without a car or a phone. A mere generation ago, such a choice, such a question, would have been unthinkable. Even top-of-the-line mobiles were pretty clunky and slow. Whether we owned a standard flip phone or a cool and businesslike BlackBerry, the grip of the mobile phone hadn't yet tightened around our collective necks. Back then, speaking or texting on the handset was fine, but you could forget anything more exotic like watching Netflix. Not anymore. There's a meme that does the rounds that says the average smartphone has more computing power than the computers onboard the Apollo 11, which steered Neil Armstrong and Buzz Aldrin to the moon and back in 1969. A cliché, yes, but one that understates the reality: it's not just a little bit more computing power but a lot more. The silicon chip processor in my now obsolete iPhone 6 is 120 million times faster than one of NASA's 1960s vintage.

Just think about all of that computing power sitting in our hands as we lie in the dark in our beds. The problem is that most of us don't think about it; we take it for granted. In fact, most of us don't even take it for granted. Taking something for granted requires at least a little bit of conscious reflection. Our smart-phones aren't something that's just there in our pockets or hands, an almost invisible natural appendage. Invisible until it runs out of power, or it's dropped and its screen shatters like ice on a frozen puddle, or its signal disappears when you're trying to download street directions at a busy intersection. *Then* it's there. And our standard reaction is not usually a zen-like equanimity. We don't shrug off the fact that we can't go online, nor do we happily switch off the phone and make a mental note to get it repaired someday or resolve to charge it sometime, maybe tomorrow, if we remember. No. It's a mini-crisis. We stare blankly at the black or shattered screen and feel both a creeping panic and an immediate emptiness. We need to get back online as soon as possible and so we reach for the expensive charger, or the pricey internet dongle or even the spare phone that we invested so much money in for just such a traumatic event.

This is perhaps slightly exaggerated, but not by much. However, it is an indication of the psychological power that this beautiful, shiny, glowing little thing has over you and me – a technological hold that goes far beyond the individual psyche and soaks into almost all aspects of social life. In the long history of human tech-nology such a command over us, a command that is strengthened every day through growing connectivity, is unprecedented. And that's no exaggeration.

A recent Pew Research Center survey found 85 per cent of respondents in the survey agreed with the statement that 'most people will move more deeply into connected life'. It is obvious to me that this observation is true. But it is also a bland statement that doesn't say very much that is insightful or important for my life or yours. What exactly does it mean to move more deeply into connected life? Indeed, what is it to be connected, and is a deeper connection better? A respondent in the same survey added a little more butter to the toast: 'The stickiness and value of a connected life will be far too strong for a significant number of people to have the will or means to disconnect.' Aha, this is more like it. Is willpower – or our lack of it – the problem, perhaps? It's a purported solution we often hear from the self-help and wellness corner of the internet. Switch off that smartphone. Get that filter working properly. Show some self-discipline. But then there's the obvious question about the rationale behind owning a pocket-sized, personal mobile device: why would you leave it at home in a drawer? And why switch it off if it's in your pocket? Such half-baked appeals to the power of the will don't make much sense in our pervasive and persuasive digital culture.

The issue with ideas about will and solutions based on its power is that it concerns you alone – you can't generalise from it. Will, like morality or ethics, doesn't mean a thing unless it's *you* either practising or transgressing it. And so, it's a deep and sorrowful irony that in this 'social' digital world, it ultimately boils down to just you – alone – with your face in front of a screen and an empty space where your soul used to reside. And that's a problem, because we're not so strong or will-filled when we're on our own, clicking, typing, and scrolling, or talking to Alexa or Siri. And this is especially so when we aren't aware that our relationship with all things digital requires that we summon the will to extract ourselves from them. Indeed, we can't conceive of the need to exercise will if we don't see a problem there in the first place.

In 2017, Facebook's former president Sean Parker said that the social media platform 'literally changes your relationship with society, with each other. It probably interferes with productivity in weird ways. God only knows what it's doing to our children's brains'. Yes, indeed. But Parker might have been rather more compelling if his dystopian vista included the brains of all of us. Facebook's business model relies absolutely on advertising revenue and on finding ways to get us online for longer, and so its critical concern is, as Parker tells us in his rather overdue exposé, 'How do we consume as much of your time and conscious attention as possible?' Therefore, the hold the online world has over us has to be one calculated by Facebook's engineers and algorithm writers.

But it wouldn't be entirely fair to point an accusing finger at Facebook alone. It is one of a handful of powerful tech corporations that grew from nothing in the 1990s and early 2000s to be bigger than anyone could have ever imagined possible, and wielding a logic of connectivity that has sunk just as deeply into the individual and collective psyche as ideas about religion, nationhood or maybe even family. Again that might be pushing it just a little, but this is the path we are set on. Alongside Facebook, most of the global bandwidth of online connectivity is sucked up by entities and platforms such as Google, YouTube, Amazon, mushrooming pornography platforms, and streaming platforms such as Netflix and its replicants around the world. All of them want our clicks to create personal profiles that they can sell both to the world's largest companies, who will micro-target you with compelling ads made by people with PhDs in semiotics and psychology, and to companies as small as the new restaurant around the corner, whose new ads about its food can hit its intended individual profile right in the eyes.

Putting economics aside, there is a rather more insidious fallout from all of this which was probably never anticipated while Google, YouTube, Amazon and Facebook have been vying for our attention. It's explained in a short YouTube video produced by the US non-profit organisation Time Well Spent. The video has high production values and is well-scripted and funny, but it makes a serious point – perhaps one of the most serious there is today. It highlights an issue that most of us fail to see as a problem – an issue that for years I certainly failed to see as a problem – because it's a sleepwalking, eyes wide shut, hiding in plain view kind of problem. But it is here, and it is now.

The video features Max Stossel, a millennial New Yorker who is hip and humorous and handsome; he's the sort of guy you might see in an Apple ad. He's in Lower Manhattan, walking down a street of brownstones and speaking to the camera in a kind of slam poetry style about his relationship with his phone. Meanwhile, he's doing what most of us spend increasing amounts of our time doing: engaging with his phone. His attention constantly flips between the camera and the phone whilst he tries to avoid bumping into similarly preoccupied New Yorkers or getting hit by a car.

He slams:

> Architects of our digital world: stop, be better.
> Because we can be, and we can see that these systems have been designed with intricacy, so that companies can keep our attention indefinitely.
> I don't want to keep crushing these freaking candies.
> I don't want these alerts to completely command me.
> I don't care if that panda bear is dancing.
> (Pauses to gawp imbecilely at his phone.)
> Well, maybe … with a hula hoop.

And thus, despite our poet's best efforts at deploying willpower, he is once more hooked to his smartphone. It's amusing and slick and ironic and knowing, and all the kinds of things that tech-savvy and hyperconnected people are supposed to be. Except they (and maybe you) are also trapped in a digital prison of constant distraction.

The creators at Time Well Spent have one main pressing concern, and it's the same one I expressed in my little prologue: time. They are concerned with the ways we squander time online and how this squandering is a direct effect of deliberate design decisions made in Silicon Valley or London or Seoul or Tokyo, or wherever the employers of highly-paid (or maybe not) tech-savvies invest lots of money and expertise to draw deeply from professions such as psychology, neuroscience and philosophy and make digital life as sticky and never-ending as can be.

But design and code and psychology are only part of the problem. It's true that these all are brought to apps and phones and servers and networks in order to orient them toward efficiency and convenience and desire. However, it's also true that the huge success of this orientation paradoxically leaves us with less time to do things and to be someone offline.

This is the zero-sum equation.

The Time Well Spent people maintain that digital design is irresponsible and immoral in this regard because it fiendishly traps us inside a digital panopticon and eats up our time in injudicious and wasteful pursuits. Time spent looking at a screen is time that is not spent in the world of fleshly people and material things and immediate surroundings: real life instead of the virtual digital version. However, what they miss, and what constitutes the other part of the problem, is that they see time – the time that's chewed up online – as something normative, as a thing or a process that we can understand through clocks and which we can quantify and translate into money. It's an understanding made simple and clear for all time within capitalism in Benjamin Franklin's 'time is money' aphorism. This is true in a superficial sense, but our digital life has made the nature of time – your time and my time – salient and problematic and something we urgently need to understand better than in a normative clock time-based way.

Let me explain.

The fact that I am so familiar with the little connectivity scenarios at the beginning of this introduction may have given rise to the suspicion that I wrote them from personal experience. Of course I did: all those and many more scenarios like it. At one time, I was hooked like the hipster poet. The difference was that unlike him, I didn't know it.

For a long time, I thought I was fine. I thought I soared above all that vulgar stuff the digital-dependents regularly degrade themselves with. My professional work is in teaching and writing about media and communications. But for a long time, I didn't reflect on my own relationship with digital technology and digital networks. The idea of chronic distraction is a pathology that I know a lot about. I understand how the connected life is, or very easily can be, a life lived in the present, where you're flitting like a moth from website to website, link to link, and device to device, bouncing like a pinball from one impulse to another in a growing confusion of going nowhere and not realising it. Millions have lives like this to a greater or lesser extent. Lift your eyes from your screen and look around you, in the train, in the supermarket, in traffic, in the street and in the classroom. And think of all those uncountable others in their homes and offices who just sit there, connected but alone.

My trouble was that for a long time, I didn't look and I didn't know that I was just like those whom I pitied: the captured, the distracted, the rude, the self-absorbed and the blinkered. The reason I am writing this now is because I managed to change myself. As I will show you, I became a different person. In a way, at least.

The first thing inevitably in questions of habit is to recognise and accept that you have a problem. One day, out of the blue, I told myself that I had a problem, and then I moved on. I didn't find God, or yoga, or a twelve-step program to recovery although who knows, these might have worked at the personal level as well. But what I did end up finding was *time*.

A central aspect of my professional work, alongside media, is the study of time. It was my specific relationship with time that I came to see as the most important feature of my digital life, and it was this that prompted me to conduct the proof of concept experiment of a digital detox that became the basis of this book.

Over the space of several years and with some effort, I eventually came to see that if I tried to go beyond the normative understanding of time, guided by a range of philosophers and artists such as Marcel Proust and Henri Bergson, then I might gain some insight into the nature of the specific problem of time within the network society. What these thinkers and writers taught me was that I was losing much more than the measured hours of the day to the online sinkhole – I was losing myself. I learned from them that the essence of time is the experience of time. Essentially, if our experience of time is dominated or deeply inflected by connectivity, then our subjective experience will be one of a constant present, of living in the perpetual moment of being always on and always available.

Ironically, it was on YouTube, whilst I was watching a band called Savages, that the connection between distraction and time became absolutely clear to me. In their song *Shut Up*, lead singer Jehnny Beth has written a spoken verse, which I had to write down the first time I heard it to get its full effect. It goes:

> The world used to be silent
> Now it has too many voices

And the noise
Is a constant distraction
They multiply, intensify
They will divert your attention
To what is convenient
And forget to tell you
About yourself
We live in an age of many stimulations
If you are focused, you are harder to reach
If you are distracted, you are available.

Wow, I thought. These artists tell us that distractions detach us from our selves. Distraction makes you available, or vulnerable, to the loss of time and the subjective experience of it. Digital distraction, in other words, occupies your consciousness and empties it of the subjective experience of time's passing. The corollary of this temporal lack is a diminishing capacity for reflection. In the zero-sum equation, there is literally less time to stop and think about yourself, your life, your experiences and what they all mean. Elsewhere, I've compared the vicious circle of a lack of time leading to a lack of reflection as a form of digital dementia, a point where we become so immersed in the present tense of connectivity that we are unable to reflect on the fact that we have no time to reflect, and so we become unaware that there might be something wrong in our life, something wrong in this shiny and smooth digital society.

I knew that I needed to break the cycle, but how? I thought of Savages' line, 'if you are focused, you are harder to reach', and turned it around to become, 'if you are harder to reach, then you can focus'. How can you be hard to reach these days? It's hard to be out of reach in the city or anywhere now, and wherever you are, the temptation to reconnect is never far away. FOMO, is what we call it now. And it's hard to tell if the users of the acronym think it more humorous than a deep problem for us all.

•

In order to understand the concept of zero-sum time more effectively, it might help to think about how we become (or rather became, as a civilisation) concerned with clockwork time at the expense of Proust's elastic time. The differences between clockwork time and what I will call lived time – and the difficulties we can experience in trying to combine them in our lives – are what I want to reflect upon here, beginning at the beginning of time (our own lived time).

When you are born you cross the threshold from one time to another. By way of the birth canal you time-travel from your mother's biological time: from the time-flow of the pulsing of her blood, governed by the beating of her heart; from the cadences of her sound vibrations as they signal the intonations, modulations, inflections and volume of her speech patterns; and from the varying tempos of her walking, running, resting, sleeping and breathing. Then you emerge, unaware and, as yet, lacking self-consciousness, from the safety and warmth of your mother's personal time that she shared with you, into the time of the world. This time is not yet your own time. It is instead just the beginning – the setting up and winding up – of an alien and unnatural time that immediately supervenes onto your new life to imprint itself and its unbending rules upon you until the day that you die.

Today is your birth day. But the time of the world you've passed into is a particular form of time, an abstracted, mathematical time; a time dreamed up by Aristotle to measure, or so he thought, what constitutes the real, the actual, the essence of what time is. His time would, in time, become a clockwork-ordered time that was given the early-modern stamp of Divine validity by Isaac Newton.

It would later become a time of geometric space that humans, according to Albert Einstein, move within as if in a universe-sized, predictably-moving mechanism – but free of any Divine influence. And since modern times, this is a time that we messy and unpredictable humans have been compelled to try to learn and to synchronise with. But we've never really mastered it. This is because you and I run on another rhythm, or rhythms: times that belong only to you and to me and which we experience differently as individuals. To paraphrase the 1960s psychedelic psychiatrist, R.D. Laing, your experience of time can never be my experience of time, and vice versa.

Even before our stay in kindergarten is over, we have had to master clock time. To do this we have to have wristwatches and phones and town clocks and radio announcers to keep reminding us that the time is … Before mechanical time took hold, however, all cultures, all peoples and all individuals in history had a different relationship with time. For some, the changing length of time between sunrise and sunset would mark the passing of a single day; days would then stretch and contract with the seasons. Time here might be measured not by minutes or hours, but by the length of time it took to perform a given task – how long to sow a field with wheat, to milk seven goats, to traverse a lake by canoe from one point to another, to grind enough millet to feed the group, and so on. Time was flux and context. It was whatever you wanted it to be, whatever you agreed upon as members of families, communities, even civilisations. And whatever worked for you as an individual. Time was what was meaningful in ways that connected you to the rhythms of life and to your environment. And so, when the more perceptive of our ancestors had the opportunity to look up from the grim and unending preoccupation of scrabbling and fighting for food and shelter and mating and territory, they would have registered a kind of rhythm and regularity in the movement of the stars and planets in the night skies. The curious, or perhaps the more ambitious of the tribe or group, might have reflected: 'That bright star was exactly in line with that point of the mountaintop when I stood on this precise spot some time ago. It disappeared and now it has returned'. Such observations would come to represent a longer-spaced time signal, a regular occurrence which marked the passing of more elongated stretches of time. Across the world, until relatively recently, human cultures would mark these as important forms of communication and they would mark us also as being human.

But, still, it's your 'birthday', a compound word in our culture that has meanings, so let's remember it and what it is supposed to mean. As you pass, as a newborn, into the time of the world, the very minute of its happening is recorded. A midwife will glance up from watching you take your first gulping breaths, to note the time on the clock in the room or on the little fob watch that they sometimes still have pinned to their tunic. They will soon thereafter chronicle that hour, as well as the day, the month and the year. You will later get a certificate to 'prove' this life-testifying and life-shaping 'fact'. Without this vital evidence of your entering into the official time of the world, all kinds of things become difficult, if not impossible, such as going to school, obtaining a passport, being counted as an official, living person, and getting all kinds of jobs. My own certificate, which is in a biscuit-tin-shaped reliquary on a high shelf in an upstairs cupboard, is evidence for all time that I did indeed pass from my mother's soothing and peaceful timescape into the time of the hard-edged, antiseptic and hard-lit delivery room that existed, along with its people, in the unerring and always future-pointing, time of the world on that day.

•

My arrival in the time of the world, at least within my particular time zone (and it was probably rounded up or down by a busy nurse), was clocked at 7.20 am. The day was a Saturday, the date the 14th, the month February, the year 1959. I was thus marked for the rest of my life as a baby boomer; a schoolchild of the sixties, a school-age teenager of the seventies, and then a statistical adult registered as either in work or out for the decades thereafter.

In this sense, the one that really matters in the cold logic of the time of the world, time is inevitably a bureaucratic process, with no indication of anything other than the relevant temporal facts. And so that reddish-coloured certificate in the biscuit tin, the Certified Copy of an Entry of Birth with the registrar's signature rubberstamped on it to corroborate that a human had in fact entered the time of the world, does not record how my mother felt about it all, or how long the labour might have been, or if the midwives changed shifts in the middle of it, or if at 7.20 am it looked like it was going to be a fine midwinter's day, or not. These are human details and, as such, irrelevant to the fact of my passing from her into the future-flowing time of the world that pours onward and unstoppably like a great river. Bureaucratically relevant also is that this time will someday end, when my own little rivulet of life leaves the great human river-flow to constitute its own little trickle that will then run to its terminus. It will then truly end when a death certificate is clipped to the birth certificate and both are placed back in the tin by some tidy-minded relative, or when a hyperlink is appended to my digital record that exists on some database that the local authority has leased (for how long?) from some data-management company.

It goes without saying that the way in which our life is date-stamped, and the way in which the world around us seems to move in time, makes a deep imprint upon who we feel we are. And being comprised of bone and blood instead of being robots, we humanise and personalise and 'culturalise' the official event in what are little acts of resistance against the hard logic of the time of the world. For example, in what is probably a universal human cultural trait, an event such as a birthday is often marked in ways that are more pleasant and meaningful than merely mentally adding another year to your age. We soften the marking off of the years towards death by celebrating it. Age in numbers can be important for children and young people, perhaps because there seems to us then to be such a lot of it still to come, or perhaps it's the pleasure of being officially a bit older than some peers. And so, these fulsome formative years have candles and cards and cake to commemorate them. In later years, we might play down the significance of (what is becoming) a superfluity of candle flame and have dinner and champagne instead. And further down the single track comes the wish that your birthday would not seem to come around so quickly. Later still, the longing begins to surface that everyone would just forget about it altogether. But even within this rather baleful late trajectory, an affirmative culture can still intervene with more small acts of refusal, or is it delusion? And so, who does not feel ever so slightly buoyed, and maybe even feel younger, when they read in some magazine that 'thirty is the new twenty' or, even better, that 'fifty is the new forty'?

We can make birthdays more meaningful in other ways by opening up the wider context of the day itself. My ordinary 14 February 1959 looked a bit more interesting when I went to Wikipedia to learn what else occurred on that day in the time of the world. A couple of events turned out to be quite uncanny little facts I hadn't known about before. I should preface my findings with one or two things about me before we go on: the process of climate change is one I think about a good deal, and I believe in the need for all of us to act and live in ways that both raise consciousness of the process and contribute as little CO_2 as possible into the atmosphere. Scrolling down the Wikipedia page, I saw that on the day I was born, and in a place far from my birthplace in the Airbles Road Maternity in Motherwell:

> The United States Weather Bureau released a report that concluded 'that the world is in the midst of a long-term warming trend', based on data gathered in Antarctica. Dr H.E. Landsberg, director of the bureau's office of climatology, said that the cause of the global warming was unknown, but added: 'One theory is that the change is man-made, that a blanket of carbon dioxide given off by the burning of coal and oil retards the radiation of heat by the earth.'

Wow. Well, sort of. Wow for me anyway, sitting at the, perhaps, more neurotic end of the spectrum of environmental activism as I do. I'm one of those who, when at home alone, switches off lights to the point where the place looks vacant from most angles at night. And during the whole of wintertime I'll drape a blanket over my shoulders rather than turn on a heater – a task that falls to whomever in my family can no longer stand the Dickensian atmosphere. And I won't step onto an elevator at any time when stairs – even a fire escape – are available. This is a psychological legacy of growing up in an indigent family, but is also temporal in its own way, in the way that 'time is money'. It seems rather barbaric now, but was normal then, that in our house in Scotland, when I was in my early teens, we had metered electricity: you put fifty pence into the meter and you got a couple of hours of electricity. We had a slot TV as well. This seems truly bizarre today. We'd feed it what little we had to watch what little was on. Periodically, a man from the Rediffusion shop in the nearest big town of Motherwell would come and empty it, take the rental cut for his company and then put the excess in a neat little heptagonal pile on top of the TV set – just waiting to be fed back in. The slot system for electricity supply was a humiliation upon the poor, but was gamed by most in our street because most in our street were poor. One way of getting your own back on the South of Scotland Electricity Board was to take a piece of plasticine, make a fifty pence impression upon it, add water, put it into the freezer, then feed the slot with the coin-shaped ice. This worked fine for a while, except we in my house were not as cunning as others who would place a candle under the metal money box to dry out the water from the melting ice. And so, one day our rented money box rusted through, and when the electric man came to empty it, it was red-faced excuses from my mum about rising damp or something, and a knowing (and understanding) look from the man from the SSEB.

Back to Wikipedia. In two more little wow moments I learn that sublime soprano Renée Fleming left her mother's time on the same day as me (adjusted for time zones); and the great jazz drummer Baby Dodds checked out (aged only sixty) just as Renée and I were checking in. Both artists have been in my iTunes library since iTunes started, and I've listened to them for a lot longer than that. Of course, these are more coincidental than eerie, but you see what I mean. The marking of time in ways that are cultural, personal and social can be as important to us today as it was for our ancestors who looked to the actual stars for a fragment of meaning to fill their hungry lives. I feel a connection with Baby and Renée and that is kind of unique – as well as not a little obscure and abstract. But then again, this is something and it can be meaningful in a personal way. What this all signifies is that the times beyond the clock, the times that we feel through direct experience of the present, or through memory, or through projecting into the future, are times that are ineradicable, something the clock cannot completely overwrite and nullify, and so therefore have meanings and importance that run much deeper than we commonly realise in our busy clock-driven (and now also internet-driven) temporal lives.

Acting as supplements to the clock, calendars also connect us to the time of the world. As the clock takes care of the minutes and hours, so do they structure the days and weeks and their rhythms. Rarely do we need to ask: 'What day is it?' However, beyond it being Monday or Saturday, we still look to the calendar for its marks of wider significance. Even in our digital age, printed calendars still sell by the millions at Christmas time, and there would hardly be a fridge without some kind of estate agent junk mail magnet calendar sticking to its door. And, in time past, the 'On this day …' feature of the humble desk diary, that critically endangered analogue species, was something that served as official notice of the significance of the date of your working day. This is an estimable tradition that Wikipedia still, thankfully, upholds. Today, for example, is the 3rd of September, but I didn't really need to consult Wikipedia because I already knew the significance of this day in history. I'm of an age where this particular date means something to me. It's the day in 1939 when the ultimatum that had been sent to Herr Hitler the day before by the British government, demanding that he 'withdraw at once' his troops from Poland 'by 11.00pm', was ignored. Then, as later, Hitler was not of a mind to listen to anybody, so his armies pressed on with their blitzkrieg and their own timetable for war. His bluff well and truly called, British Prime Minister Neville Chamberlain then took glumly to the radio waves to declare to a population, who anyway knew what was coming, that 'consequently, this country is at war with Germany'. Vera Lynn felt a song coming on, and Winston Churchill looked up from laying bricks in Chartwell and began to think his time was coming at last. Now, this fateful Sunday was a good twenty years before Renée and I would show up and poor Baby would die, but my father was around and if he didn't hear the broadcast, he was certainly reading the newspapers.

MÉMOIRE VOLONTAIRE 1

My father, William (Bill) Hassan, was born in the time of the world, 7 February 1922. That's a long time ago now, but on the day Chamberlain retracted his 'peace for our time' commitment to the listening population in Britain, my father was going on eighteen. Cool looking, with slicked-back jet-black hair, all double-breasted dark blue pinstripe and with perhaps too much of the time of the world on his hands – but time enough, I imagine, to render him bored and up for adventure. Because it was not long after that Sunday in September that he took the number 241 red double-decker bus for the fifty-minute ride through the steel and coal grime of the industrial conurbations to the navy recruiting office in Charlotte House in the middle of Queen Street in Glasgow to enlist in the Senior Service as an Able Seaman. This much I know of my dad's life, but not much more.

I have a black-and-white photograph of my father, which dates from 1943, I think. I am only guessing the year. It might be a bit later, but that does not matter. In it there are four men standing next to a big iron capstan: two men stand to the front, and the other two are positioned slightly to the left at the back. My father is front and left and looks the youngest of the four. They all look too young, but all seem to be trying to look like men and how they think men are supposed to look in wartime. The one to the back and right has a full-set beard, as they say in the navy, and his sailor's cap is pushed to the back of his head. He's smiling and looking to his left, showing his profile and looking like the man in the logo of the Navy Cut brand cigarettes of the day. The capstan puts them at a dock, but it is also somewhere warm because they are all wearing white sailor shirts and baggy white shorts that terminate at the knees. If the photograph was colour and of high quality, and I didn't know what it was, it could be a picture of a boy band embracing a gay culture in a kind of Village People parody. We tend to forget that the young men and women of that time also had their own popular culture, in music, dancing and in films, especially. Somewhere I read that in the 1930s the James Cagney gangster movies were immensely popular with film-going youth in the UK, but that the authorities were worried that Hollywood's portrayals of Cagney toting a machine gun in, for example, *Angels with Dirty Faces*, were corrupting influences for a Depression-era generation which, as George Orwell observed, had been hitherto safely weaned on sanitised fantasy life comics like *The Beano* and *Hotspur*.

I'm sure my father must have swapped his *Hotspur* fantasy life for a grittier American one and become a Cagney fan. In the photograph, he flourishes the British equivalent to the American Thompson: a much nastier-looking Lanchester submachine gun. It looks like it could blow up in your face. Google these weapons and compare for yourself. Anyway, he's also smiling at the camera, also with the sailor cap pushed back beyond the hairline, like Cagney or George Raft in their fedoras. He's half showing off and half saying 'you know this is not my gun, I've just borrowed it for the photo' – and borrowed it to show off, to look like Cagney or Raft. For added hard-man effect he also has a dagger stuck inside one of his knee-length socks, which looks positively dangerous (for the wearer). What if you fell over? Tough-man or not, over the next six years, and doubtless with attitude to spare, he saw the world through its different theatres of war. There was even a feature about him and his brother Frank, an army sergeant, which appeared in the 9 June 1944 issue of the *Motherwell Times*, and recounts the meeting of these two brothers in arms in far-away Italy. His 'voice' is there in quotation marks in the article, describing for the reader how he and Frank 'spent two hours talking and nobody listening' when they had their brief and totally fortuitous wartime reunion. Somehow, though, I get the feeling that this was the reporter telling a good story from the front line and not quoting my dad's words at all, which is a pity, but who knows? Anyway, fifteen months later he was standing to attention on the deck of his ship, HMS *Teazer*, in Tokyo Harbour on 27 August 1945, almost six years to the week after the war broke out, to witness the Japanese surrender and with it the end of the whole terrible business. Also part of the family folklore, a part which I have the vaguest memory of, is that my father used to always wear a little silver clasp on the lapel buttonhole of his grey tweed sports jacket, which the king supposedly gave to him to commemorate his presence in Tokyo on that day.

We barely consider it nowadays, but the invention of photography revolutionised public history and personal memory – and our relationship to time. Roger Fenton's Crimean War photographs from the 1850s looked not too different from battlefield photos from Anbar Province in 2003 or the outskirts of Aleppo in Syria in 2018, reminding us that war and death have not changed very much. War was shit then and now. On the personal level, and acting as *aide-mémoire*, the photograph has been an invaluable source from which we are able to fill some of the vast gaps of recorded life experience that exist inside the limbic system of all our brains. This is the stuff we've forgotten about, or the stuff that never existed, but that the photograph can still give meaning and life to. Susan Sontag wrote that photographs 'give people an imaginary possession of a past that is unreal'. But they also remember a past that is real, or real enough for me. My father died when I was young and so the few (three) photos of him that exist have a power far beyond their prima facie content. Being rare means that they are very potent and can represent almost anything I want them to.

Standing in for actual memory means that I can reconstruct that past convincingly to myself and almost at will. This is the danger. But when I write about this particular photograph, I don't make up anything. My description of the picture is as true as I can make it, because it corresponds in a very unscientific way with memory traces of my own, with discussions (usually half-remembered) with other family members, and with a general family folklore that would accommodate, broadly, my reading of it.

MÉMOIRE VOLONTAIRE 2

I'm not sure if my reading of the few photographs I have of my father is in any way accurate, or even if the story of the clasp is true or just a trick of the memory, because my father died on 17 March 1968, of complications from bowel cancer, so memories of him are comprised mostly of out-of-focus or jump-cut scenes and with no recollection at all of the sound of his voice or of anything that he said. Amidst all this perceptual fog, though, there are a few little lights of sharp and clear recall in my mind. Such as him making piles of toast for we four kids when he came back from the pub one still-light summer's night and me thinking how exciting this was – food, supper, coming from my father instead of my mother; of him rolling his own cigarettes, or smoking the ready-made Woodbines; or of him bringing home a James Bond toy gun for me that came with a shoulder holster, which meant you could wear a concealed weapon to school under the felt blazer (terrific thrill); or of him doubled-up on the floor writhing in pain and clutching at his stomach as I watched the 3.15 pm racing from Towcester on TV whilst noisily rolling marbles up and down a metal tea tray.

I have another fairly trustworthy memory of visiting him in hospital a couple of days before he died. He was sitting up in bed in good spirits but yellowed with jaundice. There was adult conversation going on, which I remember was, for a short time, devoted to the fact that a kind nurse had given my father a real sheepskin rug to put under him to make him more comfortable. And I also remember walking with my aunt back along the long hospital ward corridor to the bus and thinking to myself how strange it was to see someone with such a terrible pallor, in both skin and eyes. I'd never seen such a thing before, and I never saw him again. The day he died was significant for my family, and for me of course. I remember my mother calling me to her as I got up from my bed that morning. It was cold so I grabbed a too-tight orange polyester jumper, pulled it over my head, pushed my arms through both sleeves simultaneously, in an action I still perform today, and tiptoed toward her voice. She was standing at the stove making scrambled eggs, scraping a thin aluminium pot with a partially melted handle quickly and noisily with a metal dessert spoon, and said without looking at me, but with an odd, probably sedative-induced detachment: 'your daddy died early this morning'. She was not yet thirty-two.

Such days of death are days when Catholics draw their curtains and light candles. Living as Catholics in a Catholic area of West Central Scotland meant that I'd seen this custom often before, but it was always some other family's suffering. Now it was us with our cheap, bronze-coloured nylon curtains pulled across in daytime, signalling to all the calamity and tears going on behind them. It's rather shameful to think of it now but, in my childish and selfish mind, I remember being mainly embarrassed about his death because it meant that we were now irresistibly destined, as almost with the force of nature, to be poor. I felt victimised. When the news of his death got around, relatives would come to the house to pay their respects while those of more distant connection would bless themselves as they walked past. Some, mostly women, would stop and clasp their hands and utter a short prayer, the lips moving soundlessly. In the two or three days before the funeral, my brother and I watched the passers-by from the upstairs window. We noticed that some of the men could remove and replace their cap with one hand and bless themselves with the other, all in one move. We thought this a great laugh and practiced it for a bit with my father's tweed cap, giggling at our unsuccessful attempts to replicate this complex feat of Catholic hand-hat coordination.

On the morning of my father's funeral, Mr Ramzan from the grocery store sent his son Ali and granddaughter Shahnaz over to our house at 27B Glencairn Avenue, to offer condolences and a big family-sized box of Maltesers that he must have taken from a display of several that stood alongside a basket of green apples and an arc of Fray Bentos steak and kidney pie tins that ornamented the shop window. The Ramzans were a wildly exotic presence in this all-white, all-Catholic, all-Scottish area. I don't recall any racism at all at the time, just fascination on the part of we kids. Kids are taught to think like racists. For a kid, the man who sells 'sugar-fuel' on the way to school is always a friend. The Ramzans had bought the shop about a year before from the bald, red-faced and obese Mr McKay, who kept a filthy grocery that always smelled powerfully of cat piss from the big, fat, bad-tempered and incontinent orange tabby that used to sit (and piss) on the piled-up paper bags of coal at the shop door. Mr Ramzan's shop, however, was both spotless and catless.

Ali and Shahnaz stood on the bottom step at the door, wide-eyed and tense-looking, facing up towards my elder sister and me. Bengali newcomers stepping into an alien Celtic landscape. It fell to Ali as male, with his blustery and black glossy curls, to perform the obeisance, tripping over his words, saying that he and his family were sorry to hear the news of our father's death, and then quickly running out of any more words to say. A few seconds of awkward silence followed. Then, having scanned the overdone display of kitsch Catholic iconography arrayed behind us – statues of the Virgin Mary, crosses, and candles burning in little red jars – Ali sort of spoiled the moment when he said with a big grin, 'We thought you Hassans were Muslims!' Four little gusts of laughter rose up, condensing and mixing in the cold air. This helped to lighten a miserable day, if only for a few forever-imprinted seconds.

Wikipedia tells that in the late afternoon of the same day, down in London, some four hundred-odd miles worth of the M1 from our doorstep, 10,000 anti-Vietnam War demonstrators thronged the United States Embassy at 24 Grosvenor Square. This fracas constituted a lesser violence to that going on in Indochina at the same time; but still, 130 people were injured with fifty taken to hospital, among them twenty-five police officers.

We could play this little memory game endlessly, but you see the point. The markers of clock and of calendar, when used reflectively instead of trying frantically to synchronise with them, and to keep up with them, have a very human and very personal use. It shows that we can draw, sometimes incredibly deeply, and with practice, at will, from personal and public memory, and make all kinds of connections to fill out and give meaning to our lived time experience. This is a potentially powerful psychological capacity and constitutes almost a form of time travel. Yes. Time travel. Memory, like reflection, is the facility to manipulate time, to bend and shape and twist it in all kinds of directions. However, it is important to realise that to dwell and explore in the universe of your memory does not necessarily mean to be stuck in the past or to be a slave to nostalgia. These are wastes of time. I should qualify this a little by saying that a certain kind of engaged or active nostalgia can sometimes be both beautiful and poignant. I think of such nostalgia not as a kitsch or maudlin sensibility that 'things were better in my time': this is more like pining or whining and is immediately boring to anyone within earshot. But thoughtfully curated memory can be, as I just touched upon, a real form of mental time travel, a way to transport yourself to a time or place that may (or may not) have existed, in engaged and active ways.

These thoughts of memories and memory bring me back to Proust, whose extensive and intensive memories came with me on the *Rossini* to guide me in my own memory explorations. Proust's *Remembrance of Things Past*, which was first published in 1913, contains page after page of sublime evocation of past times where, as Proust tells it, 'memory reveals itself' to be dynamic. Our memory is able to render aspects of the past (yours and mine) alive again, or as alive as one can make it; alive enough for it to have a real effect upon you and your actions in the here and now – and alive on into the future. You can't get much more real than that. Think in particular of the famous madeleine cake memory in Proust's book *Swann's Way*, and the description of the *mémoire involontaire* of taking tea and tasting the 'madeleine soaked in [the] decoction of lime-flowers which my aunt used to give me'. Eating the madeleine cake triggers a powerful memory, where suddenly, in the narrator's mind:

> the old gray (sic) house upon the street, where her room was, rose up like the scenery of a theatre to attach itself to the little pavilion, opening on to the garden, which had been built out behind it for my parents (the isolated panel which until that moment had been all that I could see); and with the house the town, from morning to night and in all weathers, the Square where I was sent before luncheon, the streets along which I used to run errands, the country roads we took when it was fine

It does not matter that recent research into Proust's archives shows that in the first draft of the manuscript the madeleine had been a slice of toast and honey; or in the second draft that it had been a humdrum dry biscotti that went with the tea. What mattered for Proust, and what matters for me, is what is possible when 'memory reveals itself' in our lives; what matters is the acknowledgement (to ourselves) of the potential that exists within the subjective experience of lived time, time that is not displaced or numbed by the clock or calendar. Writing as he did at the height of the machine age in the early twentieth century, Proust tries, through the vector of his art, to forge an active relationship with time, one that would work against the destruction of lived time that was then being wrought through the growing dominance of the clock time of the world.

The French philosopher Gaston Bachelard also wrote a book about time, published in 1958 in English, titled *The Poetics of Space*, where he considered the fusing of time and space through memory and its powerful psychological effect upon the here-and-now. In his descriptions of 'his little room at the end of the garret' he conjures up the imagination of memory and displays its power over our faculties of perception when he writes that: 'I alone, in my memories ... can open the deep cupboard that still retains for me alone that unique odor, the odor of raisins drying in a wicker tray. The odor of raisins! It is an odor that is beyond description, one that takes a lot of imagination to smell.' Who has not been transported in time like this by a random smell, or sound, or feel, or even the particular quality of diffused sunlight or slanting shadow in a room?

We also get this powerfully vivid and sensualised memory, and even more strongly, in Haruki Murakami's novel *Kafka on the Shore*. Here, past, present and future, are all garlanded in the thought processes of memory. Quoting Henri Bergson, Murakami observes that: 'The pure present is an ungraspable advance of the past devouring the future. In truth, all sensation is already memory.' To live actively in memory like this is therefore to be intensely entwined in the present, to be able to re-render the past as real as it ever was and to shape the future as closely as possible, in the moment, to your thoughts and memories and anticipations. This is a way to think of ourselves as not being free in time, as a time that exists outside of us as in the clock time way. It is rather to be free as part of the flow of time and to think of human existence as the only form of time, as 'time itself' as Martin Heidegger argued. As a skilful novelist and a writer of fiction, Murakami, in part through Bergson, nonetheless gives the artist's insight into this fundamental quality of time, as time that belongs to you and me individually and personally.

I want to tease this idea out a little more before we move on to consider, in the next chapter, how we live in the new time of the world that is the internet – and the digital life it creates for us. We need to begin with the acknowledgement of a deep conundrum concerning the experience of time, something that we all feel, and something which goes to the heart of living in the time of the world today.

The acknowledgement is also a key rationale of this book, which is the attempt, through my period of digital detox, to separate my lived time from the time of the clock, and calendar ... and now the internet. I want to do this by considering what it is we are losing with the continual displacing and numbing of our experience of lived time through the technologies of the clock and the computer. There is actually nothing new in the mystery of time that confronts us every day in the time of the world. The puzzle was part of Western culture even before the clock came to dominate our lives. St Augustine, for example, living in the fourth century CE, wrote in his *Confessions* of the strange enigma we all feel in our lives with respect of the experience of time: 'What, then, is time? If no one ask of me, I know; if I wish to explain to him who asks, I know not.' What Augustine is saying is that we feel we know what time is, because we feel it intimately, and that this makes sense to us in our own head. But when we try to explain what our sense of time is like to someone else, it becomes difficult because we all experience the same situation in time differently. The clock is unerring and homogeneous, but our experience of time is not.

The feeling that an hour can seem to fly past, or drag, or feel like it can be a bit of both, is very common. We know also, at some level, that two people doing exactly the same thing at the same time and in the same place can experience it quite differently. My favourite example of this is to think about what happens when two soccer teams are playing in front of a crowd. As with most sports, the clock is the governing rule in a soccer match, with a game lasting ninety minutes and with usually a bit of stoppage time added on at the end. Think of a match where there are five minutes to go and the score is 1-1. For one side (my side, Glasgow Celtic), the point earned from the draw would see them win the championship; whereas for the other side (Glasgow Rangers) a single point would see them relegated, but the three points for a win would mean they would survive in the league. For the players and for the fans, too, the last five minutes is time felt intensely. In such a scenario, clock time and lived time clash, but with an assortment of different effects all bundled up in the writhing psychology of emotion – something a mere timepiece can never register. The Celtic players and fans will feel those minutes as excruciatingly long. Players will try to waste time in all kinds of ways, to 'run down the clock'; and fans will keep looking at a giant stadium clock that seems to be moving in slow motion. The Rangers players, by contrast, will be experiencing a different hell. Their experience of time will be just as acute but it will feel like it is running down faster and faster, like sand through their hands. They will run, pass and attack as quickly as they can to get a goal, to 'beat the clock' by getting the winning goal; the minds of the fans too will be racing, and they will not want to look at the clock, because time for them is moving too fast and too soon it will be all over.

Writing when he did, a learned man such as St Augustine would have had to structure his monk's life in the way that Aristotle (whom he had read) would have taught constituted time. Candles with marks cut into them at intervals would signal a passed measure of time once the candle had burned down to that point. Sometimes nails were pushed into the candle at marks measured down its length, and when the flame melted the wax at that point, the nail would fall, like an alarm, so to signal the passing of a timed period. Through such early timing devices, the day could be quantified for those like Augustine whose lives needed to be rationally organised: time for prayers, time to wake, to begin and stop work, to eat, time for reading, and so on. By adopting a mathematical routine instead of some ancient time-reckoning based upon the stars or the rhythms of the body, the seasons and so on, Augustine's lived time would have clashed with the abstract and measured time of the world that was just beginning to develop when he lived. I'm convinced that the perceptual conflict that Augustine expressed in his famous quote would have come from those different times competing for his conscious awareness of time. But he never got to the bottom of the conundrum.

It's no coincidence, from the time of the Middle Ages at least, that technological advances in time telling came from the church, to satisfy the needs of the church. It was the invention of the church bell that would ring at a regular given time to call the people of the village to prayer, for example, that inaugurated the first localised forms of social control and coordination. The geographer Nigel Thrift called this process 'clock time discipline'. As the world became more complex and more interconnected, new-fangled and increasingly accurate mechanical clocks (the word 'clock' stems from the word 'bell') were both cause and consequence of the social, economic, technical and scientific forces that would herald, eventually, the modern period. As this process of clock time discipline progressed, and the time of the clock began to dominate, the regulation of the clock began to generate, especially for those who had known little or nothing else, a clock time consciousness. The lived time of ancient culture and family and community and personal experience began to be sublimated by the abstract time of the world that was imposed by religious authority, in the case of prayer time, and later by economic compulsion, as during the Industrial Revolution when the call to prayer was replaced by the call to work. In this way, time revealed itself fully as a commodity, an article of trade. In this way, the lived time of memory and presence and anticipation were displaced throughout modern society by a system of time that intruded into our lives as a form of value, a 'thing' that could now only be saved, spent, sold or wasted. Indeed, by the time Benjamin Franklin coined his famous phrase 'time is money' in 1748, people knew exactly what he meant. More than that, this form of time seemed already to be the natural way of things.

Being born into the time of the world, with the clock as our master, means that lived time, the source of St Augustine's old riddle, is something that we tend to disregard. It requires less cognitive effort for us to imagine that time is what the clock on the wall tells us it is, and to get on with life and with the clock's mathematical version of it. By so doing, however, we fail to register an immense cost – and that is to our own self, our innermost being that exists as part of nature and as part of a society of humans. With the clock dominating our experience of time, we are denied easy access to lived time, to the subjective experience of time. That is to say, it prevents us from being individuals with full potential for (and I use this word deliberately) self-realisation. In a very concrete way, clock time is a form of external coercion that works against realms of potential that are not materially oriented. The need to synchronise with minutes and hours mobilises us individually and collectively to work towards very specific ends, to be subsumed into a (now global) economy and society that is organised to deliver a certain kind of reality, a material one consisting of things such as money, that we accept increasingly to be the basis of the only possible reality.

In Henri Bergson's much-reported and discussed debates with the equally-famous Albert Einstein, Bergson focused on the concept that time is subjective and 'lived'. Bergson argued that Einstein's defence of mechanical clock time, derived from mathematics, and supposedly comprising the ultimate form of reality, was anti-philosophical and anti-humanistic and an attempt 'to elevate a mathematical representation [of time] into transcendental reality'. And who is to say that Einstein's view has not triumphed utterly? Some, like the anarchist George Woodcock, speak of the 'tyranny of the clock', and how this, along with the present society that it made real, has destroyed completely any chance of living any other way. I disagree. For all its tendencies to govern our lives in a particular way, the clock is not totalitarian. It is a machine and a formal logic that, since the beginnings of the Industrial Revolution, we have more or less been able to work with as part (albeit a very big part) of our lives. The clock drives economy and society relentlessly, but even in the busy time of the world there were always regular down times; such as time after work, or the usual two whole days of the weekend. Then there's the couple of weeks' vacation when the wristwatch can be left on the bedside table, or the unexpected or untimely times when the clock leaves us alone for a while, alone to be free, to be with friends, with family, by ourselves, to read, reflect, to be creative and so on. In parenthesis: think about that time of creativity that you sometimes experience, and the quality of its experience, and you are getting close to your own lived time. That lived time is being displaced by clock time, to be sure, but it cannot be wiped out completely by it. We must remember that the clock is a technology, and unless and until we ourselves become machines also, the precious dimension of lived time experience is always going to be there. The trick is to recognise and nurture it.

Nonetheless things do look pretty bad, time-wise, and especially today. What happens to the clock's power over us, for example, when you make a phone call to someone halfway around the world? Not so very long ago, such a phone call would still have a clock time dimension. Being an expensive thing to do, the caller (if not the 'callee') would be calculating the passing seconds and minutes as cents and dollars. Not anymore. With the right app on your smartphone, a call to someone 10,000 miles away will cost you nothing. What time governs now? It may be 10.10 am where I am and 6.10 pm where my friend is. However, the clock and its time zones have become irrelevant because in our connecting, and in our networking more broadly, we are creating and living in not simply a new technological age, but in a new form of time – the time of the network. Just as clock time has pushed lived time aside for generations of human beings since the Industrial Revolution, what I've elsewhere called 'network time' is now making a bid for the time consciousness of you and me. This does not make the time of the clock (or even the time zone) completely redundant, of course. Seconds, minutes, hours and days still have a major part to play in our lives. But network time adds another dimension to our temporal experience; it also obscures, or buries even more deeply, the lived time that is the time of you and me. As I said, however, that time is always going to be there somewhere, obscured and latent. We just need to look for it that much harder now.

We are only at the very threshold of the digital age. In less than a generation our digital environment has already come such a very long way. I first used the internet in 1995, when I was working as a shelf-filler in the University of Glasgow Library, and was singularly unimpressed by how slow and uninteresting it seemed to be – even when there was nothing remotely like it for me to compare it with. The internet nearly failed in the late 1990s. It bounced back as all-singing all-dancing Web 2.0 around 2002 and made Facebook possible. Since then it has colonised almost every part of society, and a great deal of the life of the individual. Has this been progress? Well, you have to ask first, 'what do you mean by progress?' If it means that speed and automation and convenience and sheer computing power has given us all an easier and more stress-free life, then I don't think so. If it means that the early promise of more time for leisure and creativity and to simply be with each other more, face-to-face as human beings, then again, I have to say no. Wherever progress may lie in our post-modern world, it is not in the realms of an easier life or having more time to be ourselves and to realise whatever potential you and I individually have.

The coming years and decades will bring more changes in how we communicate, how we produce and consume, how we live, love and learn. One true and constant element, however, is the computer, the hinge technology upon which all future social change will turn. We need to understand its role and function today, especially as it affects the everyday relationship with time.

2

DIGITAL LIFE

FOR ALL DIGITAL life's alleged benefits, the thing to remember is that we didn't choose it for ourselves. Or very few of us did. Before the mobile phone became ubiquitous, I for one wasn't hankering after it. Prior to their appearance in our lives, I don't recall ever saying, or hearing anyone else say, 'I wish I had some kind of beautiful supercomputer that would fit into my hand, which I could use to see and speak to almost anyone, anywhere, instantly and for free.' Maybe kids who were addicted to *Star Trek* or the tech geeks who got the internet started in the 1970s had such thoughts, but they would have been a marginal, visionary bunch.

Mobile-phone-shaped supercomputers duly sprang upon us, as if out of thin air. They appeared in high-street shops, in supermarkets, on eBay and on Alibaba. A prospering black market in stolen or lost mobile phones grew just as rapidly. This was as inevitable as sunset tonight because there was, and will continue to be, a large and greedy market for them. Many long for the release day of each new model and then stand excitedly in line to buy them, no matter how over priced they might be. But never did we demand them, and never did we freely choose to buy them. We just have to have them. Which is different.

We acquire these products because of two kinds of pressure: economic and peer. Peer pressure is the least influential, and we can assign to this the role of brand pressure. For young people especially, the phone they display – whether it's an Apple or Samsung or Huawei or Google device – really depends upon whether they are a leader or follower of fashions. Cost feeds into this as well, of course, but there's no shortage of people who put themselves needlessly in hock to get the particular must-have phone at the time to display it to the world in order to express a particular identity. In some cases, like the choice between Nike or adidas trainers, peer pressure can make a choice seem almost like an existential decision. But it's not. And neither is peer pressure the most powerful pressure that pushes us all inexorably toward the realm of the digital: boring old economics is.

Digital life is, above all, economic life. Earlier, I made the comparison between the car and the phone as the essential item today. For most of the twentieth century, the car was the undisputed champion. Whole continents, such as North America, had their physical environment – and the people who lived in them – permanently shaped by the car. In Mike Davis's book *City of Quartz*, he explains how Los Angeles, for example, was designed with the idea that white-collar workers of the 1950s could travel from home to office with hardly any need to walk. This is part of the reason why we became overweight. But certain industries also grew from such a modern lifestyle. Corporate leviathans such as General Motors, Ford, Mobil Oil and Esso became not only the largest corporations in the United States, but some of the biggest in the world – even bigger than many national economies in dollar value terms. Nonetheless, although a car was a universal marker of success, millions of people could either not afford to buy one, or chose not to own one. One way or the other, they could still lead a normal life without a car, walking or cycling or using public transport to shop, travel, commute to work and so on.

But, as I said, it is not as easy to choose to be free of digital life. Indeed, to be part of the global flow of information is considered a fundamental human right by the United Nations, just like the basic right to food, water and shelter. And without access to digital life, it becomes difficult, if not impossible, to exercise the basic economic right to work for a living. Today, if you are an unemployed adult without a mobile phone or active social media life, then getting a job has become much harder. Employers use Facebook to find workers, and workers use Facebook to swap tips on where the jobs are. LinkedIn and a range of other apps serve much the same purpose. This is just how it is now. The choice to not have a phone therefore becomes a difficult one to sustain, even if you are lucky enough to have a secure job.

To be digitally uncontactable is to be practically invisible. The standard nine-to-five occupation has all but disappeared, especially in the new forms of work that are being created. Many workers are now expected to be flexible; they need to work online from home or from hot-desks, or are tenuously engaged on contracts, projects, and so on. All this means you need to be always on, around the clock – suddenly, that timekeeping device is no longer so important. And if you want to strike out for independence and be your own boss as a butcher or baker or artisan brewer, you will be barely noticeable – and most likely fail – without an interesting-looking website, a busy and witty Twitter account, and a much-liked Facebook page. Similarly, for the growing army of people who work in the gig economy, like those hustling in the brave new world of Airbnb, Uber, TaskRabbit, and so on, an always-on phone and laptop is the only way to stay afloat.

Karl Marx told us that the daily grind of economic life exerts a 'silent compulsion' over human affairs. This is not physical compulsion, by force, as in the days of slavery and serfdom. It's the simple compulsion exerted by the economic world all around us, the world we were all born into: the pressure to work to pay the rent, to feed the kids, and have some kind of social life – not to mention the need to be able to buy the next must-have phone or computer. What this silent compulsion does achieve, both in Marx's time and ours (though with much less fuss in our own – that is to say, without any barricade-erecting excitement from the workers), is what Marx went on to describe as the 'subjection of the labourer to the capitalist'.

Marx's phrase sounds very nineteenth century and out of date today. Our own world, you might say, is different. No longer do evil, top-hatted plutocrats stalk the planet with bags of money and silver-topped canes to beat the poor with. Google's corporate maxim 'don't be evil' supposedly expresses the new, cool zeitgeist. These guys don't even wear suits. And it is true that since nineteenth century workers rebelled against the high-handedness of your average plutocrat, life improved a lot over the twentieth century. Democratic government and organised labour brought the over-rich and over-powerful a bit more into line, even to the point of a nascent social democracy in Western Europe and North America, where the parties of the working class became the most powerful agents of change in society. So much so that by the middle of the century, Marx's subjection began to look a little more like an equal partnership. For example, British Prime Minister Harold Macmillan, himself a scion of a huge publishing house, could cheerfully express this sense of being all in it together when he told the Brits in 1957 that 'most of our people have never had it so good.' And, going into the swinging 1960s, people believed him.

But if you think about that even for a little bit, there is little sense of partnership between us and the titans of Silicon Valley today. For all their Crocs-wearing demeanor, the high-tech inheritors of the mantle of General Motors stand aloof and detached from our interests. We're kind of on our own now. Governments across the world have vacated much of the scene and outsourced economic life to the mysteries of the free market. Low-tax regimes around the world mean that the same governments are reducing themselves to fiscal beggary. They're begging for ideas, too, and feel no shame in going to Silicon Valley to solicit opinion on how to cure world poverty, or infectious diseases like malaria. What this amounts to is a feeble admission from our once-democratic institutions of the unsubstantiated belief that high-technology (or the donated profits from it) can work better than political will when it comes to improving people's lives.

Right now (and this may easily change), Apple is king of capitalism, with undeniable market power and an unfathomable product-line cachet. The tech giant is the most valuable company in the world and has more ready cash in the bank than some countries do. And not just, say, the government of Burkina Faso. That would be no contest. Apple has more debt-free dollars to draw upon than the US government itself. This is unprecedented. The company is so awash with hard cash, in fact, that it struggles to know what to do with it all.

If governments have turned their backs on the historic partnership with people and business, then unions have been placed on the endangered list in most countries as well. Workers, not least those who actually make phones and laptops, are now mainly unorganised and scattered. People can't fight back effectively even if they want to. The lack of balance or partnership is reflected in the products that Silicon Valley make and sell to us; they are like little pieces of magic – things that work, but most of us have no idea how they work. But, by contrast, Apple, Facebook, Amazon, and others know intimately how you and I work. Through their data-collecting algorithms, they are able to shape our wants and needs and fears in ways so powerful (and so secret) that the scale of it is actually difficult to gauge. Steve Jobs had no difficulty, though, in appreciating his powerful position, and was arrogant enough to be frank about it. In 1997, before the first iPod even rolled off the production line in China, destined for a world that hadn't actually asked for it, he declared, 'A lot of times, people don't know what they want until you show it to them.' Not much sense of partnership here, then.

It is difficult to prove that Silicon Valley manufactures digital snake oil. That would take a different kind of book. The key questions are hard, and they reach deep into social, cultural and philosophical matters. Anyway, millions upon millions of subjects of digital life don't think to call for a boycott of eBay, or hold mass rallies to trample upon their iPhones, as Vietnam vets once did with their medals and draft cards. Not yet, at least. In the main, people love their phones, tablets, laptops and the app-rich world they create for them. But a little research and a little reflection will always turn up little chinks of insight into what might be a more accurate state of affairs in digital life. I give you an example at random – well, not really random, but derived from my interest in computers and education that goes back a few years. It's about the Waldorf School, which, like Steiner Schools, offers alternative teaching based upon a more holistic pedagogy that gives equal weight to intellectual, practical and artistic subjects. Waldorf of the Peninsula is a campus in Silicon Valley, established in 1984. Employees from Apple, Google, HP and other local companies send their kids to this exclusive college. So what? you may say. Well, this particular school has a complete ban on digital technology in class – it even discourages its privileged charges from using them at home. It's more than a little ironic, it seems to me, that those who shape our lives profoundly through the products they design and sell want their children to have very different lives to us, even ensuring their kids avoid digital life like it was some kind of disease. As one article tells it:

> [At the Waldorf School,] ... teachers ... prefer a more hands-on, experiential approach to learning that contrasts sharply with the rush to fill classrooms with the latest electronic devices. The pedagogy emphasises the role of imagination in learning and takes a holistic approach that integrates the intellectual, practical and creative development of pupils.

Doesn't that irony just make you love your phone even more? Sarcasm aside, the point is that not many people know about this little hypocrisy. Even if they did, we seem so invested in digital life that it probably wouldn't matter much anyway. But it does matter; it matters for all of us. We have a responsibility to ourselves and our children to think reflectively and critically about digital life so to be more empowered in the choices we make about it. At the time of writing this, it was reported that the education authorities in England had axed the teaching of Art History as an A-level subject because it was deemed 'too soft'. Too soft for what? For understanding about the role and function of aesthetics in human life, a sustaining element of what it is to be human, at least since the time when our ancestors daubed their lives and culture on the walls of the Lascaux Caves in France seventeen thousand years ago?

These digital devices, which appear to be the equivalent of snake oil, in fact offer us so much – yet there is a level of insidiousness of which its creators are more than aware. All the while, we have become so entrenched in this digital life that we cannot escape it.

Now, no one would admonish people, even the well-heeled of Silicon Valley, for doing what's best for their kids. But the question arises: is there something about computers, about life inside digital life, that they're not telling us? Something that deserves more of our attention and scrutiny, something that perhaps calls for a little bit of prudence, a little bit of caution? I think there is, and we need to think some more about the parameters of freedom and choice in our digital lives.

•

Marshall McLuhan was a philosopher of media in the 1960s. He was a lanky, suit-wearing hippy before the scruffy hippies came on to the scene, and one of the very few North American intellectuals who was also something of a celebrity. In *Understanding Media* (1964), McLuhan argued that technologies act on our bodies in extremely powerful ways, functioning primarily as 'extensions' to them. A way of understanding what he means is by thinking of the telescope, for example, as an extension of the eye, or the automobile as an extension of the legs, or the hammer of the arm, and so on. Media technologies do the same. However, instead of extending our physical bodies into space, mobile phones, social media and the internet more broadly extend our minds into both space and time. That sounds like freedom, right?

Recently, I was sitting on a tram in Melbourne, on my way home from work. Looking over the shoulder of the young girl in front of me, I could see that she was on a Facetime conversation on her phone with a person who was probably her mother. They were speaking in a language I didn't understand, but if I could, I would have been distracted from what was actually going on. McLuhan is famous for his aphorism 'the medium is the message', and what I was witnessing was an example of it occurring in front of me. On the screen of her big Samsung, with amazing pixel-definition, the older woman was smiling and looking slightly downward, as if to a laptop on a table or bench. She was apparently in a kitchen at home with a tea towel in one hand, drying crockery taken from a steaming dishwasher – yes, I could even make out the steam rising from the dishwasher's open door! They were both chatting happily and (to me) incomprehensibly. What was clear to me, though, was an example of McLuhan's little maxim. The message was not the content of their conversation, which was in any case their own business, but was the medium that enabled the dialogue: the technologies they were using, and the astonishing capacity it gave them to easily traverse the planet using little supercomputers and the internet to connect with each other. This was, and is, the true message.

This young girl was reaching out and extending herself into a virtual space and a network time. However, by co-creating this virtual space and time, the media the girl was interacting with did something else, too: the technology reached into her own self. By shrinking time and space through her phone, she was changed by the action. She became a point, or node, in the sprawling global networks of communication, and was participating in digital life. Her mind effortlessly accommodated the vast physical distance between where she was sitting on the rattling tram and where her mother stood drying cups. As dwellers of this digital life, we take this astounding technological feat for granted and do not fully give credit to what is occurring every time we communicate like this. That is, we create and colonise virtual space and time, and this virtuality, in turn, colonises our psyche – colonises us.

My fellow passenger on the tram was changed by her action, as we all are when we connect to digital life. We can see this in the perceptual sense, where, with a few jabs at her screen, her mother appeared as if by magic from half a world away. In fact, magic is an interesting way to think about what is happening. I'm not thinking of magic in a Harry Potter sense, but in the way that we relate to technology, especially computers. It's magic in that we don't really understand what is going on; most of us have not the faintest idea how a mobile phone or laptop or any device actually works to shrink time and space into the palms of our hands.

The sci-fi writer and cosmologist Arthur C. Clarke wrote in the 1970s that '[a]ny sufficiently advanced technology is indistinguishable from magic.' At some level of consciousness, that's how we see computers and what they enable. In scientific jargon, they call it black boxing, and the term describes how some technologies, like computers, are rendered invisible through their own technical success. In other words, they work so well that we don't know, and don't think we need to know, about how they work beyond their surface functionality. But that attitude comes at the cost of understanding – both of the technology and what it does to us.

The technology we use transforms us in ways that we are only beginning to appreciate. Sherry Turkle is a psychologist who has spent several decades looking at what computer-based communication does to people. She has, like McLuhan, good turns of phrase that spring up in her writing in the shape of ready-made and illuminating aphorisms. One such, from her book (with an equally epigrammatic title) *Alone Together: Why we expect more from technology and less from each other*, is that the computers that construct our digital lives act as 'the architects of our intimacies', meaning that digital life gets right inside us and affects us at the deepest levels of the self. Examples from her fieldwork can sometimes induce pangs of guilt in the reader, such as when she describes children running to greet their parents at the school gate at home time. Turkle sees what we all would, if we looked: kids pouring happily through the gates only to see their mum or dad – not with open arms and big, welcoming smile – as an unfocused parent who is busy texting or browsing or talking on the mobile, and who carries on distractedly whilst shepherding the child into the car. Often, I myself have seen parents in the park pushing their child on a swing with one hand and scrolling through Instagram or some such with the other. The more you think about that, the more depressing it becomes.

There's a funnier version of this horrible non-communication at the physical level in those Windows Phone 7 ads that were screened in 2010, where people going about their normal lives are too distracted by their phones, and so walk into trees, fall over things, ignore the people they are with and so on. Their point here (and Microsoft missed their intended mark by a mile) was that their new software would make using your phone so efficient that you would have time to look up and notice the tree in front of you. But, of course, such efficiency in processing power and overall phone functionality means that we only use them more and become addicted to digital life even more.

Addiction is a strong word. But then internet addiction is a recognised clinical condition nowadays, with thousands of people around the world rendered socially dysfunctional in various ways by computer games, online pornography and other distractions. If internet addiction is not computer technology acting as the architects of our intimacies, then I don't know what is. I said before, the supercomputer in our pocket has a hold over us. It's psychological – but it's also chemical and neurological. Who has not been irritated sitting in a pub or café with a group of friends, when several have their phones out, texting or scrolling or generally not being there at all? Or, if they are less ill-mannered, they nonetheless put the phone on the table in front of them and glance at it repeatedly, tic-like, as an OCD sufferer might? Or, when it rings, they will instantly break off from what they are saying or doing, and snatch at it quickly and greedily? Maybe it's just that I am tedious company (wholly possible, I have to admit). But it's far too widespread for that; just go to a café and look around you. Apprehensive souls do sometimes push back, but not very much, and to little effect. I've seen door signs in the more traditional drinking establishments in Glasgow and elsewhere that proclaim: No Wi-Fi: Talk to Each Other! But go inside, and guess what?

So, what's going on? In our brain, the organic chemical dopamine is produced to act as a neurotransmitter – it sends signals to and from nerve cells. This process has its pathways in brain architecture and has specific tasks in the nervous system. One major role is the reward-motivated behaviour function. This creates feelings of pleasure or desire and motivates us to seek these out more and more. Dopamine is an addictive chemical. Neurologists have discovered that when your phone rings, or buzzes with a text, you get a little shot of dopamine in the brain. With more phone and social media use, dopamine loops can then kick in, where the hit of dopamine from your partner's texts or your friend's calls leaves you wanting more – so you check the phone more and more, seeking the next hit. Of course, it doesn't even have to ring or vibrate for us to reach for it. We check it unconsciously (which is a sign that we are probably in the loop). And we check it a lot. A US survey in 2018 estimated that the average 18 to 35-year-old will do it 150 times a day. Not many get this number of actual calls or texts, but we have learned to check for it automatically, subconsciously, always anticipating another hit of dopamine. And scientists tell us that neural activity is higher when we anticipate rewards – higher than when we actually get one.

I'll be devoting the next chapter to this idea of anticipation. But, to expand on how it relates to digital communication and dopamine, something interesting happens in our heads and in the loop of dopamine. The Merriam-Webster defines anticipation as 'the act of preparing for something'. That's clear enough. To anticipate is to think about something occurring in the future and to make some form of physical or mental arrangement for that event. Anticipation can generate all kinds of feelings: it can be pleasurable or it can be business-like or it can be dread-inducing.

The thing about the dopamine loop is that it affects us when we are offline; but its provenance, its trigger, is from inside digital life itself. So, both online and off, we increasingly seek the dopamine hit from digital-based anticipation. This means we are becoming constantly engaged in anticipation, waiting for a ringtone or seeking ways to ameliorate the feeling by going online in search of the hit, by making a call, checking Facebook, or scrolling through Buzzfeed, or whatever.

What are we thinking about when we are constantly anticipating? We could be thinking about anything, of course. But held in the grip of dopamine-chasing anticipation, there are things that we can't do, or can't do as well as we once did. For example, we can't easily concentrate on the present – the thing that we are doing in the here-and-now, such as greeting a child at the school gate or having direct eye-contact and conversation with friends in the pub. We can't easily concentrate on the past either; it becomes difficult to reflect upon how something worked out for you (or didn't) yesterday, or last year, or twenty years ago. To be unable to think about a conversation, or action, or promise or commitment made in the past means that these events may be lost to a relatively inactive memory. The sphere of public memory becomes problematic too. How can we be active citizens if we don't know much about politics, about history, and so on? The dynamic memory that Proust and Murakami wrote about – the memory that 'reveals itself' and which resides somewhere in all of us – becomes closed off, or is somewhere we can't go because it takes conscious time and effort. We can't go there because we are too busy, not simply with the mobile phone (this is only the bridgehead device), but with all of digital life: the virtual space of social media and work and entertainment and everything else. This virtual space is where we spend much of our time. And even when we're offline, our anticipation of it connects us to it just as if we were online. This reasoning is, for us, an interesting, but also wholly unanticipated, aspect of the zero-sum equation.

All this heightened neural activity would be good if we were in control of it. It would mean, to quote Murakami again, that, '[t]he pure present is an ungraspable advance of the past devouring the future. In truth, all sensation is already memory.' Temporally speaking, we would be free to be ourselves, away from the disciplining rhythms of the clock and the addictions of the network. But we're not. Increasingly, more of us inhabit what has been termed a constant present, where the here-and-now dominates our thinking and acting. To put it more simply, we've become chronically distracted.

It was just this kind of distractedness that prompted me to check myself into the *Rossini* and write this book on digital detox. The problem of distraction, and the information overload that comes from it, is what the media scholar Clay Shirky called a 'filter failure'. He suggested – and I agree – that all we had to do was to concentrate on getting the right mental filter in place and make sure it worked well enough to winnow out all the rubbish, letting through only what we actually need and want.

For years and years, it never occurred to me to check my own filter. And yet I was being gradually pulled into digital life and its always-on and always-now temporality. This is not exciting or productive, but uncreative and distracting. Here's an everyday example: I come into work with a plan to research something for a class, so I switch on the computer and go online to find out from Pew Research how much time, on average, people spend online (it's over 27 hours a week, and that's not counting phone time). But, soon after getting on to Google, I find myself drawn to my bookmarks, checking the news first. Same old stuff. Then I think, How did Celtic fare overnight? Lost. What happened? I skim a match report. My eyeballs then helplessly slide to the left of the screen to see an ad bursting into motion with something about a movie I watched the trailer for yesterday (yes, Virginia, there is a Google tracking algorithm that remembers these things). But the link above it grabs my attention first, so I click on that instead. It's about a drunk guy carrying a bike over a railway track. He was filmed on a smartphone, being saved from an onrushing train by a 'hero' who risked his own life by pushing the drunk guy off the tracks with about two seconds to spare. This gets me thinking about the weather and bikes and whether to cycle home that night or take the train (rain is forecast). I check the Weather.com app on my phone, again. Thoughts of bikes take me to a cycling website just to look again at a bike I've been interested in. But, of course, the website is plastered with ads. I click on a pulsating ad for cycling shoes, and a video plays with familiar background music. What is that tune? Yes, I think, it's Marvin Gaye's *I Want You* – not an original choice by the advertisers. So I Google it and, after two or three attempts that are frustrated by copyright issues, I finally click on the YouTube link and watch the video, something that 2,432,568 others have done since it was uploaded in April 2010. I watch it for its duration of four minutes and thirty-one seconds. Then I see an eBay ad for a toaster like the model I was browsing for last week, to replace the one in my kitchen that makes a buzzing sound. Google has no problems with its memory. My fire-hazard toaster makes me think, by association, of tea. This leads to thoughts of the constant spam-mail I get from T2, which makes me think about my email (that I've subconsciously been avoiding), so I switch it on and see that there are seventy-seven new messages since last night – mostly spam, but you need to go through them. And on it goes.

This is distraction. This is precisely what digital life is consciously set up to do by its Silicon Valley creators: to keep people online and keep them moving whilst there. That's how it makes money, why it exists. There's no other way that it could exist. And so, more than one hour after sitting down with the intention to work, I still haven't got to the Pew Research website. I get there eventually, but only after wasting an hour or so in shallow and empty and uncreative pursuits – doing all the things the lucky creatives at the Waldorf School of the Peninsula get to miss.

Thinking vaguely that I might have an issue, I quietly began to sound out colleagues and friends and students. Wearing the mask of a researcher, I inquired whether, by any remote chance, they experienced distraction in their online lives. They did. Almost without exception, the people I spoke to were anxious about their relationship with mobile phones, social media, the internet and digital life more broadly. I discovered from my conversations that distraction at work, of the kind I just described, has knock-on effects. I sort of knew this anyway from my own experience, but to hear it from others was both comforting and concerning. To waste an hour or three in the workday meant having to catch up some-where else in the day. So, an hour or more on eBay, YouTube and Facebook meant an hour or so emailing at night, or reading something for a class, in bed. It meant an hour not spent with your partner after dinner, or with your kids, or just by yourself. There're only so many hours in the day, so it's zero-sum again.

The zero-sum nature of measured time means that things increasingly don't get done, or don't get done properly. Emails aren't responded to, important tasks can't be given proper attention and so are done badly, or not done at all. My sociologist friend in Holland quoted a CEO of a major Dutch company to me as saying that he regularly 'sweeps things under the carpet' because he has no time for them, instead hoping they will just go away. Mostly, of course, like emails in your inbox or bills in your letterbox, they won't.

When you are distracted, there's also less opportunity to put time into face-to-face relationships, to invest the time needed to nurture and enrich them and make them a source of happiness and pleasure in your life. Just to put this idea into a little bit of context, there are indications that living distractedly in daily life has its zero-sum effect upon our sex lives too. In Japan, for example, there has been a large-scale 'flight from human intimacy' that is contributing to the disastrously low birth rates in that country. A survey in 2010 indicated that 61% of single men and 49% of women aged 18-34 were not in any kind of romantic relationship, a rise of almost 10% in five years. Another study found that almost a third of people under thirty had never dated at all. One of these reports also noted that young Japanese with 'smart phones in hand ... admit they spend far more time communicating with their friends via online social networks than seeing them in the flesh.' It goes on to describe how one interviewee for the article 'spent the past two years obsessed with a virtual game that lets her act as a manager of a sweet shop'. No time for sex when there are virtual customers waiting.

There is a short film that you can see on Vimeo (from Canada, I think), which is called *A Handy Tip for the Easily Distracted*. I sometimes show it to my students because it makes a common point about how to deal with digital distraction in a funny way. Essentially, the female character in the three-minute film makes her phone and her laptop hard to get at in her flat by placing teetering containers of liquid over them. It's a bit like the alcoholic who removes all signs of liquor from the house and avoids bars. The film is witty and my students like it, but I show it to get them to think about what it is saying. It acknowledges the problem of digital distraction but implies that it's your problem – something you need to deal with yourself. In this case, the solution is to adjust your mental filter by going cold turkey and making the phone and laptop difficult to reach. The issue, thus, quickly becomes one of personal morality, of personal weakness, of sufficient self-control, such that distraction is an individual's problem.

Is it that simple? I don't think so. The treatment of widespread addictions such as drug and alcohol is well understood in the medical and psychology fields. Even so-called internet addiction of the kind some gamers and pornography users are affected by is considered clinical and pathological, and treatments are being experimented with. But what about the routine dopamine-chase that affects millions of people in everyday life, or the uncountable masses who stress about time wasted by chronic distraction (at levels which people find difficult to deal with and even recognise in themselves)? What about turning the morality question around and thinking of the chronically distracted as victims instead? But victims of what?

What about being victims of time-theft? Time is being taken from us by systems and technologies and logic that we actually know very little about. We do know that computers can process data, in the form of bits and bytes, with great efficiency. But, as I said before, not many of us asked for these things – these phones, laptop computers, apps, and all that they make possible. What they do socially and culturally, individually and collectively, is a much, much fuzzier picture.

Something that is also understood, even at the level of the layperson, is that our computer-driven world seems to be getting faster. As the journalist James Gleick puts it in his book *Faster: The Acceleration of Just About Everything*, 'unoccupied time is vanishing.' Unoccupied time, the subjective time that we once managed to keep for ourselves, is being filled (or stolen) by digital life. It is a life where digital distraction packs so much more (online) activity into every hour, every day.

We have given computers so much latitude so quickly and so easily. We have allowed their logic to be inserted into almost every area of economy, culture and society, with hardly a serious question raised. Whatever happened to the Royal Commission into the Social Effects of the Introduction of Cellular Telephony in the States and Territories of Australia? Or the US Federal Commission into the Pedagogical Consequences of the Untrammelled Introduction of the Internet into Schools and Colleges? Nothing – they were never commissioned. Across the world, we just went ahead and absorbed technology into our lives – and were pushed from behind all the way by the data merchants who said it would all be fantastic.

Most of us acquiesce in the process because, at least at some level of cognition, we imagine that computers radiate a miraculous power in the world. The social effect of computer networks that create digital life is the real black box, the core part of computing that we know works in that it makes communication easy, but is a mystery beyond that. Though there are plenty of ideas and research in the field, it is ultimately still a mystery.

Our lack of understanding of the technology and its tendency to isolate us as it connects us leaves us in a rather invidious position; we become the weakest link in the global chain of network communication. We are the weakest link because, when we turn our face toward a laptop screen or a mobile touchscreen, we are confronting an immense technological system against which our powers of resistance are relatively puny. As Robert McBride argued in the pre-digital age in his 1967 book *The Automated State*, computers are a 'new force in society' that 'reach out' to shape it in new ways with their unprecedented technological power. This technology reaches out with the backing of government and big businesses, who create digital life and spread the silent compulsion that manages to bring almost all of us into its orbit. Alone with a screen, in bed or in the pub, it hardly matters. What matters is that we are exposed to the power and reach of a corporate-controlled digital life we neither asked for, nor constructively thrive in, as creative, independent and truly social beings.

And just when you thought it could not possibly get any worse, it can and does, every minute of every day. The philosopher John Gray, writing on the human effects of technology, argued that '[s]cience increases human power – and magnifies the flaws in human nature.' Take a minute to think about that statement. Think about the flaws in human nature that are being magnified and propagated over and across digital life every nanosecond of every day. To name just a few examples: child pornography; trolling; cyberbullying; beheading videos; predictive policing; government surveillance; phishing; revenge porn; cyberstalking; astroturfing; piracy; government censorship; identity theft; dark web illegal marketplace; fake news; deep fakes; plagiarism; online fraud; clickbait; ransomware; malware dissemination; algorithmic tracking; hate speech; extortion scams; click farms; hacking computer systems; internet gambling; the spread of DIY terrorism; virus dissemination; personal information theft; Distributed Denial of Service Attack; cyber defamation; invasion of privacy; face recognition; drug trafficking; and cyberwarfare. The list is not exhaustive and additional human flaws are digitalised and magnified and spread online with each new day. But then again, there are no days on the internet – just networked people with phones and laptops, trying to find meaning or just trying to survive.

This is digital life. This is the online environment we both create and confront on our own as we look at the screen that is our threshold to virtual life. This is what I wanted to detox from – all this, and Marvin Gaye on YouTube.

3

ANTICIPATE

LIVE ON the coast in the south-western part of Melbourne. Our family's white clapboard house is quite close to a spot where the massive West Gate Bridge stretches high over the Yarra River, casting its long shadow over the water just where it flows out into Port Phillip Bay. The bridge connects our neighbourhood to the city centre and, further on, by way of the popularly-despised tollway express, to the traditionally more upmarket eastern and southern suburbs across the bay. With an enclosed sea area of nearly 200 square kilometres, Port Phillip Bay is extremely large, so much so that it stretches, often choppily, way out from Melbourne to beyond the horizon. When its length is finally exhausted, its water opens onto an always turbulent Bass Strait at a narrow and shoal-filled neck called 'The Rip', which is a triangular area of water between the land points of Point Nepean, Shortlands Bluff and Point Lonsdale.

That little topography lesson consisted of facts I sort of knew about, but I had to look them up to make sure, because I never thought much about what existed beyond my immediate physical environs. Yet, you can live in a street, in a town, and know very little about it apart from its barest facts. You might not know much, for example, about its distinctive features, its rhythms, its eccentricities, its human and natural ecologies. It's a cliché that we no longer know our neighbours. But is it even accurate to call those living close to us neighbours any longer? Neighbours. The term evokes an arms-folded-over-a-shared-fence familiarity, where you chat about the weather, about problems with slugs, how to attract more bees, or about old Ray from four doors down, who hasn't been seen since Monday, and so one of us will knock on his door to make sure he's ok. Digital life relieves us of that particular social burden, too. And old Ray could have had a heart-attack in the meantime. In terms of our ability to manage information, this is the zero-sum game once more. Instagram, the mobile phone, Facebook's newsfeed, the black hole for time that is Netflix, and all the rest, take away the time for getting to know who's in the street.

Digital life can exact a psychic toll, furnishing consequences that we give little thought to, because we are 'too busy' or if we are more honest, too distracted. One consequence is what Paul Virilio, writing about computers and the speeding up of life, called 'a fundamental loss of orientation.' I take this to mean a lack of spatial awareness: a state of not really paying any attention, real attention, to where you live, or to what is immediately around you. If we no longer know our neighbours, then full-on digital life will see to it that we know less about our neighbourhood as well.

The general lack of spatial awareness is connected to the lack of temporal awareness. And so, I know my street and my suburb primarily as point A, which is the starting point to a point B, which could be anywhere from my university office, 21 kilometres away, to my mum's house in Wishaw, near Glasgow, which Google tells me is 16,965 kilometres to the north-west. Point A, my house, my street, is just a coordinate to the digitally toxified mind. It's a space (not a place) to travel from in order to go somewhere else, to another coordinate, this time more appropriately a coordinate, because it is, by definition, not where you live; a space unknown. My usual A-to-B travel is, like that of most people, the daily commute to work. I do it by bicycle, which has the meagre advantage of allowing me the conceit of being able to feel superior to the texting and talking and even laptop-using souls lurching along in the fuming columns of traffic.

In many ways, the bike has been a liberator. If you do it for long enough, then the process – the actual travelling and direction-finding bits, like the intricate balance that is required to ride the thing in the first place – becomes automatic. Even riding in traffic becomes subconscious. The conscious mind is then freed in that commuting time, driving or on the train; freed from intrusive media, from vacuous radio stations, too loud music, or chattering passengers, so as to think. This is when you can have your best thoughts. To work out problems, little or big. When cycling, I go into a headspace I rarely go to any other time. Often, I'll have flashes of insight into something I've been thinking about, a sudden awareness that can seem so important at the time, that I'll pull over, reach into my pocket for a notebook and pencil, or iPhone, and record it. This doesn't mean, of course, that I become all-knowing and omnipotent on my bike. Just as often, I'll look later at what I've written or said, and wonder the hell I was thinking about. But that's another story.

Being on the bike can resurrect the spatial experience as well as the temporal. It can give you more of a connection with the physical route from A to B. I remember as a kid when I first went out into the countryside with a bike. The shimmering summer roads looked and felt beautiful as I rolled along on my bright red Raleigh, which was a girl's bike, but my mum got it for free from somewhere, so what can you do? But the roads also smelled awful, smelled of something you couldn't really define until you stopped for a rest. Then you realised: it was roadkill decomposing in the heat. A hedgehog, or rabbit, or sometimes a brown fox that wasn't quick enough and had been clattered by a vehicle: each or any knocked aside to die randomly, anonymously – an everyday death registered only by the crows. It's impossible to get that acute sense-awareness when thundering through the landscape in a car or bus. Travelling through Spain in 1937 whilst covering the Spanish Civil War, Ernest Hemingway preferred the two-wheeled, self-powered mode to get around the various battlefronts. He did this not only because he was more inconspicuous to snipers that way, camouflaged with the accoutrement of a local peasant, but also because it attached him to a geography he needed to know more deeply – in order to understand it more and so to survive it better.

> It is by riding a bicycle that you learn the contours of a country best, since you have to sweat up the hills and coast down them. Thus, you remember them as they actually are, while in a motor car only a high hill impresses you, and you have no such accurate remembrance of country you have driven through as you gain by riding a bicycle.

The 21-kilometre journey to my office doesn't have any contours to sweat up or to coast down. It is pan-flat. And neither does it offer much in the way of physical danger, beyond, that is, the probabilistic hazards that all cyclists face in built-up areas from drunken, or speeding, or texting, or distracted drivers. What part of my route positively glows with, though, is a very particular aura of mystery and exoticism and promise that probably escapes the preoccupied drivers travelling from A to B and back again.

The route I take down Footscray Road runs alongside Swanson Dock, the biggest container-shipping terminal in Australia. It is about the same size as the Kobe terminal in Japan, which is the third biggest in that country. So, it's massive. Growling lines of semi-trailers, those types built specially for containers, constantly come and go through its several large gates, cutting across the main road into the city as they go, thereby adding significantly to the stop-go traffic problem. It also has a railway line butting right up against it, so containers can be lifted straight from the ship, parked onto the quayside for a bit, and then quickly yanked up again and dropped onto a waiting train that will deliver them anywhere in the country. That part of it, the 24/7 loading and unloading, and the constant computerised choreography between container and crane in all weather and with hardly a human in sight, is fairly interesting, I suppose. It's part of the high-tech cutting edge of the container revolution that since the 1970s has transformed the planet – utterly. Today, computer centres and computerised machines, working in tandem with computerised ships with skeleton crews of perhaps only twenty-five people, deliver 90 per cent of everything that surrounds us, from the computer I write these words with to the car that will take me to the shops to buy all kinds of stuff that consumer life now demands. I'll talk a little bit more about this process later. But what really fascinates me and still causes me to look contemplatively through the traffic haze towards the docks, is the container carriers themselves: those beautiful, sometimes rusting, sometimes newly-painted, always massive, differently liveried and logoed vessels (as they are properly called) that float patiently under cranes busily going about their non-stop Lego-like stacking and unstacking routines.

Almost every day I see a new line of them: blue or grey or orange vessels tied up with their sterns facing the road. Like a trainspotter, I'll often stop my bike and walk over to the security fence to peer through. They are so close to Footscray Road that you can easily make out the vessel's name, let's say it's the AS *Magnolia*, and its 'flag of convenience', which for many of them, including this one, is Monrovia, a city in Liberia, and whose flag (which looks a bit like the US Stars and Stripes) it will fly. The flag of convenience is used, of course, to save money. The shipping company will pay less tax if they list the vessel in a tax haven that it has probably no intention of ever visiting. This is not so interesting. What does provoke interest, though, is that the vessel I'm looking at as I squint through the wire has just come from somewhere, with the aura of a distant place still enveloping it, and it will soon disappear from its berth at Number 4 Dock to travel, at an average speed of 17 knots, to somewhere else, somewhere not here, and therefore somewhere necessarily mysterious and exotic.

Now admittedly, in about twenty seconds I could have checked on my iPhone to see where the AS *Magnolia* has come from, how long it will be here for, and for where it is destined. But what would be the use of that? The aura and the enigma would evaporate and I'd be back on my bike, with the act of stopping, or even looking, rendered pointless. But if you put yourself in a particular frame of mind, then those container ships, those vessels that we all have seen but barely gave a thought to, reveal themselves to be actually something rather special. The idiom 'like a ship in the night' kind of touches on what I mean. It's the sense that container ships arrive largely unnoticed, and then steal away in just the same fashion. It's as if the ship and its crew don't actually exist. They are ghost ships with a ghost crew, both of whom you never see. Ship and crew are otherworldly in that they don't form part of normal life in the way that other forms of transport do, such as cars and buses and even aeroplanes. Neither do they form part of the time of the world and the routines that govern it.

Passing these phantoms every day and, importantly, noticing them and thinking about them, I began slowly to see them as a possible antithesis to digital life and its information overload. The vague idea began to grow in me around mid-2017, that a container ship could be a perfect place, one of the few relatively comfortable places, indeed, where I could try the self-experiment in digital detox. As I said before, not exactly *Into the Wild*, or a Christopher McCandless-type effort to be in contact with nature, but sufficiently different and unusual to provide some kind of test for me and my relationship with pervasive digital communication.

Part of my interest in container ships came from my academic interest in economic globalisation, the process that went into the making of the world into a single market place to service a single consumer space. A few years ago, someone put me on to a documentary by Los Angeles filmmakers Allan Sekula and Noël Burch called *The Forgotten Space*, which is about the container ship industry. In their notes for the film they write that 'our film is about globalisation and the sea, the "forgotten space" of our modernity.' They got me thinking more about what we tend not to think about at all. We don't think about the process of container ship transportation, yet the quality of our lives depends upon it totally. And because these ships and their work is invisible to most of us, we forget about them, and as a consequence we inhabit a fantasy world where space and time take on unreal dimensions. It is total fantasy, for example, to think that physical distance has been abolished because invisible cargo from an invisible ship, from China or wherever, magically materialises in the shops for us to buy and consume. And it is a fantasy for us to imagine that time (duration) has been done away with, just because in this world of seeming plenty you don't have to wait to buy the next pair of shoes, a mango in winter, a book of medieval poetry, no matter where in the world it comes from.

Sekula and Burch tell us that in 2010, one-hundred-thousand invisible ships with 1.5 million invisible seafarers connected the world in a network that transports just about anything you can think of. In 2010 the global financial crisis was taking its toll, with ghastly economic and social consequences. But things have picked up somewhat since then, and so the number of ships and seafarers in the 'forgotten space' is probably bigger today. Nonetheless, they do not loom any larger in our collective consciousness. Container ships, moreover, are no longer built in the West. And the workers who crew them, mostly, are not people we in the West might know, because they are from developing countries, such as India, the Philippines, and Bangladesh, and are hired solely because they are cheaper and less organised than their European or North American counterparts.

Digital life, through its time-pressures and distractions, abets these fantasies and our tendency to readily forget awkward or revealing truths. As Sekula and Burch put it:

> Those of us who travel by air, or who "go surfing" on the Web, scarcely think of the sea as a space of transport any more. We live instead in the age of cyberspace, of instantaneous electronic contact between everywhere and everywhere else.

After seeing their film and being reminded of it on my daily commute, the idea of being forgotten and invisible gradually heightened my sense of what might be possible as a temporary antidote to digital life. Forgetting is a kind of release, and to be invisible is a kind of freedom. I vaguely began to latch on to the idea of using the forgotten space of container ship transport as a way to become forgotten and invisible myself. I wanted to immerse myself in what I perceived to be the container ship's strange and unknowable spaces and times; to be way out at sea, travelling slowly, where I'm unable to see the land, and where the land and its pressures and commitments cannot reach me. Moving from point A to point B on a ship that cuts me off from all forms of digital communication seemed to be a potentially good way to detoxify my digital life. More importantly, it would also give me the opportunity to discover what the experience would do to my sense of time; to find out what subjective time, time away from the clock and the computer, really feels like. As I said earlier, I had already become convinced that our waking time is stolen from us every minute of every day by the time of the world. I wanted to use a container ship as a way to go looking for that time, and to find out what happens when (or if) you get it back. But how do you go about getting yourself on a container ship? Would it be possible? Is it legal? In my backpacking twenties, people I met sometimes talked about 'working your passage' as a cook or cleaner on a ship to get from London or Sydney to, say, Bombay or Rio. Nobody then seemed to know how to go about it. Can you do that kind of thing today? I still didn't know.

Coming home from work one cold and moonless night in August, I was cycling down Footscray Road and spied three new vessels in Number 4 Dock. Their ship lights glowed yellow, and the terminal's floodlights blazed a sodium orange. Night was lit up to allow the big orange and white DP World cranes to unload the containers. I stopped pedalling and pulled over because my front tyre seemed soft and I suspected a slow puncture and needed to check. I pressed the tyre with my frozen thumb and it gave like a marshmallow. There was nothing for it. I would need to pull out the wrapped-up spare inner-tube from my shirt back pocket and change it for the flat one. I thought, equably, that I'd had a good spell of four or five weeks without a puncture, and the law of averages meant that, like earthquakes in Tokyo, it's only a question of when, not if, the next one would happen. When was now, and I didn't really mind this time because it was an excuse to thaw my fingers a little and have a closer look at the ships that had come in. Usually I make a mental note of the ships' names as I pedal past, but unlike the trainspotter, I was never enough of an

Anorak to actually write them down. Normally, five minutes after seeing a new arrival, I couldn't have told you either its name or its owner. What mattered more to me was the idle daydream about foreign ports, splendid isolation, onboard life, sleeping in a cabin, maps of voyages, secret rooms, what the crew might be like, exotic food, and so on.

On that night, kneeling at the security fence trying to lever the front tyre from its rim, I looked up and made an instant, and what seemed to me a wholly rational and long-overdue, decision. I was going to somehow get on board a ship and do what I said we all needed to do, in my book *Age of Distraction*, and escape digital life to see what I could discover. And so, with no particular plan in mind, other than to somehow make the daydream a reality, I put down the inner-tube and reached for my notebook and pencil and began writing down the names of the ships. The first of the trio, from the left, was the MOL *Emissary*, a teal-blue painted container ship flagged in Hong Kong. In the middle was the French CMA CGM *Mozart*, dark-blue coloured and patriotically flagged in Marseille, its *tricolore* flapping slowly in the night air. Third was the CSL *Xin Pudong*, a dark-green and rusting ship with China Shipping Line written in large off-white letters across its starboard and registered in Shanghai. I thought vaguely that I could Google these ships, or later ones, get an email address, and write to their captain to ask if a 'researcher' could come aboard when you are next in Melbourne, please, and allow me to accompany you to wherever you might be going thereafter.

I cupped my left hand around my right fist and blew onto the tips of my fingers, left hand then right, then back again, to get some circulation back into them. I then quickly changed the inner-tube, pumped it up, wiped the black, sooty oil from my hands onto the damp grass, and got myself home. And, deciding to sleep on it, I thought I'd try to work out the logistics in the morning.

•

A question I had pondered for years without actually doing any-thing about it, I had answered for me after about ten minutes online the next day whilst still in bed. The web, it turns out, is awash with ways and means and testimonies about booking a passage on a container ship. It was all there. Passengers who blog about their trip, how to book it, the dos and don'ts of passenger life, mobile phone video tours of the ship made by those who had actually done it, tips on loneliness, seasickness, yellow fever, piracy, and so on. These noble and exotic vessels I gazed at every day on my commute, I discovered, were not just cargo ships going about their business, invisibly or otherwise. They were also, essentially, big floating taxis for hire. You could book a cabin (it already sounded exotic) to take you from anywhere to almost anywhere, with just your laptop and a credit card. As for writing directly to the captains, they are uncontactable. Somewhat more prosaically you have to book through an agent.

Sometimes, for no obvious reason, you just get seized by an idea. For me the notion of actually getting aboard what had until now been a distant object of faint love, had quickly passed its tipping point to become a mini-obsession. That's how it was when I woke the next day. Sitting up in bed and looking out the window onto a bleak Antipodean morning, I was still tired, but my thoughts were already out of bed and leaping forward in an ad hoc planning mode, casting about for indications for what I needed to do first.

Immediately, there was the tedious but necessary logistics of extricating myself from work commitments. Did I have enough leave? When would I need it? What about all the emails and commitments that would build up when I was away (about 700 odd, I calculated)? Could I simply ignore these? What about Kate and the kids? Would they (perhaps rightly) think it indul-gent to sail away on what might appear to them to be some kind of cruise? Was the cold turkey approach to be part of the detox experiment? Should I take a laptop so I could watch movies if things got desperate? Then there was the overarching question: am I making a big mistake? I could work through all my emails and commitments when I got back to work, so that wasn't really a problem, but mightn't the whole idea actually be a massive waste of time, and not proper research? After all, I hadn't discussed this professionally with anyone at the university. Moreover, there was always the danger that I could get bored, depressed, ill, anything. At this moment, my more decisive self cut in to arbitrate in this internal dialogue and decided that this was getting silly. Sweep it all aside, I told myself, and just get on with it.

I got up. Whilst the coffee-maker was percolating, I texted the office to say that I'd be working from home today. I powered down the phone, poured the espresso, put two slices of week-old sour-dough into the erratic toaster, and powered up the laptop sitting on the dining-room table. In less than three hours, including a family conference via text and voice calls, I was done: booked, paid-for, with confirmation documents to be sent overnight to me from far-flung Marseille. I was to board the French-flagged CMA CGM *Rossini* at Swanson Dock in six days' time, taking a middle-distance voyage from Melbourne to Singapore, via Sydney and Adelaide. I switched off the laptop and made some tea. The bout of fixation I was experiencing since the night before was giving way after the morning admin preoccupation to the very future oriented temporal experience of anticipation.

It would occur to me, later, that this new psychic state, that of anticipation, was perhaps the first obstacle to be overcome in the quest for digital detoxification. Anticipation can be a form of distraction, an uncontrolled form that exists in ordinary everyday life, but is supercharged by digital life. That dopamine loop mentioned earlier – expressed in our constant checking of the phone, hoping, anticipating, that it contains a message notification, or that it will sometime soon vibrate into life in our pocket, or that it is due anytime now to sing out with a ringtone that will reassure you that you are no longer alone, that somebody wants you – feels so good. For a couple of minutes, anyway.

Even when not seeking dopamine, the rush of anticipation exists in all of us as a non-rational process and is one we often find difficult to control. We seem to want the future to come to us now, no matter what the cost. But what is anticipation, if not the slightly hysterical feeling of wishing that the future be brought forward to right now, to the present, for us to have and hold?

The Harvard psychologist Philip Zimbardo, famous for his 1971 Stanford Prison Experiment, is also known for his work on what he calls 'future discounting'. Zimbardo has shown in psychological experiments that when you are offered the choice of, say, $100 now, or $150 a week from now, the majority of us will take the money now, thank you very much. His work has been replicated many times, across many cultures, giving it an interesting universality. This seems to be what we are like. The future, if not a time too unbearably long to wait for, is at least an insecure abstraction for many of us, as far as our reckoning of its outcomes goes, anyway. We discount the future because we feel, at some level, that uncertainty is likely to intervene to make that $150 seem risky. Uncertainty means that we are susceptible to projecting negative future scenarios. There could be a sudden tsunami, the person offering the $150 could give it to someone else, you might have an accident, she may change her mind, she might not have it to give next week. Anything could happen. Irrationality quickly inserts itself in our calculations about even the short-term future.

Having paid my fare electronically, electronically scanned my passport and attached it to the lengthy electronic indemnity forms I had to fill out, I was electronically confirmed: I was

going and going much sooner than my anticipation had anticipated. It was Tuesday, and I was to leave on Sunday – less than
a week. Anticipation of the slightly manic variety was beginning
to simmer in my head, and it wasn't so pleasant. I was still in
a toxified state in respect of my relationship to digital life. And
in this very short timeframe, anticipation had become magnified,
and took the form of what the American writer Ben Fountain calls
the 'Fantasy Industrial Complex' (FIC). This is where digital life
takes hold of ordinary temporal feelings, such as anticipation, and
refracts them through the internet. It sucks up your anticipations
and whips them up into something approaching a fever pitch.

I was getting excited, and not necessarily in a good way, as things
unfolded over the coming hours and days. Irrational might better
describe it. Anticipation can be constructive only if it has time
devoted to its reflective dimension. With sufficient time we can plan,
ensure, hedge, strategise, rationalise, weigh up the chances of certain
outcomes, and so on. Even in ordinary circumstances, that is to say,
in a pre-internet world, we still could anticipate in a more-or-less
controlled and rational way. An example: not so very long ago, one
could anticipate with pleasure a favourite movie that will be shown
at 9 pm on television on a given night. There was no compulsion
twenty years ago for immediate indulgence, because there was no
technology to bring it to me instantly. The VCR, in case you're
thinking, is more about convenience, and was not a technology of
impulse or distraction. Now we can watch the movie on YouTube,
or if copyrighted watch it through BitTorrent, or any number of
file-hosting services. No need to anticipate in the normal way any
longer. Convenience is not an issue here. The FIC is geared towards
instant gratification, the sating of any desire and the informational
framing of any thought that we might have about any subject.

Documentation for the trip, headed 'Partir en Cargo: Special
Conditions' duly arrived overnight by email from France. In

the endearing French fashion, it was verbose (possibly a Google translation into English) and very serious-sounding. Most of it was Terms and Conditions-speak, but a few things stood out that did little to mollify the 'what have I done?' state of anticipation that still had me unexpectedly in its grip. Booking a flight online doesn't merit any thought. You know what's to come because you have done it before, you know what to expect. However, this seemed both too easy and too hard to know if it would work out. And this instilled in me an unease stemming from a lack of control on my part. And part of me thought that behind all this was a phisher somewhere in Lagos.

Standing out from the pleonasms of the company documents was a capitalised and bolded (and brusque) proclamation which read: **NO DOCTOR ON BOARD!** Unnecessarily apostrophised, I thought, and thought also that flaming of this sort can only cause alarm. The omen-like phrase that there would be no physician ready to attend to my merest sniffle read like a warning-off, like a thinly-veiled way of saying 'don't even think about coming – it's far too dangerous!'.

I hadn't thought about such things before; not many of us in the rich West do, much. Life is a minefield of health hazards, some might say, and as my less-decisive self actually did. As I gazed at the bold, capitalised sentence, a seeming death sentence, or if not that, then at least a very nasty medical drama unfolding with a dreadful implacability, some 200 nautical miles from the nearest landfall. Five weeks alone with only self-diagnosis and self-medication to fall back on in the event of a disaster. The 'Partir en Cargo' did say that there would be a person trained in First Aid on board. But I did a First Aid course myself, one weekend a long time ago, and I know that I would be useless if called upon to first-aid someone today. Anticipation when looking at a warning sign can change rapidly into foreboding, which is another way of letting the future control you. And so, falling down a metal stairway in a storm would, I told myself, mean a certain broken neck. A helicopter would have to be called by a special satellite phone, my logic pressed on, and a helicopter rescue, my mini-nightmare further envisioned, would be another hazard to be endured not only by me, but a none-too-impressed pilot, whose first words to me, as I was winched on board, would be: 'what the fuck are you doing on a container ship? You're not even a sailor! Don't you know it's dangerous and there's never a doctor on board?!'

The thing about the FIC-charged state of anticipation is that you don't dwell for too long on any particular calamity. You visualise all the suspected hypotheticals, much as you would browse the internet – distractedly. And you distractedly calculate the permutations of probability. Getting to the point where, as my helicopter rescue receded safely into the realm of the far-fetched, my focus sharpened on the page where I needed to get a doctor's signature vouching that I was fit enough, and that I had an up-to-date yellow fever inoculation. I wasn't worried about my fitness, but what is yellow fever? Is it something endemic to seafarers, like scurvy or seasickness? Wikipedia again: yellow fever is pretty bad. Mosquito-borne, it 'is an acute viral disease. In most cases, symptoms include fever, chills, a loss of appetite, nausea, muscle pains particularly in the back, and headaches.' It goes on to say that it usually passes in about five days. Phew. But it goes on further, and somewhat contradictorily, to note that some 30,000 people die from it each year. The 'yellow' part refers to the colour of your skin due to kidney damage. Like a slightly mad person, I was lurching from symptoms to treatments to prognoses on those medical websites that I tell myself and my family never to look at, because no matter what symptom you inquire about, it will invariably be cancer-related at some point, and a guaranteed death-sentence, to boot. I was to be assuaged by my doctor the next day, who said that the epidemiology of yellow fever did not reach to anywhere near where I was going (it rampages, apparently, mainly in Central Africa and South America) and therefore a shot would be unnecessary, and anyway, like any inoculation, it has its own potential side effects. So, no, I don't recommend one for you. Phew again.

I'm one of those who never reads the small print of a document, any document. I cannot count the number of times this has gone against me, but there you are: a character flaw, or subconscious will-to-self-destruction, or maybe simple laziness. But I do know that if I am in the zone, I can look at a page of writing and be able to pick out the parts that I need to, or that my unconsciousness tells me to, without having to actually read the whole page. I can scan a page in two seconds and decide whether to flip to the next or not. Turning quickly over the last pages of the CMA CGM legalese, the noun 'piracy' leapt out, as if by means of some invisible spring, to hold my gaze. It was part of a short sentence stating blandly that maritime piracy was a growing phenomenon worldwide, etc. etc., and that although the risk is small, the company cannot be held responsible, etc. etc. This was something else I hadn't thought to worry about. Primed only by having seen the movie *Captain Phillips*, the Tom Hanks flick – based on a true story – about a container ship captain who surrenders his vessel, Maersk *Alabama*, to a band of Somalian desperadoes 440 kilometres out to sea from the port of Eyl, this was even less reassuring than the absence of a doctor, or the hypothetical presence of yellow fever. I reached for the internet again.

Google fetched up a website published by CNBC.com, the US cable television channel. I clicked on it and it shrieked the headline 'Crime on the high seas: The world's most pirated waters'. This didn't refer to the distant blue waters off Somalia, as I had hoped as I scrolled down, or to somewhere equally off my radar, but to exactly where I was headed, to the Singapore Strait and Strait of Malacca, where half of all the piracy attacks on the high seas take place, apparently. At this point I was sitting on the couch, half-watching TV, with the laptop battery icon showing red. I instantly lost any remaining interest in Eurosport's preview of the upcoming Vuelta a España and went to the next room to plug in the laptop. The CNBC scare story began:

> SINGAPORE – The *Ai Maru* steamed alone under night skies on June 14 when a speedboat slipped in from the darkness and overtook the tanker about 30 miles off the coast of Malaysia. At 9:15 p.m., seven men with handguns and knives clambered up over the side, smashed through doors, tied up crew members at gunpoint and bashed the Ai Maru's communications equipment.

Surely, I reasoned to myself, this would be a case of some decrepit old vessel with no safety procedures, and with a locally based crew who are all probably in on the scam? I needed more context, more evidence. I then Googled 'CMA CGM' and 'piracy' and the robots dutifully served up this as first choice, dated only a few weeks previous:

> The chartered 4,300 TEU container ship CMA CGM *Turquoise*, under way from Lagos, Nigeria to Douala, Cameroon was boarded in waters about 30 nm off the coast of the Niger Delta. The captain activated the SSAS and the crew retreated to the citadel, but two were captured and kidnapped before they could enter.

US Navy Seals came to the rescue of Captain Phillips. Do the French do that sort of thing, too, I wondered?

•

Henri Bergson, the principal *fin de siècle* philosopher of time said, 'One should act like a person of thought and think as a person of action.' He uttered this near the end of his life, in 1937, at a conference on René Descartes, the seventeenth century philosopher who is famous for his 'I think therefore I am' line. Descartes was also celebrated for his ideas on the human body as being a kind of machine, and the machines that were being devised in his time, at the very beginnings of the age of modernity, he saw as mirroring human bodies. He considered the human heart, for example, as a kind of furnace, and the veins and arteries as analogous to the pipes of a machine. On its face, this is fairly sensible and natural, but others such as Bergson, and many more today, viewed such a cosmology with alarm. For Bergson, machines may augment our muscles, but they take something from our humanity, too. More pertinently, the clock, he saw, takes away our experience of time, replacing it with a mathematical abstraction that has little or nothing to do with how you or I live it at the subjective level. Today, computers redouble the effects of the abstraction. Digital life consists not only of what I referred to in the first chapter as 'network time', but also a pervasive automation of machines and their processes, which make us increasingly redundant as producers of physical and intellectual labour. Digital life disempowers us and leaves us vulnerable to all sorts of digital effects, not least a manic form of anticipation.

It is not always easy to keep in mind that the social world is a construction. Each of us carry around in our heads what is called in German a *weltanschauung*: literally a world view. This is formed and shaped and reshaped by social life: family, school, peers, media and so on. Moreover, and more powerfully today, is the role of technology in this process. It has often been attributed to Marshall McLuhan, and it is the sort of thing that McLuhan would have said, but it was his contemporary John Culkin who, channelling McLuhan, provides us with an on-the-money aphorism to make a horrendously complex process of our relationship to technology seem stark and simple, when he wrote that: 'we become what we behold ... we shape our tools and afterwards our tools shape us.' But this doesn't mean that we are stuck in a kind of suspended animation, unable to change our mental conceptions of the world. Structures like the clock, which we are obliged to synchronise with in everyday life, cannot stop us relating to clock time differently, of seeing what it is and what it does, and to make pushing back against its logic an aspect of how we live our lives. We can behold who we are in a different way. We can begin to consciously exert as much control over the clock as we can and experience the times that are released as a consequence. But the pressures of daily modern life constantly work against autonomy from the clock. For example, every now and then, the governments of South American countries such as Peru or Ecuador launch what they call 'punctuality drives': media campaigns that try to promote the need to be punctual, to buy a watch, to actually be somewhere when you said you would, to synchronise their lives with what the authorities, in their fawning appreciation, call 'English time'. I think that the social construction of 'English time' should be undermined as much as possible, and not just by the English. We all need to instead embrace more the 'Latin time' of untimeliness as an expression of a temporal freedom and a refusal to be synchronised by a machine – every minute of the day.

This is the digital detox aspect that I wanted to behold on my voyage. Going cold turkey as far as connection to mobile phones, to the internet and its distractions. And apart from the mealtimes specified on board the *Rossini* that are administered by the clock, time, too, will have a minimal regulating temporal effect upon my life whilst on board. Mental conceptions of the world, that which are derived from institutions such as the clock, are fairly easy to identify, but more difficult to exert personal control over; more broadly, cultural mental conceptions, such as those derived from digital life, are actually rather more difficult to behold because they are so densely interlinked. But if we stop and think, then the function of the internet and mobile phones can soon become manifest and we can begin to assert our subjective selves over these forms of time and discover our own time. This allows us to see that anticipation, that psychological state that affects us all, can become more human, more manageable, and more creative. Strands of revisionist European Marxism, such as that of Leszek Kołakowski, argue that before the era of modernity (the era created by the clock) humans had no real conception of the future, beyond that which religion provided. Enlightenment and modernity gave us the idea of progress and certainty, which was a future of more and better and improved and so on. As Zimbardo's $150 experiment shows, this has broken down, and we are now mostly afraid of what seems to be a mist-shrouded future (with religion bringing much less comfort than it used to). But to clear away the insistence of clock time and accelerated network time, even for a short period, would allow a new perspective on the world: a reformed mental conception of the world that might allow me to 'act like a person of thought, and think as a person of action.'

Let me try to articulate what this anticipation of a new way of anticipating might be like: to consciously deconstruct the time of the world and digital life might mean that my thoughts may become more subjectively temporal; I would be living predominantly in my own time. The act that stems from this new state may itself be purely reflective, to explore memory voluntarily and instead of 'involuntarily', as Proust has it. The present may be experienced and understood for the moments in which it is passing, reflecting upon what I am doing and where I am doing it. This state of mind positions me in the world, vis-a-vis the future. And my context (the place in which I find myself and the state of mind that accompanies it) is the basis for a new world view, where the future, short-term or long, may still be vague and unguaranteeable, but at the very least my sense of it will be more authentically mine.

Having gone through this thought process of making my time more salient by calmly thinking through the process of pre-detoxification, I felt much better. It didn't even take me very long. In fact, it was during a bike ride on the Thursday, around part of Port Phillip Bay – to Sorrento and back again. And there was a strong wind against my back on the way home. Four and a bit hours later, I was in a hot bath and feeling kind of elated. I'd thought it through, and the manic worry of digital life anticipation had dissipated. I hadn't even needed to stop and write any thoughts down or record them on my iPhone. I'd calmly thought it all through and cleared my head in the process.

4

WAITING

WHAT'S THE DIFFERENCE between anticipation and waiting? Well, waiting, if viewed as it normally is in the time of the world, is, or usually is, a negative process. Waiting rooms come immediately to mind. My default memory when I think of waiting is of my visit to the local employment office when I was sixteen. It was my introduction to waiting. I had newly left school and was newly moving to the lengthening national register of unemployed; this was when I signed on for the first time.

It was June 1975. My God, so long ago. It had been a warm start to summer and the final term at Our Lady's High School in Motherwell had fizzled and died. 3C's last ever lesson was geography during which, if I remember right, we learned the virtues of baseball from Mr Hill, the exotically American import with the red beard and blonde shoulder-length hair and grey 1970s suit. Afterwards, my cohort pushed and shoved each other out the classroom door, stormed down the worn steps and fanned out across the playground before funnelling through the heavy russet

Victorian iron gates, only to fan out once more to every direction on the compass, never to come together as a group again. But where were we going? For some, it was to more education or training at another institution in September. But the majority in this high school – those streamed for manual labour at best by the scandalous eleven-plus system – faced a void. Most had no plans and no expectations, and no expectations of adopting a plan. But we were young, the nights were short and it wasn't cold, so the looming chasm was something I didn't register initially. What I did register was a slightly giddy feeling of freedom. There were no more teachers and no more books, and that was the main thing.

Too soon after stepping out into these sunlit uplands, after playing football day after day until it got dark (11 pm at the end of June), and swimming and skimming stones in the pollution-rich Calder River at a bend called the Sandy Bottom during the hottest of these days – which peaked, incidentally, at an extraordinary 28 °C on 25 June – it was time, according to my mother, to become a dependent adult and to go and respectfully request that the state support me financially. She pushed me along this path expecting, as all local mothers did in similar circumstances, a good-sized and non-negotiable 'digs money' cut of the almost thirteen pounds per week which was apparently my due in the then semi-socialist Britain. This sum floated up in my mind's eye as a previously unheard-of quantity to someone who never possessed more than a Friday night's pound in pocket money. Signing on seemed like an adult plan of sorts, even if it wasn't my plan, and with no school or anywhere else to go to I was now an adult.

The walk from Glencairn Avenue to Quarry Street in nearby Wishaw took about half an hour and during my stroll past the drab shops on Shields Road which connected this particular A to B, I was already spending the free money in my head: Nazareth's *Hair of the Dog* LP from Round Sounds record store and perhaps a couple of pounds toward a pair of adidas Samba trainers from the Littlewoods catalogue, which stood in as our family Bible in those locust years. I found this was a pleasant mental exercise and so, as I went on toward the pot of gold, I began to spend more fictitious sums on various luxuries for the weeks and months ahead: more LPs (perhaps Pink Floyd's *Dark Side of the Moon*, which I possessed only on a bootleg cassette tape), Dr. Martens boots (black, twelve eyelets high and with yellow stitching around the soles), and maybe even petrol money put aside for a mooted road trip to Morecambe, Lancaster, with John McGuigan, my very recent 'old school friend' and the only person I knew who was my age and had a car (a dark green Cortina Mk II, fuzzy dice and all, and the envy of all who saw him scoot around in it).

In 1975, the local employment office was a 1945-vintage complex of prefab offices that had sprawling Rorschach blots of green lichen and powdery white seagull shit covering much of its asbestos roofs and walls. It's now a Tesco Warehouse, which I discovered through Google Street View. My first visit to it was on Monday, 30 June, a day on which I also noticed that my current favourite song, *My White Bicycle* by said Nazareth, had only moved up one place over the past week from number eighteen in the BBC charts. Its ascent to classic status seemed to have stalled, I thought, as I listened to the chart's rundown on Noel Edmonds' Radio 1 Breakfast Show before setting out. This may have been a portent. I was about to discover what 'to stall' and 'to stall early' meant in my own life. I was about to experience what waiting in the grim bureaucracy of the time of the world could consist of.

In what is an eerie synergy, the inside of the Quarry Street dole office resembled the mean-looking and always dark Ladbrokes and William Hill, the betting offices of the period which cornered the market for legally fleecing the poor. One gave the money and the others took it away. Quarry Street Department of Health and Social Security offered the unwanted experience of dingy, low-ceilinged rooms filled with a constantly thickening cigarette smoke haze. The room's day-to-day workings produced a waxy grime that clung to every surface – chairs, windowsills, handrails – signalling months if not years of close and repeated contact by uncountable hands, backsides and elbows. Young men and old men milled and filled forms in the smog that floated at the back of the room. Soon they would take their place in queues that only seemed to lengthen out from the row of six booths at the front of the room from where women, who projected a female power I hadn't seen before, processed the docile line of males.

Taking my cue from those around me, I read a pinned-up cartoon sign inviting me to fill in a form, which I did and then joined a random queue and … waited. A little while later a gap must have opened up ahead and so, synchronising with an unconscious collective movement of the whole line, I took a half-pace forward. My knee connected with the back of the leg of the guy in front of me. I assumed, in what was until then a physically unconstrained youth, that there had been some kind of incident along the line – someone had probably tripped on his flared jeans, but he'd be up in a jiffy, laughing self-consciously at his clumsiness, and on I'd quickly go to face my new alma mater, who'd smile at me through the perforated glass and smoke and welcome me to a new world of lots of free time and free money.

But no. It was a half-pace at a time. This was a physical and psychological time I hadn't reckoned with before. It was as if a big hard palm with stiff fingers was spread across my solar plexus and stopping me from getting on with my day. I risked losing my place if I stepped out of the line, and the line was moving at a pace I hadn't previously experienced: slow. We wanted to move forward, but we were all thwarted by the unseen yet all-powerful force of the state. I just wanted to be back out in the sunshine and fresh air with money in my pocket and to have tea with a happy mum who would smile as I handed over her share of socialism, made possible by the trading of subjective acquiescence and passive waiting for fortnightly subventions of state cash.

Extracting the scene from my memory now, I can picture the face of the woman at the counter when we at last came face-to-face. I thought then that it was the mark of an adult, but the woman's face must have been that of a youth or young woman because a terrible topography of dark purple acne covered her forehead and cheeks, and active pustules congregated around her chin and mouth. I'd rarely seen this before. My own skin, then like a tanned peach, would undergo a similar though less cruel trauma just a year later. But I realised that her scarred countenance embodied what was to me an unjust authority over my time in a way that was previously determined by teachers who anyway cared little if I came to school or not. I removed the green card that I had filled out and placed in the breast pocket of my Levi's jacket and offered it to her. She took it, stood it in a grubby little pine wood box to her left, and wrote something down on a white ruled card of the same size which she placed next to the green one. She then looked at me in the eye for the first time. She looked friendly.

The card I gave her was only a preliminary registration, she informed me. I would need to join another queue further down and make an appointment with an employment officer, which would probably take place next week. At that interview, she went on, her eyes downcast now, as if she was reading from one of the cards, I would be assessed for suitability for such work as was available. If there were no immediate vacancies for me to occupy, then I would need to make a formal claim for unemployment benefits by filing a UB40 form, which would take another two weeks to process (all things moving along as they should, that is). I can't recall if I gave any response, or if I just contemplated the pressurised pimples on her chin and mouth. Anyway, she pulled out a sheet of A4-sized blue paper and applied her orange Bic to it. I must have been waiting for the moment of proper ending to this encounter, and she must have sensed this, because she looked up after writing no more than a word and said: 'Are you Laura Hassan's brother?' 'Aye,' I said. 'She was in my class at school,' said she. She then looked indifferently past my right shoulder and called: 'Next.' Laura was eleven months older than me.

My first encounter with the state was a shock. The shock being the sudden knowledge of what it felt like to have to wait – to be physically and psychologically constrained by forces outside my control, to be trapped by waiting and to be waiting without knowing why. All of us, in our lives, deal with versions of waiting. But there is a larger picture that gives some context to my little tale of woe. As I write this on my laptop, a check on the UNHCR website tells that there are 65.3 million forcibly displaced people in the world. This dreadful figure says nothing about the lot of a displaced person, which is to experience waiting of a much more terrible kind than I can imagine. The forcibly displaced endure traumas that will seem to many of them to have no reason or end. It does no justice to describe what these souls experience as waiting; perhaps it's languishing. Whichever, it's an utter powerlessness and a pointless waste of their human time, a waste of their human lives. Nonetheless, for you and me in our own worlds, a sense of powerlessness and wasting of never-to-be-returned time is a universal feature and a seemingly necessary price to be paid for being born into the modern time of the world.

Before moving on to the *Rossini* detox proper, I want to spend a moment showing that we can mitigate the experience of the stultifying wait that distorts and magnifies the time of the world. This is important. Waiting can become positive and it can have affirmative aspects that don't need to emphasise a lack of power in a given situation or drive home the fact that your time is being squandered by powers over which you have little or no influence. If we turn our attention to our subjective experience of time then, with a little reflection and the exercise of free will, we can move, as Henri Bergson put it, from 'state to state' – from a negative waiting to a positive waiting. We know that we can move the physical state of our bodies from cold to hot, or with perhaps more difficulty we can move the psychological state of our mind from sad to happy. However, by being mindful of how we relate to time – at any point in time – we can move beyond the particular qualities of physically and mentally waiting, and place ourselves in what is another state of waiting – a waiting that is a conscious state beyond negative waiting, and from there to inhabit what might be experienced as the antithesis of waiting, a non-waiting, or of waiting that feels like a kind of freedom.

To reach that time, we need to become attentive to the experience of time. To illustrate this idea and its possibilities to my students, I play a little game with them. I call it Time Moving – Ego Moving. On a PowerPoint slide, I show them the text of an imagined email. It reads: 'Next Wednesday's meeting has to be moved forward by two days.' Then I ask them which day the meeting would be and get them to write it down on a piece of paper, which I collect. What do you think? Very often there's a rough split between 'Monday' and 'Friday', and students are usually surprised to learn that someone else would have a different answer to them. Researchers who have studied this phenomenon say that those who answer with Monday, which was also me when I first did this experiment, are said to be 'Time Moving' individuals, meaning that they perceive themselves to be standing still with time (the future) moving toward them. The Wednesday meeting thus moves forward toward you, landing on Monday. To answer with Friday indicates that you are an 'Ego Moving' perceiver of time, meaning that you move with the flow of time, like floating on a river toward the future. Wednesday's meeting then flows two days forward in the river of time to be held on Friday. Get it?

Time Moving and Ego Moving are not fixed states. They are shaped by culture, language, and context. We can move from one to the other. Bergson, in his 1910 book *Time and Free Will*, argued that time is comprised of individual conscious experience, and that this is a state that we can tap into if we clear away the clutter of daily living and the chronological time of the clock (and the network time of digital life too, perhaps). Bergson draws from John Stuart Mill's work on free will and determinism. The latter constrains the former, but in the case of time, Bergson believed we can assert free will against the determinism of the objective time of the clock. We can choose to connect with the subjective experience of time and place ourselves in the flow, or river of time, to be a part of it, and 'go with the flow' as we say today, and let the time of the world 'go'. Bergson wrote that, 'the free act takes place in time which is flowing and not in time which has already flown.' Time that 'has already flown' is the time that comes to us in the Time Moving state, a time that comes to us from a future, and comes in its own time as a determining force. Bergson's 'time which is flowing' is where we want to be when we are waiting. And waiting in such a conscious state can become a free act where we can embrace waiting and experience the time of waiting as a positive act. This may simply mean going with the flow in a queue at the train station, or passport office (or dole office); or, more powerfully, perhaps, it can mean to free yourself from the stress and tension and emptiness of waiting for a future event that will come. But we do not have to wait for it to come to us; we go freely to it.

The Ancient Greeks understood this. They called this deeper involvement with time Kairos. This translates from classical Greek as 'the right moment', or the 'opportune time' or, better, 'the moment of transition'. It is contrasted with Chronos, which refers to sequential, ordered and rigid time, as with the clock. Kia Lindroos puts the idea of the asynchronous element of Kairos very well:

> The cairologic approach neither searches for means of measuring or understanding movement through temporal continuity, nor attempts to control the dynamics of time and action through freezing them. Instead, this approach emphasises breaks, ruptures, nonsynchronised moments and multiple temporal dimensions.

Kairos always carries with it a positive element, meaning that when Kairos appears, the 'time feels right' to do something, to go somewhere, to say something. The negative process of waiting doesn't come into it, because negative waiting means that the moment is not (yet) right; it might never be right, and the right moment might never come. Within Kairos, however, that's ok, because to accept Kairos means that the possible stress or frustration of waiting is not there. Yes, you can make something happen and bring the right moment to you and to the present, but that is something else again. That is active participation with the future, not waiting. However, if waiting is present, then turning it from its negative to positive state is to involve the acceptance of Kairos and to 'go with the flow'. The secret of acknowledging and using Kairos is knowing that the first step – as the mountain climber Manuel Schneider put it in reference to recognising when the right time comes – is to recognise also that you are 'waiting for oneself.' And so, when you are ready, you will know when the moment comes. And when it does, there is a good chance that it will be the right one for you.

Of course, acknowledging and choosing Kairos and the positive state of waiting is not always maintainable. The times of the clock and the network are strong and powerful, and we often find it necessary to synchronise with these times, or to at least try to. The important thing is to know that we have this potential as temporal beings and that we can inhabit temporal states which can ameliorate negative waiting, at least for a time.

•

On the day before the *Rossini* was due to dock, I got a terse-ish email from the owners' local office. A Monsieur F. Barthez instructed me to present myself to the security at the front gate of Swanson Dock three hours prior to departure time. The name on the email looked French, but also seemed suspicious. During my research, I'd heard of various and more-or-less plausible scams in operation, such as online 'agents' taking money for trips and ships that don't exist – ghost trips in ghost ships. Could the F stand for *Fabien* as in Fabien Barthez? Why choose that name? Surely it couldn't be someone's wicked sense of humour to evoke the former Manchester United player; he of the shaved head and close-set eyes who helped France to victory in the 1998 World Cup? A wave of alarm ran through my, up until then, zen-like waiting mode. However, the fact that I could see the *Rossini* as a blip on the screen, and that it was still en route to Melbourne, suggested that my fare had probably not gone to a Nigerian scammer. And in fact, as I quickly reassured myself, my 'agent' from New Zealand had written just the day before with a piece of unsolicited advice concerning seasickness. I put thoughts of fraud out of my mind.

Three hours prior to departure meant 3 am. To counteract the alarm, a fleeting sense of elation at doing something quite outside of the temporal routine moved in. I would be out at 3 am with a purpose – not coming home, as was once the case in an earlier nightclubbing existence, but going out and not coming back for a month. Sunday morning about 2.30 am would be my own departure time. It was now Saturday night and the *Rossini* was floating, becalmed in Port Phillip Bay. Its blip had been stationary now for a couple of hours, waiting, I imagined, for Berth Number Four to become free. After checking my email for the last time, and scanning only for emergency-looking subject lines, I powered down my laptop and deposited it in the linen cupboard, covering it with towels. My phone was already in a drawer, now dark and mute and unreceptive, no doubt sulking that it hadn't been invited either. The detox was about to begin.

Taking the place of my phone and laptop were a Sony ZX100 MP3 player, six cheap 148-page Daiso notebooks, a box of twelve exam standard HB pencils and a high-end German-made sharpener. As an afterthought, I took a Victorinox Swiss Army Knife 40-in-1 that I bought for a cycling trip to Tasmania a few years ago but never used. I still hadn't used it, but you never know. I also impulse-packed a small pair of National Geographic birdwatching binoculars which I suspected would be hopeless but, again, you never know. The largest item I packed was a 100-teabag box of matcha green tea, which I hadn't tasted before. My reading material would be four unread hardback books and an old and yellow and aromatic paperback from my bedside table. *The Physicist and The Philosopher* by Jimena Canales, *Gray's Anatomy: Selected Writings* by John Gray, *Proust and the Squid* by Maryanne Wolf and *Grand Hotel Abyss* by Stuart Jeffries created a stiff base for the small no-name black sports bag I'd bought for my stuff. The paperback was Volume Three of *Remembrance of Things Past* by Marcel Proust. It had been a started-and-stopped book whose spine illustration of Count Robert de Montesquiou had stared at me accusingly for years from its spot underneath a lamp. These books were all concerned with time, and I hoped they would serve as a spur to my thinking during the detox period.

It was now after two o'clock on Sunday morning. From Kate's phone I could see that the blip had moved into position at Berth Number Four. I'd already said goodbye to the kids, who were now asleep, and was waiting with Kate for the taxi to come.

I really wanted to cycle down to Swanson Dock, travelling my normal route to work as a route towards what would be an abnormal few weeks at sea. At sea. The idea still hadn't penetrated. No land on the horizon, and no appointments to keep or people to see, and, most intriguingly of all, being out of reach from the whole world and its time. My NZ agent told me that crews tended to be pretty sexist and unless the 'paying passenger' was female, then you'd probably be seen as someone in the way of their work and someone who should probably keep out of the way altogether. This suited me. Gender-based isolation and cold turkey detox meant no lapses of borrowing phones, or laptops or anything else that could connect me with my land-life and my routine time of the world.

I could have chained my old bike near the docks somewhere for a month, but it might have got stolen or, worse, got rusty from exposure to the winter rains. It's a sky blue 1979 Peugeot Competition bike, which I'd found on eBay from a seller in France. It even has a vintage bike-shop sticker on it which reads: 'M. Bidart, 6 Rue d'Ossau, GAN.' Google Maps shows the address now to be a nondescript but tidy frontage, next to number eight, which has a sign saying 'Cabinet Gérard Bourdeu' outside. There is something too revealing about the all-seeing Google eye. Looking at 6 Rue d'Ossau now, I can imagine the day that someone somehow saw that beautiful, shiny brand-new bike in the narrow shop window sometime during 1979, bought it, wheeled it out the door, and took off excitedly toward the high passes of the Pyrenees, via the nearby town of Pau. Vintage sticker aside, the reason I bought the bike was that it exactly matched the one I had as a sixteen-year-old, purchased with an early wage packet, from the Wishaw bike shop. And so, for $70, its French cousin became mine at auction – the only bid – and for a further $115, it was delivered to Melbourne by post. I couldn't leave it alone in the cold and wet for all that time, so an unromantic taxi to the docks would have to do. I said goodbye to Kate, who waved and said, 'Don't get washed overboard!' as I walked out to the waiting taxi.

Big wharves like Swanson Dock never stop, never slow down. The pace, noisily efficient, is maintained 24/7. Even when there are only a few ships in dock, the container handlers practice their skills in the art of stacking and unstacking the boxes again and again in a large space where the trains come in. Overhead, many dozens of huge orange sodium lights throw down vast circles of colour to illuminate points of action on the ground. Vans and cars with flashing orange lights on top signal humans going about their business in a three-dimensional scenescape. On my arrival, this scene reminded me a little of the alien landing pad in the movie *Close Encounters of the Third Kind*. Being there at 3 am on a freezing Sunday felt surreal and also as if I was doing something illegal, like I was not meant to be there – similar to the Richard Dreyfuss character in *Close Encounters*. The taxi driver had it in his head that I was a sailor. My Scottish accent and the drop-off point suggested to him that I was returning to my ship and then on to some distant part of the planet. 'What's your ship?' he asked, taking the fare and the large tip I offered. 'The *Rossini*,' said I with, I hoped, the air of a practised sea-dog. 'Where to next?' he asked, smiling at the tip as I clambered out with what turned out to be a heavy sports bag. 'Singapore,' said I, returning the smile and feeling inwardly mortified at the pointless economy I had just practised upon the truth.

While I was walking over to the gate, I could see the heads of three turbaned Sikhs sitting behind a long counter in a scruffy

white portakabin. Their disinterest suggested either that processing paying passengers on container ships was a routine chore
for them, or that they would have no idea who I was, or how to
assist me. It was neither. The Sikh man in the middle took my
name, picked up a phone, spoke for twenty seconds, then told
me that the minibus would meet me in five minutes at the other
side of the security gate behind the portakabin. 'Take your bag,
walk over to the gate, and I'll buzz your through,' he had said.
I walked and he buzzed. I was now waiting in a 'Restricted Area'
and needing to piss. From where I stood, Berth Number Four was
about a kilometre away, and obscured by mountains of stacked
containers. Vans and cars were whizzing about, here, just as I'd
seen them hundreds of times before from the other side of the
fence during my daily commute to and from work, on Footscray
Road. Any of them could now be coming for me, I thought. Apart
from the pressure on my bladder, I was enjoying the wait because
it was so exciting, so unlike a dismal and antiseptic and strictly
scheduled airport wait. This was uncertainty and grubbiness and
cold within a hideous orange light. I waited hardly more than two
minutes. A battered white Toyota minibus rolled slowly past me,
then stopped. Its red reverse lights came on and it began to back
up toward me with its beeper sounding. I turned to the portakabin
and the middle Sikh was giving me the thumbs-up and nodding
his head. This was my lift to the ship.

The driver was an old guy who didn't look interested or friendly
and simply asked, 'Berth Number Four?' I said thanks and got in.
Two or three minutes more of weaving through container can-
yons and bumping over the rail tracks of the container cranes,
with orange, red and white car and van lights flashing on all sides.
Suddenly I was at the side of what seemed like an impossibly large
ship, with the CMA CGM logo painted on its dark-blue hull, in
gigantic white capitals. The driver stopped his van under the letter

A. From this spot, a long and also battered aluminium ladder ran at a 45-degree angle from the dockside way, and upwards to a little gate that had been opened at the gunwale at the middle of the ship. I stood at the bottom and looked up for guidance. Should I just walk up? The minibus had already zoomed off.

I picked up the sports bag and stepped onto the steep and unsteady ladder, immediately triggering a response in the shape of a silhouetted figure who began to gallop down the stairs, obviously adept at this, and waved his hands as if to communicate 'Stop!' or 'Don't!' I stopped and didn't do anything except wait for him to arrive. I was thinking, as he descended, that I must have breached some strict customs regulation, like stepping into an international departure lounge without a passport, or crossing a busy runway on foot at Melbourne Airport. Anyway, he reached me and said a bit breathlessly: 'Mr Hassan? I'll take your bag, sir.' He snatched the bag, pivoted, and was off, back up the ladder, two steps at a time like an ibex. 'I'm Salva Cruz, your steward!' he shouted, without looking back. I fixed my gaze on the company logo on the back of his Hi-Viz fluoro-green vest and darted up after him.

Salva Cruz was even shorter of breath when we reached the gate at the top. He turned to face me, smiled, and gently placed my bag at my feet and took a gulp of oxygen as he rose. 'Breakfast is at seven,' he told me. 'I'll see you then,' I replied. Maybe it was the unexpected tinge of deference, but I felt like Prince Philip stepping aboard the Royal Yacht *Britannia*, when the Windsors still had it. Another smiling face, this time wearing faded blue overalls, a white safety hat and no fluoro, appeared next to me and gave me a clipboard with a list of names on it. 'You'll need to sign in,' he said. I found my name on the list and penned a squiggle next to it with a ballpoint that was sellotaped to a piece of string tied around the hole in the steel clip. He took the clipboard and the sports bag and said, 'Follow me, please.' In about four strides we passed through one of those steel doors that you see in submarine movies and, behold, I was inside the ship, actually inside an actual working ship.

We were in the lower deck, and the sound of engines, or some kind of roaring machinery, seemed to fill the air from all around and with no apparent source. It was also clammy. My scalp began to itch. I guessed that this was the deck where the day-to-day running of the ship and ship's crew was organised and coordinated. I followed the man into the first room on the right of a long corridor that ran to another steel door at the starboard side. It was a large, windowless room space and seemed to be a kind of operations room, probably where crew came in and out all the time. Right now, it was empty. Big, heavy, and oily Hi-Viz jackets and safety hats hung on hooks around the walls. Gumboots were arrayed underneath. Four old and heavily smudged desktop computers glowed at the far wall, under the yellow strip lights that were fixed to a very low ceiling. Dozens of blue CMA CGM-logoed ring binders, some open and some closed, were arranged untidily on the desk fixed to the wall and on the shelves above. 'The First Officer will come to take you to your cabin in a minute,' the man said, and then he disappeared.

I was alone and not feeling like Prince Philip any longer. I thought I sensed a faint smell of scrambled eggs. With my foot I slid the sports bag toward a free-floating long table covered with papers and clipboards and yellow rubber torches. A big box containing, according to the label, 192 bars of Toblerone was piled on top. I sat down and began to feel hot, so I took off my coat and sat down with it on my lap. I looked around. On the wall at the end of the table I could see a large framed photograph of the *Rossini* looking brand-new and glorious, full of evenly stacked CMA CGM containers, and sailing through a smooth dark blue sea under a clear light blue sky. Next to it I spotted the universal symbol for male toilets and so I jumped up and took my chance. When I re-emerged, a man who looked far too young was standing there and asked, 'Are you Mr. Hassan, the paying passenger?' I said yes, feeling as if I'd been subtly insulted. 'I am First Officer Enzo Bourget. Follow me, please, and I'll show you to your cabin,' he said. He didn't offer to carry my no-name sports bag. He was, I think, part nervous and part demeaned: he was a French Officer in the third-largest shipping company in the world and having to conduct a paying passenger on some kind of folly, to his purchased accommodation. His problem, I thought.

There was a lift in the *Rossini*, in the middle of the corridor. Like the lifts in the cheaper French hotels, it was slow to come, a squeeze to get into, and slow to rise to the fifth floor of the ship, which was just before the navigation deck and apparently where my cabin was. Enzo smiled uneasily in the lift when our eyes met, and so we both fixed them onto the floor numbers, which were going up slowly and achingly from D to 5. Eventually, we arrived and stepped out into a corridor with gleaming cream-coloured walls and a strip of brown carpet atop a gleaming cream-coloured rubber floor. Someone obviously worked on its shine every day. Enzo fiddled in the breast pocket of his white shirt and pulled out a key. 'Here is your cabin,' he said, again with that nervous smile and with a sweep of his hand, toward the door. We walked a few steps and stopped at number six – the 'Owner's Cabin' it said in a green plastic plaque above the door. Enzo handed me the key. 'Breakfast is at seven,' he said. He handed me the breakfast menu from his clipboard, along with another sheet indicating the mess room location on A Deck. 'Have a good day,' he said, in what sounded like a John Cleese impression of French-accented English. Slightly unkind, I know, but that's what flashed across my mind as he spoke.

I went inside, put my no-name sports bag on the floor, turned around and closed the door. I felt for the light switch and then, turning to the room, I noted an odd-looking analog clock on the cabin wall, which said that it was 3.25 am. All of a sudden, my eyelids decided they'd had enough of being open and wanted to close. There were two beds in the cabin and part of me wanted to crawl into the closest one and go to sleep. But how could I sleep when breakfast was at seven and when, as I pulled back the thin and short green curtains, I could see containers swinging up and down and to and fro hardly two feet away from my nose, in the orange-lit darkness outside?

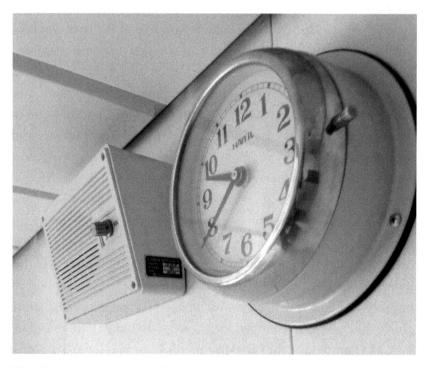

'The clock is everything in a ship': Captain Calment

The room was far bigger than I had expected. In retrospect, the notice on the door seemed accurate. If this ship did have an 'owner' then I'm sure this would be where he or she would be when on board. It was too much, and too big, and I felt that there must have been a mistake. Two large beds were connected at their tops by one long couch that ran under the double windows that sat smack-bang in the middle and the top of the ship – just under where I imagined the captain must stand when he's steering. Short of me squatting in the navigation deck, the position and view could not have been better. A writing desk and office chair were positioned to the right, and a large coffee table stood in front of the couch. The beds had deep drawers underneath and there was a built-in cupboard in the wall at the end of each of them. The shower room was smallish, and next to its door was a waist-high platform which had on top a mini jungle of pink, white and green hardy-looking plants – the kind that scarcely need any attention. A new-looking fridge full of plastic two-litre bottles of Zilia eau minérale was stowed in a cabinet underneath the foliage, as if a source of life for them through some weird hydroponic system that they had on ships. I knelt on the couch and peered outside. Through the orange glow, I could make out an LED lamp atop a kind of lookout tower right at the prow of the ship, and beyond that, another docked ship with a name I could not make out in the distant gloom.

If the operations room had been hot, then the cabin was cold. I spotted the air conditioner control next to the door, and turned the dial up as far as it would go, and then began to unpack my things. That took five minutes. I put my hand in front of the air flow from the ceiling unit and it still felt freezing. I took off my shoes, kept on my socks and coat and piled the bedding from one bed on to the other. I got in, pulled the blankets up to my nose and lay there staring dully at the strange clock, which registered 3.45 am. When it got to 3.46 am, I shut my eyes and opened them again a minute or so later to look at the clock once more and then to look around the room without moving my head. Then I closed my eyes again and fell asleep until my eyes opened to see the clock was approaching 7.10 am. I hadn't moved a millimetre in between those times.

7.20 am, A Deck mess room. No one around. After about ten seconds, Salva Cruz appeared, looking like a different person in his steward's garb of a waist-length white jacket with a mandarin collar and five gold buttons down the front, and black trousers above scuffed black shoes. He said good morning cheerfully and then disappeared back through the swinging aluminium galley doors. Breakfast was fit for a tourist in France: pots of brewed coffee, little baguettes, cheeses, jams, butter and fruit, a help-yourself affair from a buffet table. Wonderful. My name and status, 'M. Robert Hassan: Passenger', was written in ballpoint on a folded yellow card that was placed upon a brilliant-white tablecloth on the table next to the door.

There were five similar tables arranged in a row from the galley to the window. From what I could guess, the senior officers sat at the table at the window, then me, then the other ranks. I was to sit on my own, it seemed, between the ranks. It felt kind of strange. I loaded my plate and filled my mug and meekly took my designated seat. As crew members came in for breakfast, they would look at me and say 'bonjour' with the same familiarity that Salva Cruz had displayed, as if I'd sailed with them for a year, and then they'd make for the buffet. Maybe that's what sailors are like, I thought. Eventually, the captain, the tall and balding and authority-radiating Monsieur Calment, came in and introduced himself to me, saying 'Good morning' in Cleese-English. Actually, he was very nice – formal and distant, but perfectly measured. 'Please have a coffee with myself and the officers after breakfast in the Officers Mess,' he said. 'Yes of course,' said I, repressing the thought that he was like a gallic Sid James and I was an extra in *Carry On Cruising*.

Half an hour later, I was in the relative luxury of the Officers Mess; small but with the plushness of rank, which seemed to consist of prettier curtains and five or six leather tub chairs around a large round plywood coffee table. The dominant feature was a vast flat-screen TV fixed to the wall and a games console on the table below it, which had enough FIFA and shooter games to last for days. I sat in one of the tubs, having what might have been my fourth coffee before 8 am, this time from a Nespresso machine, and explaining myself to the captain and four officers who faced me with mildly expectant expressions. 'I want to experiment with the experience of time. To be cut off from communications, from the web, from mobile phones, from the time of the clock, and reflect upon the experience and then write about it sometime,' I said. 'You've come to the wrong place then I'm afraid, *Professor*,' Captain Calment said, with an emphasis on the rank and a slightly malevolent look. 'The clock is everything in a ship. Without it, we cannot do anything.' This was to be his final word on the matter. He got up and made for the Nespresso machine. The other four nodded slowly in agreement and beheld me with what felt like silent pity for my having undertaken such a rapidly aborted trip.

I was back in my still-cold cabin around 8.20 am. The day was now bright and sunny, but it wasn't as if I could slap on some sunscreen, put on some sensible walking shoes and go for a walk around the shops and local places of interest. I could still see my breath in the air in front of me. The first thing was to get warm. After fiddling with the air conditioning to no discernible effect, I decided to forego my usual concern for the planet's resources and stood under a hot shower for at least fifteen minutes.

We were still tied up and floating at Berth Number Four. Outside my windows, overlooking the whole of the ship, the crane activity continued. The ship was being filled from its very depths way down below with the regulation-sized boxes. The dexterity and speed of the crane operators was impressive, but very noisy and dangerous-looking. Several times as I watched, boxes would swing past my windows so closely I was certain that they would come through the window or into the wall. But instead they were dropped, almost by the weight of gravity, onto the preceding box, with a tremendous crash. Again and again they would be dropped, with hundreds of boxes being swallowed up in the hull and gradually becoming visible up over the sides of the ship. Workers in Hi-Viz jackets and white hats lashed the boxes together with ten-feet-long and inch-thick diameter rods, which they then screwed tightly into place with large spanners. Enzo, the First Officer, told me later that the containers were placed in a computer-designed arrangement, with heavy boxes at the bottom, lighter ones in the middle, and empty ones being kept for the top. They were also spread out evenly to stop the ship from listing or being too heavy at any point. By 9.00 am, the workers looked like they still had a long way to go, but at least my view remained clear. I hoped more avidly

The view from the cabin. *Latitude: -36.445037 Longitude: 129.725307* (In the middle of the Great Australian Bight, 9th August)

than was reasonable that my cabin wouldn't be blacked out by a big box containing Christ-knows-what being dropped and secured in front of it.

Captain Calment had given me a folder with a bullet list of dos and don'ts for the paying passenger. For example, alcohol was readily available – a carafe of Beaujolais at every lunchtime – but, the list advised, it is not wise to get drunk on the open sea. More germane right now was that during bunkering operations (loading and unloading), it was forbidden to go outside onto the decks where a swinging container could foreshorten the paying passenger's life. That made sense – it certainly did not look safe out there, and not all that safe in my cabin either. A bullet point about halfway down the list was more positive. It said that for the paying passenger, the navigation deck was always open. I could walk in anytime but I had to be respectful of the fact that it was a very important work space with sensitive navigation equipment, computers, gyroscopes and the like, which should on no account be touched. The bullet point also inferred that I should speak to crew only when spoken to. I was happy to oblige and more than happy to spend time on the navigation deck to look and to be just an observer – both of the workings of the room and of the fantastic and ever-changing (once we got going) 360-degree view of the ever-changing world that it offered. Giving up on the air conditioning, I got into bed again to get warm, opened the pristine copy of Jimena Canales' book, read half a page worth of the preface, closed my eyes, and woke up three hours later.

12.20 pm. Lunch comprised of quiche, green beans, rice, baguettes, apple pie and a banana. It was beautifully prepared and needlessly itemised (there was no choice) on a photocopied A4 menu, which had a bit of artwork consisting of a suitable picture (I think it was an indistinct clump of gum trees, perhaps in my honour) dragged and dropped from the web to decorate the bill of fare. Plus there was a carafe of unbranded Beaujolais. Sitting on my own and professorially writing not very much on a new Daiso notebook with a sharp pencil, I ate every bit of the food and drank the entire carafe, which equated to nearly a full bottle of wine.

Seeing that everyone seemed to be eating and going in a working-lunch type fashion, I decided to get out as well. Suitably fortified by too much wine too early in the day and with too little proper sleep, I felt intrepid enough to walk up the five flights of stairs from A Deck to the navigation deck at the very top of the ship. It was unexpectedly dark where the last step met the last landing. A heavy-looking, electronically locked steel door was all that was left in front of me. I knocked hard on the door, too hard for my knuckles. Nothing. I knocked again more softly and said 'Hello!' in a loud voice to compensate. Silence. The Beaujolais emboldened me to lift the lever and pull on the door. It opened. Expecting an armed response, or to be rugby-tackled by a French sailor who was once a prop forward for Clermont, I kept saying 'Hello! Hello!' like an idiot, as I stepped into the navigation deck. But there was no one around. It was completely deserted. They were probably all too busy with the bunkering. So I just looked around, feeling a bit tense in case someone should be surprised to find me there. Nevertheless, authorised by the bullet point and buoyed by the wine, I soon relaxed and then felt curious. It was just like Captain Phillips' deck in the movie, with its computers and the matching green panelling of the walls and control housing.

That didn't interest me so much as the traces of culture that were dotted all around the room. In the two rear corners there were long-stemmed succulents that grew and spread like thick vines. They were tied up by strings and seemed to be in a more or less healthy-looking state, having been sustained from dry-looking soil packed into large Super Croix Hydro laundry powder tubs. The plants, despite all outward appearances, were interesting to me. They were alive, unlike the computers and the mysterious-looking controls. I thought of these succulents and the travels they must have witnessed. They could have been years old, perhaps from the ship's maiden voyage in 2004, and unlike the sailors who have set routes and who come and go, these plants could have been to every corner of the planet many times. I was looking at the only true living companions to the *Rossini*, I thought – the real crew. I squinted at them and looked as closely as I could for some evidence, I didn't know what, of the adventures they'd been part of. I thought of the thousands of sunsets and sunrises that had lit and shaded them in their little corner settings; of their presence during long days in the calmest of seas, and in the terrible dark winter crossings of the Atlantic – a passage so dangerous that paying passengers are not allowed; and of them feeling the chill through the windows from the freezing air on the Pacific routes north of Japan and the USA; and of them shrinking from the same windows that bake in the oppressive heat and slow pace of the Suez Canal in July–August.

To the left and rear of the room, there was a modular seating area with well-worn and grimy dark red upholstery that had seen a lot of overalls; another Nespresso machine sat on a wide window ledge, and underneath there was a steel sink that could have done with a scrub. Next to it was an equally dirty IKEA dish drainer stacked with mugs, some of which bore the surviving coffee streaks from a careless rinse. To the left again, English-language technical books on navigation sat handily for crew to study whilst having coffee, but they looked long undisturbed on a neat, tall bookshelf. All around, the view from the huge outwardly slanting windows was still Swanson Dock and my bike route, but promised to soon change and to reveal a great deal more in the coming weeks.

The best thing thus far was the very large chart table where a very large chart for Port Phillip Bay sat atop a lot of others. It looked beautiful in its blue and yellow and grey colours, especially with the drawing and navigation instruments just lying on top, as if they were placed there five minutes ago, *Marie-Celeste*-like, and with the pencilled lines and marks and numbers and mysterious symbols of the actual passage of the blip I'd followed on the website. Analog reality, I thought, wins over digital virtuality every time, at least as far as aesthetics goes. It struck me then that my dead laptop and sulking phone, and the digital life that lay behind with them, were already very far away. Notwithstanding this happy proto-detox state, I could still almost see my house from where I was standing over the chart.

The door suddenly swung inwards and someone in blue overalls and wearing Ray-Ban Aviators stood before me, expressionless. I put my hands up in surrender, identified myself and confessed that I was a simple paying passenger who had only just come onboard. He moved his Aviators to the top of his head, gave a wan smile and said, 'That's ok. My name is Jesse. Navigation Officer.' He then busied himself with something at one of the computers. He sounded Filipino. His relative disinterest emboldened me to ask if it was ok to step outside to the large viewing spaces at either end of the deck. 'Sure,' he said without looking away from whatever he was doing. I walked over to the right-hand door, struggled with the heavy up-turning lever, leaned on it and stepped outside.

The wind was blowing in gusts and I had to close the door once outside to stop it swinging. There wasn't really much to look at beyond busy cranes and containers and, further afield, the town of Newport squatting in amongst the trees, out of the wind. I decided that once we were underway, I would come out here as much as possible, just to look. The familiarity of the too-close and crowded horizon caused me to study the ship itself a bit more and to examine what was immediately around me – to do what we increasingly don't do. I saw that I was standing on what is called checker plate steel. This is the steel flooring that you see in, for example, steps and walkways in factories or warehouses. It has lozenge-shaped bumps on it to stop you slipping. You don't see a great deal of this stuff in sedentary office jobs. After not having thought about it for some time until now, the checker plate triggered the outlines of one of Proust's *mémoires involontaires*. The sight of this grey painted steel, together with my presence on the ship, flashed a memory before my mind's eye, a memory of reading a newspaper at lunchtime in my first job, and noticing an advert for workers needed in Australia. I held it there in my brain and began to remember.

Over the coming days and weeks, and with the time to reflect and with pencil and paper in my hands, I recovered much more of this memory that had lain totally undisturbed for decades. I realised with more clarity than I'd ever experienced before why I first came to Australia.

MÉMOIRE VOLONTAIRE 4

My new life on the dole in mid-1975 did not last very long. My mother worked as a cleaner in the offices of a nearby company called Lanarkshire Welding. They built lots of things with checker plate. Anyway, not bothering to clear it with me first, my mother asked her boss if they were needing anyone for anything. Yes, was the answer, and so the deal was done. When she came home she mentioned it casually whilst putting a couple of Findus Crispy Pancakes on to fry for tea. This information interrupted me as I was watching (or have a strong sense that I was) an episode of *The Tomorrow People* on TV, a teenagers' show about people who could time travel. You can still watch it on YouTube, and it holds up rather well. Regarding the job, after I felt an unexpected and unwanted jolt of responsibility, and also annoyance at not being consulted first, I began to feel quite excited but also quite perplexed. What would I be doing? How much would it pay? Would it be exhausting and dirty? Would I have to be there every day? And so on. Well, I found out on the following Monday at 7.30 am, when I turned up at the little office that evidently my mother hadn't yet cleaned, and was told by Sandy McDonald, the works manager, that I was to be an apprentice welder. I came to hate Sandy McDonald. His father, Sandy Senior, owned the company, which boomed from Mulberry harbour contracts for D-Day in 1944. The company had fallen into his son's (also) fat lap, as had the Jaguar XJ6 that he'd get my mother to clean and polish for him, and which he'd change every year, to a different colour, and probably as a tax write-off from the car business 'McDonald Motors', which had also been given to him by Sandy Senior.

I can't remember how much I was going to be paid, although I do remember feeling that I was going to be even richer than before. But the job turned out to be exhausting and dirty and smoky and noisy and boring, and I occasionally got choked by fumes, flashed by the intense UV light from the welding arc, and burned by hot metal (I still have a scar on the top of my right foot from when a globule of molten metal slid down my boot). However, it was a trade, as my mother kept reminding me, and tradesmen will never want for work, she always added. I did that bloody job for eight years, and I still have recurring dreams – semi-nightmares, actually – of still working there, trapped in the 1970s with the haircuts, clothes, cars and all. The TV series *Life on Mars* gets it exactly right on this score. But one day in my sixth year of being repeatedly choked, flashed, burned and bored in the service of Sandy McDonald, I saw an ad in the *Daily Record* for welders at a place called Cockatoo Island Dockyard, in Sydney, Australia. To cut a short story even shorter, I applied, not knowing anything about Cockatoo Island, or Sydney, or Australia, or applying for jobs.

A month later, I had a ten-minute 'interview' with two Australian men in a Reo Stakis hotel room in the centre of Glasgow. They sat on the ends of their beds, facing me, and I sat on one of two occasional chairs that had been pushed underneath an open window. A strong smell of chips cooking in oil wafted up from the kitchen below. The interview must have gone well, because about a fortnight later I received a letter saying I had the job, and could I be there (in Sydney, expenses paid) by June. This was in March and June seemed eons away, and I had little in the way of possessions or connections, so I said yes, and was put in contact with the Australian consulate in London to sort out the details.

I was the very first of about sixty welders who the company had hired from across the UK. I duly arrived at Cockatoo Island, just a little way away from Sydney Harbour Bridge, as promised, at 7 am on Monday, 8 June 1981, at 7.00 am. I was met coming from the ferry by a very old man in dirty overalls who held a card with my family name 'HASSAN' hand-written on it with a black marker. The old man assumed an unconvincing air of importance to nullify what I could immediately see was his lowly rank, and led me to the stores. Here I was given a pair of washed but used overalls, new boots and gloves, and a used welding visor. I was then told to report to the nearby office of an Egyptian chap named Claude, who was the delegate for the Amalgamated Metal Workers and Shipwrights Union. Claude was short and burly, with a dark complexion and hazel irises that were magnified to an unusual degree by powerful spectacles. He informed me, as I recall, that I should forget what I had learned about the work process in the UK and to synchronise with my fellow welders – everyone was to work at the same pace, he said. I nodded but made a note to myself that I'd find out if this was an order – and if he could give me one – and what it meant. Perhaps it was because I was the first of the UK hirelings to arrive, but I got a visit on my second day from a couple of men in suits who came down to the shipyard from the management complex of offices up on the hill, where they had a panoptical view of the eastern part of the island. Perhaps they were curious about the nature of imports they had acquired. They spoke to me as if to a child for two minutes, about nothing beyond the barest pleasantries, and then they left. I wouldn't speak to another man in a suit on the island again.

Back to the pace of work: initially I thought that I might need to improve my game and work like a dog in the smoky and noisy interiors of the ship that I was engaged to weld, the HMAS *Success*. But the opposite was the expectation. It became clear that I should work as slowly as possible and to learn all the ways to appear hard at it when charge-hands or supervisors were around. Unofficial union policy was that my foremost duty was to find places inside the hull of the ship to hide until the shift was over. Actually, the change of pace was hard going as I had to adapt from working at a natural pace to doing virtually nothing for weeks on end. Many of my workmates thought they had found the perfect job, but I hated the boredom, the needlessly elongated days and the sense that the pay packet – pushed out to us every second Thursday from an unsmiling paymistress – a surly woman behind a steel grille – was unearned.

The working day soon became long and depressing as I tried to figure out how to fill the hours. The tabloid newspapers could be digested over morning tea, but there were long interludes between breaks to kill. After some days, I began to see workers – the work-force was largely made up of new migrants from about a dozen different European countries, as well as Canada, Argentina and even one man from Japan – with paperback books stuffed in their overall back pockets or slid inside one of the large breast pockets. For me this was something unusual, something I never saw in my working life in Scotland.

Books presented me with my first challenge and my first opportunity in Australia. I was practically illiterate when I ran through the gates of Our Lady's High School on my last day. I was now twenty-one and had read only one book that I could recall – *The Wizard of Oz*, and not even the L. Frank Baum version but a large-print film edition with big pictures of Dorothy and the others. However, in the noise and smoke-filled hull of the slowly-taking-shape HMAS *Success*, with its uncountable compartments and hidey-holes, a vast literature circulated. Reading material passed discreetly from hand to hand like *samizdat*. After making some appropriately diplomatic inquiries to one or two book-holders, I was admitted into the network. It began with eager offers of glossy pornography magazines, often German and of the vilest kind – so vile that it seemed to me to be unbelievable that you couldn't be jailed for possession of that kind of stuff. After refusing these, lots of the much more sedate *Reader's Digest* came my way, and I would read them cover to cover in a glassy-eyed sort of way.

I quickly sought out other networks of literature of a more challenging sort and was passed a frayed and thumbed 800-odd page copy of *The Don Flows Home to the Sea* by Mikhail Sholokhov. I loved it. Its vivid detail of characters, scenes and plot seemed to me like watching a movie. *And Quiet Flows the Don* by the same author flowed to me and kept me awake through many a shift. Within this little communist-inspired network, I graduated to *The Brothers Karamazov* and *Crime and Punishment* by Fyodor Dostoyevsky. There were also blue Pelican 1971 reprints of E.H. Carr's three-volume *The Bolshevik Revolution*, and an outlier blue Pelican by George Woodcock called *Anarchism*. For light relief, lowerbrow networks would distribute novels by Harold Robbins, Sidney Sheldon, Stephen King and Frederick Forsyth. With so much time on my hands, I got to know the people, the distribution channels and the genres passing through them. I read for several hours a day, often passing on a book with a short critique for the next reader: crap, quite good, interesting.

One day in the lunch room, I was handed the 1980 Penguin edition of George Orwell's *Homage to Catalonia* by a weedy North Londoner called Paul who never forgave me for trying on his sunglasses in the lunch room one day and putting them glass-down on the tabletop. Subsequently, I too developed an irritation towards this malpractice, and to this day I think of Paul whenever someone puts the specs glass-down in a pub or cafe. Anyway, his succinct advisory was, 'Faacking brilliant.' I read it, re-read it, kept it and still have it. It would get me into university about ten years later when I was asked, as part of an entry requirement, to write a 1500-word essay on one of a selected list of classics.

Much of what you've just read was new to me. Like the other stories I'll recount later, I 'found' these vignettes and people in my memory. They had always been there, recorded from the experience but never retrieved, because I, like most of us, didn't have the time to explore what's inside. I spent hours and days kneeling on the couch in my cabin and staring out the window at the middle distance or horizon. I spent unregistered time lengths tracing and retracing a long-dried and wobbly brush stroke of paint on the cabin ceiling. I walked around the deck of the ship or stood at the very point of the ship with the wind howling. All these moments and more allowed me to explore my memories. It seemed to me that I would begin in a memory which had a context and which was more or less contained. However, with effort I could move from a particular context and start seeing what was next to it: a new detail, another piece of dialogue, another person, another context. With some practice and yet more time, I could establish myself as a disembodied presence within these memories, seeing myself in them and then moving myself like a supervening force to a new part or a new adjoining context. I would keep doing this until I felt I had exhausted its store.

•

I peered into the navigation deck to see that Jesse had gone and the place was empty again. I went back inside, feeling more relaxed and confident, and thinking about HMAS *Success* and the *Rossini* and the fact that in both cases, the welding for the most part is shoddy. I knew why this was the case for the ship I worked on – it had a completion timeline of three years and it took seven. But the *Rossini*'s weld work was rough, too. I'd heard all the stories about the super-efficient yards 'in the East' that were taking 'our' jobs in Scotland and Australia, but the *Rossini* had been built in South Korea, and I could nonetheless see the evidence of slapdash metalwork. I told myself that workers, welders – people – were pretty much the same all over as far as waged work is concerned.

I went downstairs to my cabin and saw that my door was open and Salva Cruz was in there making the two beds that I had disordered. I told him not to bother and he said it was no bother and we left it at that. I wanted to get back into one of the beds. Before Salva left, I asked if he could call me when the ship was about to depart because I wanted to be back upstairs for the event. 'Fifteen-thirty approximately, we depart, sir,' he said, smiling and clattering his metal trolley on the way to the door. Before he disappeared, he asked me if there was anything I needed. I asked if he could find me a little teapot, any sort, for the green tea I'd brought along. Then I fell fully clothed into the newly made bed, put on a playlist of the Cocteau Twins on my MP3 player, and heard only the first few swinging, jangling bars of *Pearly-Dewdrops' Drops* before blacking out again.

I was woken by a rapping on the door, followed by the papery sound of a note being slid underneath. I sat up and rubbed my eyes and face, making spirals on my temples with my middle fingers and feeling slightly hungover and trying to remember if I'd brought paracetamol. 'We are underway,' the note read, in a blunt pencil mark presumably from Salva Cruz. It was seven minutes past four according to the clock, and still light and sunny. I was very pleased that I had a straight and unobstructed view from my windows to the prow and could see that we were coming up to the West Gate Bridge, the opening to Port Phillip Bay. Four paracetamols later and I was outside through the exit of the port side door on my deck. I sat on the green checker plate steps and watched in slight amazement as my normal cycle-route under the bridge floated by. It looked like a nondescript road wending toward a (if I'm honest) nondescript suburb. I'd never thought of it like that before. Maybe it was the hangover. I was also cold again. I could see the navigation deck up above from where I sat, and so I climbed up the checker plate stairs to the viewing space I'd stood in a few hours previously. Embarrassingly, the door to the deck was closed from the inside and so I had to knock on the window to ask to be let in. Captain Calment was sitting at what I assumed was the captain's chair. I was pleasantly surprised that he simply smiled, said welcome, and introduced the local harbour master, whose name I now forget, who would guide the ship out from the docks, over the bay and through the tricky shoals that guard the infamous Rip at The Heads.

This was the beginning of a full three-hour vigil on the deck. In that time, not a word was spoken to me by anyone. I just watched and listened and moved periodically from inside to outside and back again, to get some air and to soak up the atmosphere and look at the views. People often say that sunsets observed from an airplane are magnificent. They are. But so are the sunsets that are part of our life every day. We just don't notice them enough – especially in the city, where you have to make an effort to get to a vantage point – and so in the end they stop being part of our conscious experience, like the immense galaxies above our heads that are veiled by a screen of light pollution. However, at sea (or Port Phillip Bay in this case), the sunset gives plenty of notice of intent. It was

The sun sets over the Rossini. *Latitude: -2.822859 Longitude: 107.200884* (Off the Bangka
Belitung Islands, 30th August)

utterly dazzling to see the slow, sumptuous sinking of the disk and
the colours that it radiated onto the sea, sky, clouds, yachts and
anything else in its path. Windows onshore, which were set at just
the right angle, would suddenly burst with a laser-intense orange –
utterly dazzling. And I knew that the rooms behind those windows
would be filled with the last slanting golden light of the day.

As the *Rossini* slowly sailed away from the city, the sun dropped
further to the west behind it and a cityscape began to glitter in the
blue darkness left in its solar wake. The lights in the vast circle of
the bay began to reveal themselves, too – low yellow and white and

sometimes red pinpoints of light stretching for 200 or so kilometres right around in my 360-degree view. I didn't want the experience to end but I was consoled by the iron fact that the sun gives us this most primal of rhythmic displays, the time of the natural world, day after day. I was witnessing a kind of natural Kairos, where the time can only ever be right because it signifies the deep time and rhythm of nature unfolding at its own pace. I began to get a tiny glimmer of understanding of the reasoning of those ancient tribes I mentioned before, for whom the movement of the sun was the very basis of a cosmic time and order and who were certain that this was the most important thing in the sky and the most import-ant thing in nature and thus the most important thing in human life as an integral part of that nature and that cosmos.

I slipped back inside through a deepening twilight. I imagined the sailors would likely witness the light show routinely and would be less overawed by the luminous transformation that just hap-pened in front of their eyes. They were all busy working. Four men were carefully steering the *Rossini* as we neared the hazardous reefs lurking at The Rip, where The Heads of Port Phillip come to a narrow point of contact just wide enough for ships to pass through. Since the 1800s, hundreds of vessels have come to their end here or hereabouts, and it occurred to me that just a few metres below there must be the ancient remains of ships, sailors, passengers, prisoners and cargoes. To this day, you can go paddling or snorkelling among many of the rocky shorelines in the bay and find sea-worn, smooth-edged and brown cracked fragments of blue Willow crockery made in Stoke-on-Trent, England, that were shipped out to Australia but destined to never grace any table.

There are no overhead lights in the navigation deck. It's lit by the sun during the day and by computer screens and one or two small desk lamps at night. It was now almost totally dark inside. A long horizontal streak of deep red where the sun used to be was still visible outside and behind us, and little guide lights were appearing in front of us as the ship moved forward though its designated channel. By sea law, Captain Calment must cede control of his ship until it gets beyond the danger zone, the zone that the local harbour master has intimate knowledge of. Monsieur Calment sat in his usual captain's chair, but for now the real authority was with the harbour master, who regularly moved between the radar screen and the outward-slanting windows, peering ahead through binoculars. Enzo was standing over a computer in the shadows to the back of the room, and Jesse was at the left of the harbour master with a seemingly special role of just listening and looking – perhaps his role was to observe the process. This is where sailors' training comes into use. Enzo would later tell me how much he loved the training school in Marseille, and how much he loved the process of navigation.

After standing at the back of the navigation deck for a few minutes, I could sense the concentration and the tension in all of them, and it took me a while of observation to figure out what was going on. The process of steering was precise and had its own rhythms. In the background, sitting on top of a shelf above the chart table, was a noisy little printer. A thick ream of paper fed a continuous stream of print-outs, which I later learned was the data from the echo sounders that were scanning the sea bed for the same rocks that had ripped the wooden, iron and steel hulls that lay below us. Every few seconds, the printer would rattle into action and its print-head would screech back and forth across the blue-lined pages until that particular batch of information had been recorded. Then it would stop, then go again, then stop. Taking his cue from the radar screen, the harbour master would call out a number that Enzo would key into a computer. This would then guide the *Rossini* in a micro-shift change in direction – left, right, back, or even pause.

The harbour master calls, the captain repeats, the first officer confirms and keys in the data, again and again. In the dark, it sounded almost like a mantra. The Australian accent, the French accent and the French accent once more, then another sequence of numbers and a shift in direction. It was like vespers by numbers: monotone, with each listening ear straining to ensure the number and the direction, its repetition and its confirmation are all exactly the same. Maybe that was Jesse's role, I wondered, his silence being the required confirmation that all was correct. All the while, the printer intermittently screeched and then fell silent in the background.

In addition to his experience, the harbour master was guided through the narrow channel by little floating lights that formed a distinct pathway. At one point, he turned from the window and signalled, with a flapping of the four fingers of his left hand, for Captain Calment to come to him, and then pointed to the biggest radar screen: 'Let me show you something, Captain,' he said. Captain Calment jumped up from his swivel chair, and they both dipped their faces into the green glow of the radar. A short time later, at a pre-arranged point, the *Rossini* stopped. The harbour master's job was done, and he was about to be picked up by a waiting tug-boat. Underneath the port-side windows in the dark, men were unspooling a rope-ladder to a little tug bouncing on the unseen waves and banging its rubberised gunwales on the hull of the container ship. The last part of the navigation would belong to Captain Calment. The Australian put on his life-jacket and was escorted out the door by another officer. 'He's really good,' said the captain of the harbour master, addressing no one in particular. I took this as an opportunity to leave, too. Three hours of standing and watching had gone past in what seemed like hardly any time. I said thank you and good night. Enzo, who was standing next to the door, said to me in what was his first act of informality, 'The big waves will now begin', and then he gave me the wide-eyed, fake-scared look of a dad who is about to put his son on a funfair rollercoaster for the first time.

5

TO SEE

As Enzo had predicted, burgeoning waves were waiting for us as soon as the *Rossini* cleared The Heads. Before I left the navigation deck, I drew a copy of our route from the large-scale chart of Australia and its coasts that Enzo had been working on and which still lay on the big chart table. No one had told me what the exact route was, but from the chart I could see that when we cleared The Heads, we were to turn left and steer toward Sydney, a thousand kilometres away, to drop off and pick up containers. Then we would double-back down the coast again, retracing our route, only to pass Melbourne without stopping and make for Adelaide, across the delicate curvature of the Great Australian Bight. From there, five days hence from Adelaide, we would turn right at the bottom-left corner of the continent and then head north-west, 104 degrees NNW, up and across the Indian Ocean to the Sunda Strait gap between the islands of Java and Sumatra, and then bear left and north-east toward Singapore via the Java Sea.

A smooth and golden flow had characterised the route out from Footscray. As soon as The Heads was behind us, however, the *Rossini* began a rolling motion that was unexpectedly intense.

The differing temperaments of these connected waters were striking. I had to touch the walls, left and right, as I walked down the corridor to my cabin. Let's see how it goes, I told myself once inside; it would surely calm down soon. Seeking some distraction from the portents of a swaying cabin, I looked around to ensure that nothing was going to roll about and get damaged, although I'd brought practically nothing, and nothing breakable, with me. One puzzle was solved straight away, however. The reason for the mysterious red plastic cable that hung from the inside of the leg space of the writing desk became apparent: it was to keep the chair from lurching backwards when the *Rossini* pitched to its port side. I was supposed to hook the chair inside the desk's leg space when not using it. I discovered later, that when actually sitting at the desk, depending on the direction of the roll, I had either to dig my heels into the carpet when the room sloped to port, or apply the brakes with my toes when it went starboard. This was a kind of exercise for the legs, but not really conducive to writing.

It was time to stop distracting myself and look for hard evidence of the extent of the roll. It was dark outside so direct apprehension was no good. An indication of sorts came from one of the bottles of Zilia that I'd opened. It was three-quarters full and sitting on a little ledge above the writing desk. I could see from the water surface that the pitching of the ship looked pretty steep – but then what did I know about what was steep and what was normal? The to-ing and fro-ing of the water level was given another dimension by the vibrating of the ship, which I hadn't thought about until then. It made the water surface bounce up and down in thousands of little droplets, like rice grains on a drum. The combined effect was curious. If I picked the bottle up, its fizzing and see-sawing would subside. Put it back on the shelf and it would start up again. I picked it up and placed it on another surface, on the coffee table in the middle of the room. Would this be a more tranquil part of the cabin? No. What about the cute little shelf above the beds? No again. The entire cabin was vibrating and pitching equally. Randomly, I thought about what this might do to beer in cans. Do they have beer on container ships? Maybe they only serve wine for this very reason: cans might explode when the ring was pulled. But thinking back to earlier in the day, I saw, or thought I saw, a Coke Zero can at one of the tables at lunch …

We had been travelling north for a few hours now. I'd even been to dinner at 7 pm on the dot, eating my way rapidly through *pasta al tonno in bianco*, rice pudding of the sort you get from a tin, with peaches also of the sort you get from a tin, followed by cheese and biscuits. Salva Cruz had placed another carafe of Beaujolais on my table, with a white napkin tied around it in a kind of cork arrangement, but I left it untouched, took what was left of the litre bottle of Zilia on the table, and went back upstairs to the cabin. A full stomach and feeling fine. I even tempted fate by considering, for a time, the way in which the water in the toilet bowl reacted to the ship's rolling. When it rolled to starboard, the water would disappear completely down the S-bend for a few seconds, and then when the pitch moved to port, it would gurgle back up again in a kind of reflux action, coming dangerously close to the rim and threatening to spill out over the floor. It never did. I went to sleep and never did feel sick, despite my rolling on the bed.

•

I hadn't really thought about the mechanics of the digital detox in too much detail. The process itself, as far as I had actually reflected upon it, was to simply cut myself off from the time of the world, to think about what it was to be free from the clock and from the network, and then to experience, in a more conscious and salient way, the subjective time of duration that exists somewhere – in you and in me – struggling to break out from the shackles of clock and computer. But what does that mean in practice? I wasn't sure on my second day what I was supposed to do and feel. Digital detoxification is something I could have done anywhere, I suppose. I could have taken a month's vacation and turned off all my devices and stayed at home or gone to a beach or a forest or a mountain and lay or walked or climbed. But I reasoned that an ordinary attempt at freedom from the digital would inevitably be infiltrated by temptation and distraction. Even if I could resist these, their relative availability or ease of access to them would likely prey on my mind. Like the recovering alcoholic who would be wise not to keep vodka in the cupboard 'just for guests', it seemed to me that to do something a bit extraordinary, actual cold turkey, would plunge me, so to speak, into a new realm, into a form of isolation, one by no means extreme, such as in a prison cell or McCandless's bus, but enough to throw me back onto myself, for once. I would be compelled to work with this; to explore in a heuristic way, and see how time 'feels' when the clock, the computer, the time of the world, and the digital traps are let go, for a little while, and to see what happens.

Isolation was the first feeling. When I woke naturally the next day, without the prompting of the 'slow rise' alert on my iPhone, there was nothing to do, no one to see, and no role to play. Moreover, my position as paying passenger meant that I could not simply go and be a part of the life of the ship and its crew. They had their jobs to do, and I didn't. But what is isolation? It sounds like desolation, but it's not. Desolation connotes a despondency and misery, and is a political subject-position, an extreme state, one that does not come into the reckoning here. There is a term regaining currency in the age of Brexit and the general crisis of nation-states, and it is 'splendid isolation'. It was first used in the nineteenth century to describe Britain's policy of avoiding foreign imbroglios and alliances, and to 'go it alone' as much as possible. That went well, didn't it? The isolation envisaged by the modernising Victorians such as Benjamin Disraeli, was to be one that gave a freedom of action and a freedom from commitments, and possibly made some sort of sense at the time. But the world then was already globalising and so isolation, splendid or otherwise, became impossible. It is well-nigh impossible for us today, too, both as individuals and as members of a society. But it is still possible to create the context for it for a time, and within that time discover, hopefully, some things about ourselves and the world we live in. Isolation was, thus, both a prerequisite for what I wanted to find out, and also an opportunity to use those conclusions as possible ways for changing myself, even if in a small way, through new understandings of what it is to live in the time of the world, and with the technologies that govern it.

It was Theodor Adorno, the German cultural theorist and Jewish refugee, who wrote in 1944 that 'Communication establishes uniformity among men by isolating them'. He had in mind things such as the private car, but was also prefacing thoughts about technologies such as the television and the computer and the mobile phone. All connect us as points of communication, but at the same time isolate us physically, causing us to become cogs in the machine or nodes in the network. I mentioned earlier the psychologist Sherry Turkle and her book *Alone Together*, which says essentially the same thing: the more we connect, the more we become isolated – physically isolated in front of a screen, or with headphones over our ears, or a head-up display wrapped around our eyes, or wearing a full-body immersive suit technology that is claimed to deliver a virtual reality. Adorno and Turkle see isolation from flesh and blood people, which militates against the formation of traditional communities. This is unarguable. But also in this view, the isolated individual still has the connection of the network: they still communicate, albeit at a denatured and abstracted level. To be really isolated in the particular (non-desolate) sense that I wanted, is to eschew technological communication, that is to say, media, itself. And so, being on the *Rossini* isolated me from people in the normal sense, but it also isolated me from the distractions that isolation through communication brings, which for me was the key thing.

Ok, so now what? Well, I was thrown back onto myself and to my resources, to my senses, fundamentally. I could use my eyes and read. Pick up the books and writing materials I had and get busy. That was my first thought on this new day in this new context. But I wanted to ration those. Anyway, to read my books about time and to write about it would not be to experience time, but to use it in a conventional way. Alternatively, I could use my eyes and look around me. More focused looking is natural when in new contexts and situations, but I wanted to go beyond that and look at my surroundings in a way that we never actually do unless through a conscious willing of it. Looking is underrated or taken for granted in our culture, notwithstanding the fact that almost everything depends upon it – in individuals' lives and in the collective life and coherence of society. Indeed, where would digital life be without the visual dimension? Those who are blind or visually impaired can access worlds through the invention of Braille, but the worldwide web has little functionality for those who cannot see well. Marshal McLuhan argued that with the coming of print and literacy, the human 'sense ratio' shifted from the aural, where we imagined our world through hearing stories, to the visual, where seeing dominates. In everyday conversation, one never says, 'hear you tomorrow' or 'look forward to hearing you'. And so, in digital life, there is competition for those eyes, for our attention, so much so that we are never allowed to have them rest for too long on any particular aspect.

Look at people on a train or bus in their commute. Not so long ago, the eyes would be on a newspaper or book, or unfocused, on the middle distance, in thought or contemplation, or out the window, or on the head of the person in front, or simply letting the gaze softly wander. There was a relative calm and attention accompanying the movement of the eyes of previous generations. Not anymore. I once went to a seminar where a researcher had visually represented real-time Twitter communities in Australia. Up on the big projector screen, blobs of colour dilated and contracted and bled into one another. It looked like a moving Damien Hirst spot painting, or a 1970s *Dr Who* outro. If someone somehow could rig up an eye-tracking device to follow the movements of commuters today with their smartphones and tablets, and then visually represent all this action, the effect would be something to see, I'm sure. The chaos of information, as I imagine it represented, would be like fifty-thousand kids running around and waving sparklers in the dark.

But to look closely and with attention is to experience both visual information and time in a different way. Gustave Flaubert, the nineteenth-century writer of *Madame Bovary*, the great novel of observed French bourgeois emotional life, is said to have remarked: 'For anything to become more interesting you simply have to look at it for a long time'. Hmm. 'Anything' might be stretching it a little, but the point is a good one. In an essay titled 'The Concept of Experience', the cultural critic Mark Greif introduced me to this little insight into the experience of experience and how to make experience and the time of experience a salient aspect of the practice of daily life. Greif observes:

> Life becomes the scene of total, never-ending experience, as long as the [looker] can muster the intensity to it in this way. We all have the power to find the meaningful aspect of a thing by going onto or into it; by spreading the surface world with experience and pressing your imagination and emotions into any crack. You must let it into you, too.

This shift of emphasis is partly just old-style reconnecting with your environment or surroundings – something we all do from time to time, when, for example, you enter a favourite room, or corner at a familiar bar, or a regular table at a café or restaurant. You do it because it is pleasing and comforting, and it can relax and calm you. It's familiar and restful because over a period of time, you have looked at the surroundings in a way that allows you to know it, to be in a sense a part of it, and to have a purely subjective relationship with it and its aspects. But to look is also to connect for the first time with the new and the unfamiliar, or perhaps with the overlooked aspects of the 'surface' of your world, to zoom-in on them and consider what you see. As Greif emphasises, and as I tried to convey in the previous chapter, this is a matter of will, and the free exercise of that will to 'muster the intensity' to trouble yourself to look – and look more closely for a change. By going into and onto your surroundings, to map it with experience, means to see the world in a different way and also to experience the time of the world in a different way. In fact, to 'press your imagination and emotions' – and I would add memory – into and onto your physical surroundings, means that for as long as you can 'muster the intensity', then the time of the world dissolves from consciousness, and the subjective time of individual experience emerges.

To write about looking does not properly convey what looking can mean for the subjective experience of space and time. What David Abram called the 'unfortunate side-effect of the alphabet' intervenes to place abstraction in front of direct perception, in front of the direct perceptual mapping to give you a vicarious experience. Text can be wonderful, and under the writerly spell of a good observational novelist, the reader can be transported to other places and times. Another French writer, Alain Robbe-Grillet, took writing about looking to the micro-level, down to the level of dust. This is from the opening page of his 1960 book, *In the Labyrinth*:

Outside the sun is shining, there is not a tree, not a bush to give shade, one has to walk in the full sunlight, hand shielding the eyes that look ahead, a few yards ahead only, a few yards of dusty asphalt where the wind traces parallels, curves and spirals. Here the sun does not enter, nor does the wind, nor the rain, nor the dust.

The fine dust that falls dulls the horizontal planes, the varnished tabletop, the polished parquet, the marble of the mantelpiece, and that of the chest of drawers, the cracked marble of the chest of drawers, the only dust here comes from the room itself: from the gaps in the parquet possibly; or from the bed, or the curtains, or the ashes in the fireplace.

On the varnished tabletop, the dust has marked the place occupied for a while – for a few hours, a few days, minutes, weeks – by small objects since removed, the bases of which are clearly outlined for a while longer, a circle, a square, a rectangle, other less simple forms, some of them partly overlapping, already blurred or half-erased as if by the flick of a rag.

Time (and dust) permeates this fine-grained (and dusty) description of the mundane and the overlooked, raised to an intensity by the writer through looking and writing about looking. But this is a mediated looking, a vicarious looking from the perspective of someone else's eyes, and then mediated once more through the alphabet. This is well-honed writing, nonetheless, and it is possible to enter into a narrative like this and go with its time and flow and lose yourself in it. But it's not *your* time, it's secondary and so the experience can only be secondary and diminished, or if not diminished then of a lesser intensity than that which could be attained by looking at oneself. You need to do it yourself.

My reading and writing would be, henceforth, rationed whilst on the *Rossini*, and I made a decision, then, to shift the sense ratio

from the standard and distracted looking that might character-
ise not only my looking but that of the majority of us in the
screen-filled world that is digital life: no screens, fewer books, and
more focusing on the surfaces of the world around me. This ship
was a small world, to be sure, but all of it was totally new, and
totally exciting once I began to look at it.

•

Day two. Not seasick. Or hungover. And, therefore, a breakfast
of brewed coffee, several two-bite-sized croissants, Bonne Maman
strawberry jam in jars whose tops were too wide and generous,
and a large ramekin that Salva Cruz had filled with amazing,
more-white-than-yellow-coloured butter, which one would have to
finish because any remainder would be thrown away. I was at my
table by 7.03 am and so could observe the crew as they wandered
in from their differing shifts, dressed in either a crisp white officer's
shirt for the navigation deck, or the Hi-Viz jacket from being out
and about in the sea air. People whose names I would never know
continued to nod respectfully and say 'bonjour' as they simultaneously scanned the buffet table's offerings. Direct eye contact,
apparently, was no longer necessary after the first greeting.

I noted that the seat in the middle of the officer's table, with
its back to the lace-curtained window and directly facing me, was,
officially or not, reserved for Captain Calment. He is one of those
characters – a charismatic, who has a bit of an aura that shimmers
around him when he enters a room. I got the feeling, however, that
he was still working out his relationship with his fellow officers.
Enzo mentioned to me later that he was new to the company, having made his career in oil tankers, which was considered a superior
occupation compared with container ships. He was also said to be
rather bad-tempered. Possibly, it was a combination that meant
when he approached the breakfast table and hovered at his seat,

a tremor of deference ran through those already seated. Tipping back their chairs as they did so, one or two would half-stand in their obeisance, usually the younger ones, whilst more experienced and more senior officers would remain seated in a minor act of mutiny that the looming Calment would ignore. A time-lapse camera of the scene would show that as the captain sat, the table would soon clear, and Monsieur Calment would be left alone to eat what I saw would become his usual breakfast of too few Coco Pops floating in too much Nesquik. Perhaps the deserting French officer class could not bear this daily act of *trahison culturelle gastronomique*. But now with a clear field of view, the captain could offer me a smiling nod of acknowledgement before plunging his spoon into the bowl.

At these southern latitudes during August it was generally cold, especially in the more open areas of the vessel, so it was good to get back to my cabin after breakfast. Already, I had the feeling of a voice and tongue unused, and unused to unemployment. With no one to speak to, and no digital distractions to compensate, looking and acting became the salient modality, the new state. Acting was physical movement, partly to keep warm, and partly to have the kind of order I thought necessary in my surroundings. Making the bed, folding clothes, putting away shoes, picking up pencils that had rolled to the floor, etc. I had also resolved to continue keeping fit and to use the little gym-room on B deck that Enzo had shown to me the day before during the little familiarisation drill. Gloomy and unused, it offered a stationary bike, a cross trainer, a treadmill, and various weights and bars arranged in the corner. It even had a porthole with a view to starboard, above a lost-looking table football game.

Today I was going to explore the *Rossini*'s lower D Deck, on the outside where I'd first come aboard in what already seemed like much more than the couple of days ago. Before I set out, the cold obliged me to don a pair of thick light grey sweatpants, an extra-large thick grey sweatshirt of exactly the same shade and grade, thick grey Japanese woollen socks, which were slightly darker, and the only pair of trainers I own, no-names, which were a darker shade of grey. Plus, a red Italian merino scarf. Red scarf aside, I'd never worn such a monotonous combination before, and I felt like I was in prison garb, or like Sylvester Stallone running up the steps in one of the *Rocky* films. Of course, there was no one who would notice or care, anyway. To go down the five levels to D Deck using the stairs was to experience the clueless kitsch of corporate identity, but I came to enjoy it in the dozens of times I would use the stairs again.

The *Rossini* was named after the famous Italian composer, but there is also, somewhere on the world's oceans right now, a *Mozart*, a *Bellini* and a *Berlioz* flying the *tricolore* for CMA CGM. There was nothing particularly Italian about the *Rossini*, except for a pride-of-place framed daguerreotype of the great man, on my deck. Fat and smiling wanly, the operettist stands holding a cane in his right hand, while the thick knuckles of his left are digging hard into a book lying open on a table. The knuckles are a giveaway. For some reason, Signor Rossini looks uptight.

Apart from the strange choice of photograph, the company's interior designers had also tried to portray an internationalism of sorts. The narrow landing of each deck was fitted with a gold-framed poster reproduction of a majestic CMA CGM container ship, idealised as a friendly visitor to enchanting parts of the world. On my deck, next to the daguerreotype, the stairhead displayed a *Rossini*-like ship in a reproduction of a poster-paint rendition of Hong Kong Harbour, with an Oriental woman, under the shade of a red Japanese umbrella, looking out toward the ship and giving a clunky wistful effect to a tableau named 'EUROPE-ASIE'. The same one was in my cabin, screwed onto the shower-room door. There were similarly clichéd scenes on the different deck levels, titled 'AMERIQUE DU SUD, TRANSATLANTIQUE, EUROPE-ANTILLES', and at D Deck, in a re-inscription of the general tone, a monster-sized CMA CGM ship was depicted sailing into the sunset, and titled 'TOUR DU MONDE'.

The stairway was in permanent semi-darkness, but the lighting on the framed posters gave the sentimental scenes a cosy allure that grew on me every time I went up and down, to and from, the cabin and navigation deck. To have one of these kitschy artefacts in your office or room would be to occasionally dream of those mythic places, or those idealised voyages, but here I was actually experiencing it in the normally abstract space of the open sea. The pictures themselves, however, in a strange space-time logic, were continually travelling to their own destinations.

Stepping outside for the first time through the submarine-type doors on the port side of D Deck, and sufficiently prepped by the poster scenes, I half-expected the smell of the sea and other natural elements to contribute to the overall impression of something exotic. What hit me, however, was the bouquet of burning oil, and a fast-flowing gauze of soot that stung the eyes as the wind and the ship's motion carried the particulate from the ship's funnel, down the length of the *Rossini*, and out over the stern to sink into the wake. My disappointed half-expectation gave way to the other half and the remembering that this was an industrial ship, part of what Sekula and Burch saw as the 'maritime economy' that inhabits the 'forgotten space' of the open seas. The other mini-shock was the vibrating of the ship from the outside, which was noisier and far more intense than inside. The power emitted from the engines made literally everything tremble. As I made my way down the narrow checker plate walkway, a violent rattling noise, different from the engine's vibration, seemed to stay with me as I went. It was the sound of the thousands of long lashing rods that kept the containers in place by means of bolted twistlocks. They vibrated continually, like what seemed to me to be inch-thick guitar strings, only their sound was not musical. Mild shock at this new and unexpected context, however, soon gave way to something like awe. The industrial smells and sounds of container shipping sank back into a deeper part of my consciousness, because there was so much else to see in the half light of this grey day.

Blue-overalled welders with white safety hats were stationed here and there. Some were doing mysterious things with hand-held tools, which looked ship-specific; others were chipping at rust or daubing a deep red paint over newly welded metal patches, to where time and salt had holed a wall or a floor or a ceiling. Rust, like the succulents in the navigation deck, was a constant companion of the *Rossini* on its never-ending voyage. The welders were mainly Filipino and Bangladeshi, smiling politely and making way for me as I passed them. In the coming weeks, I got to see them regularly and discovered that they, like me in another life, also found places in the ship where they could hide from the Bosun, a Frenchman named Jean-Claude, who would make his predictable morning and afternoon rounds to see what was what in his domain. In contrast to the smooth lines of the ship's hull, the deck had all manner of mysterious corners and ropes and pulleys and boxes and pumps and bevels and chains and diagrams and hooks and numbers and doors and pipes and chairs and passageways and noises and lights and written instructions that presented themselves to me at almost every step I took. Outside in the wind, though, it was easier and warmer to keep moving and stop only where there was a little shelter – and this was in the spaces between the containers themselves. A Hapag-Lloyd-owned box would find itself underneath one from Maersk, which in turn would hold up another from P&O, and on it would go, stacked up to twenty-five high from the bottom of the ship. With a hint of jealousy in his voice, Enzo once mentioned that their great rival, Maersk, holds the record of 17,603 containers stacked within a single (immense) ship, the *Mary*, sailing from Algeciras, Spain, to Tanjung Pelepas, Malaysia, in 2014.

At each end of each container at eye level in front of me, there were stickers and sometimes papers, flapping and quivering in the wind, affixed to them. These signified, presumably, the origin and/or destination of the container. The stickers were different shapes and sizes and colours, and I spent a couple of hours in the morning looking at them, things I'd never thought to examine before. Why would you? I chose one to draw in my notebook because of its especially beautiful colour and size: an Yves Klein blue with a dark blue-grey trimming, and with the diameter of a large dinner plate. Curving around the top half of the circle were the words 'PRE-TRIP INSPECTION' and coming up to meet them at the bottom, 'ALEXANDRIA + 002035842528'. Within the top half of the space of the circle was a logo of some sort with straight white lines intersecting a dark blue dot. Beneath that, there were two white blank spaces, like cells in a computer form where you fill in your details. The top one said 'OK DATE' on top of the space, and the space itself had been left blank. Underneath, there was a smaller blank space with 'temperature' printed in lower case above it. On the white space was the sloping and irregular black ink-marker signature of 'Khaled'.

This was like a little archaeological discovery. A faint trace of humanity. No date, but the sticker looked fairly new. Maybe this was its first trip to Australia: an anonymous container picked up in Alexandria, Egypt, and given the good-to-go imprimatur by Khaled. As I looked at his name, I conjured in my mind's eye an image of the man. He was in his Hi-Viz and hard hat as he wrote in the unthinking way that most of us write our name, never projecting much into its destiny as a mark. But his personal mark, like that of a painter, is a part of him, and that part of him is represented in the sloping and uncertain mark of someone whose first language and script is probably Arabic. So it might be his self-translated mark, his globalised identity, that can be found here deep in the southern hemisphere. Alexandria is on Egypt's Mediterranean coast and was a centre of protest in the 2011 uprisings that toppled the Mubarak regime. When things are quieter, its catacombs and many Roman-era fortresses and baths attract the tourists. Alexandria could not be more different than Melbourne, except that both cities share a sea link, and together they form part of the network of container terminals and container ships that feed and clothe and shoe and entertain the planet.

Walking around the ship, I still had that lingering feeling that I really shouldn't be here. I half-expected to be suddenly bawled at by someone for straying into a radioactive area, or that I was about to step onto a hidden trapdoor that would carry me down and out through the back of the ship. Apostrophised warning signs and danger stickers seemed to decorate passages and openings and stairs every couple of metres. I moved slowly through this potential minefield to the stern, and finally stood next to the large French *tricolore* that had wrapped itself to its limit around the flagpole, which was set at an angle, out over the *Rossini*'s wake. It was a large flag, and fairly new-looking. It had a tiny 'Made in Taiwan' tab in the inside corner and was made of 100 per cent heavy-duty nylon. I wondered if this was to stop it fraying so readily, as cotton flags do, or if it was just a question of cost.

Standing next to the flagpole, I had to lean over and stretch my upper body quite a bit to be able to see the long way down to where the propeller drove the *Rossini* along. The immense horsepower devoted to the churning of the sea by the propeller seemed dangerous in its awesomeness. I'd never seen anything like it. Not only did the power that burst from the engines shake every millimetre of the ship, twenty-four hours a day, the sea was also being agitated by the gigantic propeller blades. To look from above at the work of the propeller was to look at a kind of watery hell, with an utterly inhuman mixing, breaking and slicing up the natural order of the marine world with every low-pitched *thoom, thoom, thoom* of the blades. The foam produced by the action was a brilliant white and boiling. Millions of sea water droplets flew constantly upwards from the churn and sparkled in the air like machine-made snow being forced through a massive blower. The curling and twisting water that roiled just underneath the spray was, to my surprise, a beautiful green, the very colour of Listerine. The thing was, the sounds of the bubbling and hissing from across the wake couldn't be heard above the roaring of the wind. Stepping back, I unwrapped the flag and let it go, with the wind-gusts collecting it immediately. It flew straight and stiff, and its rapid flapping and snapping, I imagined, would likely make short work of this 100 per cent nylon, Taiwanese-made symbol of French *mondialisation du commerce*.

Making my way up the starboard side, through a maze of more warnings and advice about how not to get electrocuted or gassed or maimed in some way, I came to a flight of checker plate stairs, twelve of them, which led to a doorway in a bulkhead, which then entered onto the forecastle of the *Rossini*. This is the pointy end of the ship and is where the pole with the red light that I could see from my cabin is located. There is a winch in the centre of this open space that pulls up the anchor, presumably stored in a compartment underneath my feet somewhere. Again, at eye level, there were signs. Here they were even more obscure and looked like early twentieth-century modern art in the geometric shapes and colours that were evidently a sort of maritime code. The one painted on the wall to the left-hand side of the door I'd just stepped through was a long yellow triangle against the grey paint of the ship, with a black dot at its top point, and a black dot in the middle, with both dots joined by a thin black line. At the top, over the top dot, it was written 'POINT OF BREAK' and at the base it said 'SNAP-BACK DANGER ZONE'. I had not the slightest idea what it signified.

At the very point of the ship, just about where the figurehead would be if modern ships had them, was, and I had to look twice, a metal seat welded into the apex. Walking around this closed space, and slowly making for the dark blue painted seat to look at it more closely and try it out, I was aware that something had changed. I couldn't think what it was, but this space felt different. It felt a little warmer, but that wasn't it. When I reached the blue seat, I turned around and sat down. Both knees suddenly ached from their being pressed too heavily at the writing desk in the cabin to stop the chair from sliding to and fro. Then I realised what had changed.

One of the Rossini's many warning signs.

There was no wind. In fact, there was hardly any sound either. The wind that rushed up from the surface of the water toward the prow of the ship blew right over the top of this little spot, like smoke going over some aerodynamic thing in a wind-tunnel test, rendering it wind-free and a perfect place to sit. Was that why the seat was there? Who was it for? Not for the welders, surely. It seemed an illogical thing to do on this ark of human exploitation and industrial efficiency.

I stood up, turned around and stepped up onto the seat – immediately the ongoing gale almost blew me backwards. Stepping down again it was silent and still once more. It was as if you could turn the wind off and on. I made a mental note to come down here sometime soon with a book and perhaps a pillow or two from the cabin. I stepped up onto the seat again and looked around. I saw that it was possible to step up again onto a welded ledge, which took the gunwale of the ship to below my waist, enabling me to experience the full effect of standing there like an eighteenth-century carved figurehead, with what felt like a 125mph wind ripping through my hair and distorting the skin on my face, like I was on a sky-dive. I shouted at the top of my voice but could barely hear myself. I looked around, with the wind slamming into each of my ears and cheeks, alternately. I looked upwards, almost falling backwards again, and shouted once more, registering even less of my own voice this time. I slowly looked around. The sky and sea were exactly the same colour as my sweatshirt and pants. There was no horizon to make out, and there was no longer any land to see for 360 degrees. Where were we? I sort of knew we were in the South Pacific, heading north to Sydney, but it didn't really matter. It was completely grey all around, with just a pummelling wind that stung the eyes and got deep inside the ears.

MÉMOIRE VOLONTAIRE 5

Sitting down again in this little sanctuary, with my throbbing knees at my chin, my thoughts began to search to when I last was on voyage unable to see dry land. I combined that train of thought with that of the ubiquitous checker plate under my feet, and suddenly my memory was in the mid-1980s. I was seeing a photograph I have at home of another horizonless moment, the only horizonless moment in my life until now, and a photograph I only ever glance at when I occasionally flick through the old album that lies at the bottom of one of my drawers. It's a cheap photo from cheap film. There are four of us in it, standing on the green checker plate in front of the white railings of the *Antrim Princess*, which used to sail between Stranraer in Scotland and Larne in Northern Ireland. Eventually it went the way of many of the world's vessels today: to the world's largest graveyard for decommissioned ships, which is the salvaging beaches in Alang in Gujarat on India's west coast.

At the left on the photo is Pat Ferris, to his left are the brothers George and Martin Wylie, Michael McGuire (who posed with us briefly) then me. A weak January sun is glowing low in from our left, putting half of our faces in bleaching light, and the other halves in dark shadow. We can hardly be made out; and my hair is cut off through inexpert composition, as is Pat's. The Wylies were shorter, and so they and their *de rigueur* mullet haircuts can be made out in silhouette.

A smooth sky-blue sea behind the railings fades into white as the eye ascends the photo. Due to the limitations of cheap film stock, you cannot see much of anything behind us, but I know that there was no land to be seen around us because I recall saying to my companions that this was the first time that I'd actually been 'at sea'. My friends are all wearing a mid-1980s uniform of tight Wrangler jeans, Dr. Martens shoes (black) and crew-necked woollen jumpers

Pat, George, Martin, Michael and the author aboard the *Antrim Princess.*

of different colours – black, grey, cream, respectively. Each jumper, however, has a two-inch bar of singular colour, red, red, red, running across the chests. (I'm coincidentally wearing a grey sweatshirt again, but with the logo 'LONSDALE' written across the chest.) I'm also the only one with a jacket, a padded Japanese army surplus which I'd bought in Tokyo at a stopover on the way home. All my friends have their arms tightly folded at their chests, either as some protection from the January temperature, or tense from the changed relationship with me: I was now someone who didn't live with them any longer. They are all thin, and with a pinched look. Martin looks positively wolfish – he always managed to look both predatory and hunted at the same time. My hands are in my jacket pockets and a black camera case is looped around my left wrist. I'm smiling weakly, probably because the photo was my idea, and they think I'm wanting to have my photo taken with the natives.

It had been my first trip back after leaving for Australia. It had only been three years, but as a young man it seemed to me like a lifetime. Nothing had changed. Why would it? Craigneuk, Wishaw, the Catholic area of my childhood, which I spoke about in the beginning of this book, was still a Catholic area. For decades, it had been settled by alternating surges or trickles of Irish immigration to work in the steelworks, in mining and in related industries. There was segregation, ghettoisation and discrimination of the usual kind against both the family that had just got off the boat and their Scottish-born and -accented descendants. Surname and creed remained, fixed and indelible and obvious, like a tattoo on the knuckles. My own street was thickly populated by ethnic Irish. As I write, I'm mentally going up Glencairn Avenue, house by house, toward St Matthews Primary, my first school. I pass by the unvaryingly green doors: the Reillys', the Higgins', the McGuires', the Foleys', the Meechans', the Gallaghers', the Fearons', the Wylies', the O'Preys', the McKelvies', the O'Connors' (Pat, Joseph, Mary, Edmund and John), the Kellys', the McCaffertys' and the Hughes'. Danny O'Neil and Sammy Corrie from the Avenue would find minor fame as rock duo The River Detectives around the mid-80s. Pat Ferris from the photo lived in nearby Flaxmill Avenue. And there were others, whose green front doors I can see, and whose 1970s faces I can summon, but whose surnames and Christian names have gone. Our own relatively unusual surname, once thought exotic and Middle Eastern was, in point of dreary fact, from County Londonderry. I suspect my forebears thought they could escape the brunt of the inevitable discrimination with a name that was not, on the face of it, all shillelaghs and shamrocks. But there was still our Catholicism to live with (and through). In Craigneuk, Celtic Football Club was the only option for a Catholic looking for an identity and a team to support. Following Celtic was, and is, a form of ethnic and religious organisation. It is also organised entertainment in the shape of supporters' clubs, which blend Irish heritage, Catholic religion and a feeling of persecution. And naturally, this led many to support the Irish Republican Army in ways that could go beyond the rhetorical.

The trip aboard the *Antrim Princess* was, for me, a jolly way to catch up with old friends. But for Pat, George and Martin, it was a piece of serious business. They were going to Derry as members of the Wolfe Tone Flute Band and were to participate in a commemoration march for the 1971 Bloody Sunday killing of thirteen protestors, held by the British Army. Flute bands inhabit a highly sectarian world in Ireland and Scotland, and for many from Craigneuk, it's all that they have. On YouTube, if you type in the keywords 'Craigneuk' and 'Wishaw', you will find little else other than iPhone capture of flute band marches, dozens and dozens of them, Catholic and Protestant – all with the comments section disabled to stop the inevitable flaming and hate-speech. In their world, this identification with Ireland, Irish culture, and Irish persecution is their *raison d'être*. Pat, George and Martin would all identify as Irish, first and foremost. I didn't, and that was a part of the problem. In fact, the trip almost didn't happen for me because the night before in the local, the Era Bar, in Craigneuk, I said something uncomplimentary about Pope John Paul II, and was lucky to avoid a punch in the face.

In my time away in Australia, I had reinvented myself as a photographer, and armed with a Zenit Praktica 35mm that I had bought for twenty dollars in Sydney, I pleaded with them to be allowed the role of unofficial documentarist. This wasn't so easy. Three years had been a long time for them, too. They were astonished to learn that I was no longer a welder, abandoning the trade that had gotten me away, and I could tell that they thought I'd abandoned the working class as well, with a January tan and a strange-looking jacket bought in Tokyo, a place that to them might as well have been one of the moons circling Mars. Thinking back to that photo, I realise I was on probation for them on that day.

The date on the back of the photo is written '25.1.1985'. This was the Friday before the march in Derry. When we got to Larne on the Friday afternoon, a red-haired and much-freckled guy in a much-driven and hand-painted orange Ford Transit picked us up and took us on the hour-long journey, past Antrim, to the town of Dungiven, where we were to be billeted. Sitting on the floor in the back of the van and drinking from the two-dozen duty-free cans of Harp Lager, Martin, the eldest at twenty-eight, led an impromptu tutorial for me on the significance of Dungiven. It was here that Kevin Lynch, one of the ten IRA hunger strikers who died in the 1981 prison protest, was born and had lived all his life. The IRA men had demanded to be treated as prisoners of war, or political prisoners, and not as criminals. And Lynch, like the others who eventually starved themselves to death, was held in quasi-mystical reverence by my friends. I made a mental note to keep any opinions on the hunger strike, which I had actually followed closely in Australia, to myself, and nodded my assent at the right moments. Like me, my friends had little time for a neglectful school system, and none of us had very much formal education. But I was struck by their fluency in matters concerning the complexities of the Irish struggle. Sieges, dates, banners, people, flutes, bandoliers, marches, drums, battles, wrongings and rightings, bravery, flags, songs, foggy dews, blindfolds, firing squads, persecution, persecution, persecution. It was history and they lived in the time of history.

The beautiful but bleak and barren hills we drove through on that January afternoon were their world and their environment. It was not just the lager having its effect, you could tell that this is where they felt alive: in the northern Irish landscape filled with what Winston Churchill disparagingly called 'dreary steeples', and (for him) overfilled with a problematic people with problematic beliefs. But for Pat, George and Martin, this is where they really came from and belonged, not the actually dreary streets of Craigneuk and Wishaw, where unemployment was now stubbornly high, and where the policies of Thatcherism were beginning to seep into the roots of a culture, and poison it. Peering out the back windows of the van at the low treeless rises and blackening sky, as the Wylies dozed and Pat practiced his drumming with the sticks by rapping a military beat on the metal wheel housing of the Transit, I felt somewhat jealous of their affinities and almost embarrassed at having been able to escape what was once our shared culture. In one sense, they were lucky. Their culture and attitude meant that they were time travellers from the past, from many pasts, and the present for them was simply a way of living those real or invented or distorted pasts.

We spent the evening in the Arcade Bar in Main Street, Dungiven. Drinking was a major pastime for my friends, and I sometimes think of them now when going to a pub on a cold night somewhere. The thought brings to mind also a line in James Joyce's 1905 book of short stories, *Dubliners*, which conveys superbly the attraction of a certain kind of pub in a certain kind of climate, to a certain kind of person from a certain kind of culture. In the book's 'Counterparts', Joyce narrates the story of the hapless and alcoholic character, Farrington, leaving work after a bad day, suffering under his dictatorial boss's bad temper, and desperate for a drink: 'The dark damp night was coming and he longed to spend it in the bars, drinking with his friends amid the glare of gas and the clatter of glasses'. There were no gas lights in the Arcade, but it was as Irish as Joyce, and what might be called a republican pub. It was also hunger striker central, with republican drawings, paintings, photographs, framed and bare, covering the maroon flock on the walls. Kevin Lynch had pride of place, of course, as a local lad now local hero. The Northern Irish accents, the flute and the bodhrán drum playing in the corner under the window, the crush around the bar, the sticky carpet and slippery tiles, the smoke and the Guinness, constituted a present existing in the past. The one-arm bandit and television and jukebox took nothing away from this archaic scene. We sat at a big curved bench, boxed into a corner, and I was introduced to everyone, above the noise, as Robert 'from Australia'. It felt like someone had just pushed me out of a children's huddle in the schoolyard. No offence was meant, but everyone was silently registering, my friends and their friends, that I was not one of them. The Irish have a history of emigration, not least to Australia, and it is said that when you take to the boat or plane then you are gone, forgotten.

The next day we were informed that the Wolfe Tone Flute Band were not to be granted permission to march on the Sunday. I forget the reason, some kind of infringing of the Bands' Association rule. Internecine politics and none of my business. So, the band paraded around a wet and windy Dungiven on the Sunday morning instead. Lashing rain and a freezing wind whistled over the grassy hills and swept the sounds of the drums and flutes eastwards, toward the Irish Sea and back to Scotland. Afterwards we went to the Arcade again, to warm up, dry out, drink, and to curse the Bands' Association bureaucracy, to listen to more music and to sing the by now familiar songs of Irish republicanism. I had taken photos all morning with my Zenit and a roll of 36 was already used up. Walking up Main Street to the bar, however, a soldier with a London accent pushed me up against a wall, took the camera from me, opened up the back, pulled the film from the roll and said, with a menacing grin: 'Get some nice ones, did you?' After the initial shock of the minor violence perpetrated on me, I felt secretly quite glad it had happened, despite my outward displays of anger and outrage. Everyone saw it, and everyone saw it was unprovoked harassment. I'd earned a tiny bit of credit with these people.

On the *Rossini* and sitting in the little wind shelter at the prow of the ship, somewhere in the South Pacific, thinking about the hunger strikers of 1981, it occurs to me that what Kevin Lynch must have done was to experience time in the most intense way, in a way I could only scratch the surface of here in my benign isolation. His was a battle in time and for time. Lynch and his comrades had been waiting to die but waiting in the positive sense

I discussed earlier; a form of waiting wherein they were in control of their time's concentrated unfolding. In a cell in solitary confinement, or later in a hospital bed, they waited, and they experienced waiting and the intensified time of waiting through the experience of personal duration. In a real sense, they were free. They had decided to strike through an act of free will, and through this act of will they freed themselves from the experiential aspect of physical confinement. Through the act of slow starvation, they had commandeered their own lives and their bodies by choosing to kill themselves. To hang oneself from a cell window would barely register as a political act; it's over in seconds, and is invisible, and is past-tense. However, to draw it out, to live in the long shadow of a death through starvation that is reported daily by the media and anguished over by family and doctors and priests and supporters is a political drama that only heightens with time. How long will it take to die? They must have asked themselves this again and again. To act, to exercise free will like this, is to move from 'state to state', as Bergson put it. The hunger strikers must have known this, they must have discussed amongst themselves what it meant to act, and what it meant beyond the purely symbolic.

When the decision was taken, Kevin Lynch and the others were no longer living in the present because the political context had structured it for them, and they were no longer dwelling on the past, because their movement did. They had transported themselves to some unknown time in the future. They existed at the point of the estimated time of their deaths, and had become actors in the political and personal consequences of their deaths. Their action and their time that was running out was not negative or futile, but for them a positive weapon wielded against a State that had oppressed them. But it now no longer could, because they had escaped the present of their gaol and gaolers. The time of hunger, and of the growing weakness of body and mind, was their own time that they were living. No one could take it from them or force them to live it any other way (force feeding was dropped as an option by the British government in Ireland in the 1970s). Kevin Lynch from Dungiven was free for seventy-one days from 23 May 1981 until 1 August, when he died. Those seventy-one days were his guarantee of immortalisation. Seventy-one days that may last for a thousand years in books, in oral histories, in murals and, more ordinarily, in the lives and memories and lists of grievances of Pat, George and Martin.

Google Street View can take you down Main Street in Dungiven, and there you can stand virtually outside the Arcade Bar as it was scanned by the 360-degree Google camera in April 2016. The Arcade stands on a gable-end, next to a public library. Its gable-end wall is given over completely to Kevin Lynch, depicted in the mural tradition of Irish republicanism: Kevin Lynch as shinty sporting hero, Kevin Lynch as hunger striker, Kevin Lynch's grave. There is a large painted inscription, too, which speaks about Kevin Lynch's resolve to die for an idea, and about the centrality of time for the hunger strikers and their aims:

> I'll wear no convicts uniform, nor meekly serve my time
> that Britain might brand Ireland's fight 800 years of crime.

YouTube can take you inside the Arcade, too, to let you see its patrons doing what they have been doing for maybe 150 years: singing republican songs, hailing republican heroes and remembering republican struggles. The Wolfe Tone Flute Band is also still going, with the band and its members still marching and practising and practising and marching in venues around West Central Scotland and Northern Ireland. A particular YouTube video depicts the Wolfe Tone Flute Band in Dungiven, doing what they do with the drums and whistles. A phone camera scans the main bar, back and forth, where everyone is seated and drinking and singing, or going to or from the bar with glasses. We see the singers and a lone flautist rendering a low and sombre tune (most of them are melancholic). Through the grain of the pixels I can see Pat, for the first time since 1985. He looks trim and fit. He's sitting across the table from a man named John Fearon, whom I have not seen for even longer, but he's unmistakable. We used to walk to primary school together. In the wintertime, I'd go to his house earlier than necessary because his mum would always have a bright and radiant coal fire burning and I could stand there getting warm and drink sweet tea whilst she dressed John (and this was fascinating to me) who would stand in front of the fire with his eyes closed, still half asleep, lifting his feet as his mum got him to step into his school trousers, and lifting his arms as she pulled his jumper down over his head. John today looks just like his grand-father used to. George Wylie is in the Arcade video, too, standing at the bar in conversation with someone I don't recognise. Martin is not there. He died in 2006 of a heart-attack, and I only heard of it four or five years after.

•

I'd been outside in the cold for maybe four hours now, looking and writing and looking some more. The horizonless sky and the checker plate had taken me to Ireland, in my mind and without distraction, and I had been able to remember things and people and places that resided somewhere deep in my memory, somewhere in my consciousness, a reservoir of real and imagined memory that I think is bottomless in all of us – we just need to tap it. Writing about Martin's death triggered another memory I hadn't re-run before: the last time I had seen him. It was July 1996, when I stood on a vast slagheap – maybe a square kilometre of it – that was once a part of my childhood, a mini-mountain of coal spoil that was known locally as 'the Bing'. For some reason, this appalling black mound was able to sustain trees and thorn bushes and various grasses. These had quickly taken root in the 1950s when the heap was established. No more waste had been added since the local council built St Matthews Primary School next door in the 1960s, so it had become a little forest, a secluded place to drink illegally as teenagers, a place to plan the long days in summer, and a short-cut to Wishaw to go to the pubs, when we were finally able to look eighteen.

On this July day, however, it was a vantage-point from which to watch the controlled demolition of the cooling towers of the Ravenscraig steelworks, under whose literal shadow I grew up. What was once the largest strip mill in Europe, had been deemed 'uneconomical', personally, by Margaret Thatcher. She got to choose between either Ravenscraig or the Port Talbot steelworks in Wales. But the Conservatives never got in votes in Scotland at that time, so there was no point in pandering. You can see collapsing towers on YouTube, too, taken from the Bing, and just metres from where I had stood, watching, and waiting, with dozens of others, for zero-hour. This was also the scene of my last reunion with Martin. He had recognised me, had strode up to me, a crushing shake of the hand, and a 'how's it going, Bobby?' As the towers crumpled and the dust rose, I got the feeling that he imagined I had just flown in again from somewhere he wasn't, and hadn't ever been, that I'd flown in just for the day, for the entertainment, to see the explosion, and to watch the tower collapse, and to wipe out another aspect of a time I lived before I left. And if he thought that, then he was right, I think now. I'd left. I could come and then go. And I would leave again that very day. But this was his life and place of work that was being dynamited. And I'm not sure if he ever worked again in the ten years that were left to him.

6

DISSOLVES IN WATER

SEVENTEEN DAYS HAVE passed since that first walk out into the wind, and things have changed. The *Rossini* is through and out of the squalls and the grey clouds and seas of the South Pacific and Great Australian Bight. Several days before, we had turned the bottom left-hand corner of Australia where the currents of the southern Indian Ocean mix with those of the Bight and the freezing northerly streams of the Antarctic Ocean. Enzo, with whom I've become friendly, mentioned at that time that this was a notoriously rough patch of water, with gigantic seas at this time of the year, and so the vessel would need to steer around it by means of a series of delicate, radar-informed manoeuvres to avoid the worst effects of the converging waters. He evidently saw this as a welcome break in the usual humdrummery that is the life of a navigation officer. He seemed to relish telling me about how, when all is said and done, even big ships like the *Rossini* are ultimately at the mercy of the unfathomable caprice of ocean weather systems. Ships are lost, lose cargo and lose people 'all the time' he had said, with an insouciance that did nothing to reassure me. When we were alone on the navigation deck, he took the opportunity of being in sole charge (apart from the computers) of the vessel to continue on talking about the manoeuvres that would take place that night, giving an animated description of the operation itself, via screen and map, which he walked me to and from several times. I had detected the octave-higher note in the register of his voice and wondered if he was actually as nonchalant as he wanted to project, or if he was as apprehensive as I was becoming – or if he was just excited, like the kid he still actually was.

After this little induction into the dangers of seafaring in this part of the world, I retired to the cabin, half-expecting to be called to the lifeboat before the sun was up. This was one of the lifeboats, by the way, that I had been shown by Enzo the day before in what I assumed was another of his scheduled *familiarisation* exercises. But it now felt like a presentiment. If worst came to worst, he had explained then, as we sat on the lifeboat seats, peering out the tiny little port-holes toward the ship's hull, then half the crew would have to cram into this sealed little container made of heavy-duty orange fibreglass. The rest would need to scramble for seats in the only other lifeboat. Captain Calment would be in charge of one, and his chief engineer, Monsieur Lassel, would be supreme commander of the other. Both would have powers of total authority over those in the lifeboat. Handing me a floppy plastic bag of water to examine, which he'd taken from inside one of the seats, Enzo related a fascinating little aspect of the life-or-death power invested in the senior officers: none of the precious water supply would be distributed (personally by Calment and Lassel) until after at least twenty-four hours had passed, because drinking it any sooner would bring no benefit to the body. You just piss it out. You need to wait until you are *really* thirsty before the water bottles are opened. This news reminded me of the scene in the Robert Redford film *All Is Lost*, where Redford plays a yachtsman, alone somewhere in the vast Indian Ocean, his little boat half-wrecked and stricken after hitting a semi-submerged container that has fallen from a container ship. Redford's character drifts for many days and becomes half-mad with fear, hunger and thirst. He becomes almost demented when he discovers his very last ration of water has become contaminated with sea water. 'Have you seen it?' I asked Enzo. 'No,' he said flatly, and carried on with his *familiarisation* monologue – moving to the topic of the immersion suit that would be worn in case of abandon ship: a full body rubber suit, replete with flashing light and peeping whistle, that would protect the wearer from hypothermia for an unspecified time.

After the *familiarisation*, and back down in my cabin, I lay on the bunk with these thoughts in my head – along with a dozen different lifeboat scenarios from bad films, where things *never* seemed to turn out well. I supposed, however, it would be boring, drama-wise, if it was scripted that everyone in a lifeboat scene was usually uninjured, calm and well-disciplined, and that a passing ship with warm blankets and cocoa on tap picked them up after a couple of hours. In the *Rossini* script, as it turned out, I slept soundly that night through non-existent storms and capsizing seas.

And since then we have been sailing north-north-west toward the Sunda Strait and are 230 kilometres west of the Western Australian town of Carnarvon. Now it's significantly warmer, the sky is blue all day, and the constant rolling of the ship has stopped.

The context is all wrong, I know, and we're at the other end of the world as well, but in the humid tranquillity of the Indian Ocean, Mendelssohn's 'Hebrides Overture', that most evocative of sea songs, is what comes to me every time I wake and look out the window. Indeed, I can look out the window properly now and this has been a recent revelation.

Two days ago, I noticed a thick metal rod hanging on a chain behind the window curtain. Kneeling on the couch at the window, I held it and pulled on its short length, wondering what it was for. It wouldn't come off, so I looked around at its short radius of possibility and saw that it could only reach a thick bolt located at the base of the window, which I had assumed previously was to keep the window shut permanently. Well, no. The bolt had an eyehole on top, like a needle, and the metal rod fitted snugly into it. My eyes closed and I smiled when it dawned on me what both rod and bolt did in combination. I slowly turned the rod anticlockwise, and up came the bolt, opening the window at the same time. In fact, the bolt was able to come out completely and the window could now open fully inwards, where a little latch on the wall at the other side of the window held it in place. I screwed the bolt out fully, pushed the window all the way back and latched it, and let the sound of Mendelssohn rush in with the soft tropical air. I let out a whoop of joy.

Such expression of emotion is not really like me, and I told myself this as soon as I did it. But I knew also that something had changed, and it was not just the weather, or the billowing of fresh air into my cabin for the first time since leaving Melbourne. People talk sometimes of this or that experience as being 'life-changing' for them. That expression always seemed rather too dramatic. Maybe it's just me; maybe my life has been too uneventful. But I really can't imagine what lightning-strike type of incident it would take for me to say 'my life has just been changed'. And yet. I felt different. I felt it when I became mildly ecstatic at the discovery of a window that would open. And I felt it when warm salty air, with a hint of seaweed, drifted past my face and filled the cabin, rippling the sheet on my bed and caressing the plants on top of the fridge, which now began to sway naturally as opposed to the micro-vibration from the engine that had been their unhappy lot since Melbourne. The nearest I can come to describing the feeling was that I felt like a child with no responsibilities and no worries.

It had been a gradual accretion of happiness, I think. Objectively, I knew that there were many, many unopened emails sitting in a server with my name on them, and many, many things existing in the time of the world that would be there waiting for me when I returned. I knew this. But I also knew that here and now the time of the world and its demands did not matter. This was not denial; they actually didn't matter to me. There was an increasing distance that I could feel between me and them, a distance that lengthened as the *Rossini* steered further north-north-west toward the equator. Time and demands were actually me. But I'd let them go, forgetting about them to such an extent that they had 'dissolved'. I think that over the past couple of weeks, that's what I've been doing: watching the time of the world and my connections to it dissolve, or fade, or dissipate, or lose their negative energy because I have not been sustaining them. So, it wasn't a Damascene moment, or even series of moments that changed me, just a letting-go, through a process of forgetting – forgetting to think about the time of the world and its demands and distractions, as opposed to expelling it all suddenly with a bolt of lightning. This forgetting was mainly due to the isolation that I sought on the *Rossini*, and the new digital detox environment it provided for me. And so the uncharacteristic emoting of joy was myself reminding myself that I was changing, and was becoming someone who, like his surroundings, was different, yet becoming familiar with time.

People often say that they could not live without their smartphone, or the internet, Facebook, whatever. I believe that many people actually believe this of themselves. But when you are able to apply a little will and step out of the time of the world and let go the kind of person the time of the world makes you become, then it is surprising how quickly you forget the digital connection. It seems to me that the negative dopamine loop that keeps users tied to their phones can be replaced by a more positive loop of forgetting and dissolving of those aspects of the self that are created by, and are trapped by, the worlds of time and computers and the constant need for efficiency in everything. I'll come back to this idea of the self.

•

It was Christopher Hitchens, the journalist and anti-theist, who, summarising Mark Lilla, wrote that 'Human beings are pattern-seeking animals who will prefer even a bad theory or a conspiracy theory to no theory at all, and they are thus ... by nature "theotropic," or inclined toward religion.' I think he's being a bit too anti-theist, here. I agree that we have always sought patterns in the natural world, in the heavens, in what happens around us, and in our personal and collective hopes and fears. But we do not necessarily have religion or metaphysics in mind as an explanation for that which appears unexplainable by reason, or by the laws of physics. At the subjective level, we can, through identifying and adopting patterns in our life, derive meaning from them, and these give meaning in our life. Meaning could be religiously oriented, but equally it could be anything that has meaning of whatever kind, and for whatever reason provokes it. The biologist Richard Dawkins had it right when he said that science allows us to understand the nature of the world, but if we are looking for meaning in the world, then we can only make it up for ourselves. What are patterns, anyway? In everyday life, they may simply be routines – regularised processes that give some scaffolding to the day: a way of routinising the flow of time in a way that you yourself choose. Since my first full day of feeling slightly at a loss as to what to do, I decided that, along with engaging with my ship, sea and sky environment through looking and mapping experience onto my surroundings and engaging with whatever caught my interest there, I would also establish a few routines, just a few, and not rigidly so. And so, aside from my morning and afternoon walks around the entirety of the ship, and the dusk visit to the navigation deck, and aside from the non-negotiable (and always anticipated) routines of breakfast, lunch and dinner, I decided it was time to enact my promise to myself to frequent the abandoned little gymnasium every afternoon for an hour to get the endorphins flowing instead of the dopamine.

The twice-daily circumnavigation of the ship via its slate-grey checker plate walkway soon became a bit like stepping out into a narrow street in a small village in some remote place. And as the days went on, and as I began to write and read more, the walks became more like after-breakfast or lunch constitutionals. I would see certain sailors at certain places and after a while we would half-expect to meet each other. I'd stop and talk if it felt appropriate, and if the Bosun, Jean-Claude, was not around. One of the Bangladeshi welders, whose name was Yunus, was always ready and happy to talk. The fact that I'd once been a welder seemed to act as a little bond between us. Every time we'd meet there would be (for me) an awkward encounter with the fist bump protocol. I would invariably get it wrong, by doing a high five instead, and then the next time we met he would try to compensate by high fiving, just as I would simultaneously offer the fist bump. It was like a twice-daily game of rock paper scissors that always ended in my discomfiture. However, Yunus's sunglasses and toothy grin belied a desperate homesickness and also a stubborn and essentially racist inequality that is characteristic of life on board many container ships. For example, the workers such as deckhands and ordinary seamen, those who weld and paint and oil and grease and cook and clean, have their own, and rather grubbier, mess room, which I was rather shocked to discover one day, when walking into it by mistake. I creaked open the door of what I thought was the Officers Mess, one breakfast time, and a whole table of about eight men turned to me with big, amused smiles and pointing signals, directing me, almost apologetically, to where I should be.

Shipmate Yunus *Latitude.* -24.219571 *Longitude:* 109.794359 (Off Canarvon, Western Australia,

24th August)

It felt like an apartheid-era scenario, with me the white liberal simpleton, accidentally walking into a *slegs swartes* restaurant in 1960s Johannesburg.

Through speaking with Yunus before, I knew that he didn't mind his job so much, but he missed his family. All his wages went to feeding them and building a house in Bangladesh, but he feared that he would only enjoy spending time with his family as an old man. His eight-year-old daughter, Samreen, he said, was growing up without him, losing time with him that could never be regained. To regain time, one needs to have memories, but Yunus and his kinfolk would have relatively few shared memories. The French officers work two months on and three months off. This would (or could) be difficult, for many reasons, and Enzo had mentioned the complications of maintaining a relationship with his girlfriend in Marseille. But Yunus and his fellow non-unionised workers are required to work six months on and one month off.

Yunus and Enzo had their duties on the *Rossini* to preoccupy them. They also had psychic ties that stretched across the seas to their separate homelands. This was a preoccupation, too: longings, frustrations and regrets that disconnected them from what I spent most of my time trying to connect with on board – my surroundings and myself. This was a wonderful opportunity for me as a writer and researcher, but it also made me feel a little guilty about this gap between us.

It was getting dark, and dusk, whenever it began to prepare itself in the skies, was my cue to go up to the navigation deck in the room above mine. I was never quite sure who would be on watch duty when I pulled open the heavy steel door that would sometimes be shut, sometimes ajar. However, after a couple of days of doing this, it wouldn't matter who was there, as there was no need for me to say anything to them, or them to me. It had become a routine. I'd usually walk to the right-hand side of the deck and stand at the part of the window where a pair of powerful nautical binoculars was always left. I'd pick them up and look around, but it always felt as if this was a secondary and mediated way of witnessing the sunset and the 360-degree canopy that staged it. The naked eye was easily the best way to take it all in. In the built environment, dusk comes unnoticed, obscured by electric light and buildings. We unthinkingly add to this non-event in our modern lives by switching on lights in rooms, in cars, on bikes, on streets and so on, in order to see our immediate environment better. But what we see by artificial light grows in direct and inverse proportion to what we miss in natural light: as the day colonises the night, modern culture expunges nature.

On the *Rossini*, I was at the threshold of nature as city dwellers no longer experience it – surrounded by a vast, darkening sky at the cusp of transition. To take the three or four steps from the window to the door would be to cross the threshold and into nature itself. The overture of colour and shape in the sky would change each night, depending upon the atmospheric conditions. Air pollution, sadly, makes for more spectacular light shows. But still, I'd get to see gigantic flat and diffused altocumulus clouds of pink, orange and red one night, and a cloudless sunset that resembled a Mark Rothko painting, the next. I saw a cloud, a five-thousand-foot column that rose up, brilliant white, from the pale blue ocean and into the dark blue sky – like a nuclear mushroom cloud without the mushroom on top. I gazed at it for some time, wondering what in nature could have formed it. I then became distracted by a light on the horizon and wondered whether it was a star or ship. I went inside to get the binoculars, but they proved no use in deciding the matter, so I turned around again to look at the column of cloud, but it had vanished. After just five minutes, how was that possible? Where did it go? Was it a trick of the sunset light, or had it evaporated? Standing outside on the viewing deck, whilst the officers were busily and silently working inside, I often had to repress a shout of rapture at the experience of what I could see. With no one else seemingly interested, it was as if the sunset belonged to me. All I possessed was the ephemeral experience of the event, and yet this was enough, because I knew also that although this short overture would pass quickly and be lost for all time, it would give a different rendering of itself tomorrow.

To be distracted by lights that might be ships was common in the first weeks. This was because other ships were noticeable by their absence. In the South Pacific, the Tasman Sea, in the Bight and in the southern Indian Ocean, the *Rossini* might go three or four days without sight of another vessel either going our way or heading to where we had come from. I couldn't understand it. Port Phillip Bay was always full of ships coming and going. Where did they disappear to? I mentioned it to Enzo: 'Why no ships in the day or the night?' I asked. His answer was partly obvious. 'It's the other end of the world, down here,' he said. And he surprised me by following up with a grasp of the Australian colloquial image of being trapped by the tyranny of distance: 'You call it Down Under, don't you? Actually,' he volunteered, 'no one likes to come here. It's too depressing, too empty.'

I could see what he meant. When standing on the blue seat at the prow, when on my walks, I would scan all around, trying to make out the horizon where sky meets sea and hoping to see something, anything, that I could fix on and wonder about. When I did see a ship through my surprisingly good National Geographic birdwatching binoculars, which I kept in my coat pocket, it felt like looking at the *Rossini*'s mirror image. Always and only a container ship, or tanker, usually some distance off and going about its own globalising business. I thought of the vessels' captains: both peering at each other through binoculars, and perhaps sharing information on VHF radio about the weather or gossiping about something or other. I also thought of the steward Salva Cruz's counterpart, doubtless somewhere on one of the decks, either making the beds in the cabins, or in the galley slaving for a French or Danish or Chinese cook. And I thought about Yunus's compatriots, welding or painting or skiving, or in bed sleeping before the next shift began. In my conversations with the officers and workers, I got the impression that they were mostly incurious about the other ships, about the sea and the skies, about the fishes and the birds, and also about their location, unless it was instrumentally connected to the *Rossini*. Yunus and Salva Cruz and others had no interest even in going ashore when in Sydney or Melbourne. 'Too expensive' was Yunus's explanation. I could see his point but couldn't fully understand why you wouldn't. Why not go ashore and just look around? Buy an ice cream? Take a photo?

For some reason those on duty on the navigation deck became a little more relaxed when it became dark. Perhaps it was the knowledge that Captain Calment would unlikely be around; or perhaps it was due to the fact that, since there was no longer anything to see outside by way of potential hazards, they were driven to their radar, to their charts and to each other. I had gone up to the navigation deck the previous night after dinner, when it was already dark. Enzo and Jesse, the unforthcoming Filipino Navigation Officer, were on watch duty. I just nodded to Enzo, who nodded back; Jesse simply looked at me, and then back to whatever he was doing at the radar screen. I felt no hostility from Jesse, simply a lack of the slightest interest in me. That's ok. It was a neutral stance that I didn't feel put out by in the least.

In the darkness, the deck was lit only by desk lamps and screen glow. Enzo was stooped over his charts, working with Captain Calment's antique brass dividers, and walking them point-by-point over the pencil track he was plotting for the next part of the route in the north Indian Ocean. A shelf CD system had Steve Miller Band's *Rock'n Me* playing. It was barely audible. I thought it strange that these two young men would have such ancient middle-of-the-road tastes. The big doors were open at each end and warm air flowed in through one and out the other, caressing the succulents as it went. I walked to the deck on the left-hand side, past the plants in their plastic laundry-powder-box homes. Poor things looked more neglected than ever. With a nonchalance earned through nearly three weeks of nightly visits, I went to the recycling bin and picked out an empty Zilia litre bottle and filled it from the tap at the sink, walked back to the succulents, soaked their cracked soil to nearly overflowing, and hoped that the drying leaves might pick up a little. I tossed the Zilia bottle back into the bin, retied the loosened string that held up some of the succulents' long, searching stems to the window frame, and went outside.

As usual, the containers were creaking and rattling out there, unseen in the darkness. Now and then, for some reason, a single lashing rod will make its own sound above the rest, a sudden and alarming rat-a-tat-tat, like a machine gun, then fall back into line. Like a frog that will suddenly raise a note above the cacophony, then rejoin the communal chirring. Enzo once told me that container ships, like tall buildings, are built to flex and twist. It's a vital aspect of their hanging together in one piece. And even up high on the outdoor part of the navigation deck you can feel it. The surface of the sea is smooth, but the ship's heavy, invasive presence stirs it up underneath and seems to demand a response from it. The pliant sea has no option but to push back, and the pressure from the disturbed currents act like a massage upon the hull, which writhes and bends as its solid core of a propeller shaft drives it on.

The mood seemed to have brightened amid the darkness of the navigation deck. Standing almost nose to nose at the Nespresso machine, Enzo and Jesse were positively gossiping about another officer. 'He just refuses!' said Jesse, with a mischievous smile that indicated that there would be repercussions, perhaps from Captain Calment, from this business. 'No!' said Enzo in mock disbelief, his eyes widening and his mouth staying open after sounding the vowel. I walked past them toward the chart table, to savour the beauty of the charts once again and to get an idea of where we were. Enzo and the usually glum-looking Jesse seemed cheered by the story of the fellow officer and by the anticipated contretemps that would make their *Rossini* routines more bearable.

Enzo must have been disc jockey for the night. Steve Miller had finished, and Enzo picked up a stack of loose CDs and shuffled through them like a deck of cards. He settled on *The Very Best Of* by the Eagles, and I wondered again at the source of his taste. He clicked the machine to his required track and turned up the volume: it was *Hotel California*. Enzo sat down at the radar screen and patted his thighs in time with the opening drumbeat: 'On a dark desert highway …' I don't know, maybe it was an in-joke thing for them, but when the lines about checking in any time, but you can never leave came up, both sang along loudly and badly in their respective French and Filipino accents. This was a completely different side to both of them. According to Enzo's map calculations, we were now a day or so from Christmas Island, en route to the Sunda Strait.

I mentioned before that Salva Cruz provided a carafe of Beaujolais with every lunch. It was always tempting to down a glass or two in order to better endure the solo dining experience. I never drink alcohol during the day (and anyway it still feels like morning when lunchtime arrives on the *Rossini*), and I wanted to be able to go to the gym-room in the middle of the afternoon. I'd decided that the clock would govern every minute of the hour I spent between 2 and 3 pm in there. If nothing else, it would keep me in touch with the time discipline of the time of the world, and serve to remind me that I had not gone irretrievably too far toward any contemplative zen state. I mentioned also that this little gym-room (number B.03 on B Deck) looked pitifully underused by a crew that were either too busy or too lazy. This suited me. No need for small talk with whoever might be there. I would therefore adopt this orphan, feel happy within it, and be a little protective of it. And a little territorial, too.

Gyms in the regular world can be mini gladiator arenas where complete strangers, or that person whom you've never spoken to but is always there when you are, will vie with you for dominance in unspoken, but mutually understood, contests: who is fastest and longest on the spin bike; who can lift the heaviest dumbbells through the most repetition; who, even, can sweat most profusely. This kind of modern competition can feel like the expression of a deep-set trait in humans, a culturally evolved form of what was once fighting over the carcass of a woolly mammoth, a physical prowess that indicated the good genes that would attract the most mates, and so on. But the roots of the competitive drive in sport are of more recent origin, coming with the rise of industry, to be precise. Moreover, the fact that most sports are contextualised, or are decided in some way by the clock, is intimately connected to this. The German sociologist and theorist of time Norbert Elias maintained that sporting competition today is not like sporting competition even in ancient Greek culture, for example. There, just as in prehistoric battles over mammoth meat or territory disputes, deadly violence was integral. Modern sport, however, Elias argues, has closer parallels with industrialisation. Potentially lethal violence is channelled or sublimated towards rules, discipline and control, primarily. This is because violence is not productively efficient: dead workers can't work. Moreover, productive efficiency in the workplace is predicated upon temporal efficiency: faster is not only better but cheaper, too. In sport, time is the ultimate value, either in a beat-the-clock competition, such as in running or swimming, or it is framed 'efficiently' by the clock, such as in soccer or basketball; and many sports are simply skill combined with endurance – a competition over who can prevail over the longer term, such as in tennis or cricket.

If 'The clock is everything in a ship' as Captain Calment reminded me in our first conversation, then the gym in B.03 was no exception to this ship's life-rule. Like gyms everywhere, LED clocks attached themselves to much of the exercise paraphernalia.

Looking around on my first visit, with trainers and a towel, only one of the gym's assortment interested me: the stationary bike. At just before 1500 hours on this first visit, I stood over it and examined it with the critical eye of someone who has built and ridden many bikes. It was not all that impressive. Cheapness would have been a primary consideration for the CMA CGM employee, perhaps at his desk in faraway Marseille, who would have furnished this little gym from a list on a supplier's catalogue. The bike was branded an **EMPEROR EN551** and was made in the Philippines. It was constructed from thin black metal tubes that looked and felt so flimsy, it seemed that I could bend the frame with my bare hands. It had handlebars that were simply tube-extensions, and not like something you'd see on any bike on the road. The seat was badly fitted and was sloping up horribly, and would need a spanner to adjust it. The wheels consisted of four rubber blocks that were connected to the stabiliser tubes that ran to the floor. It was missing the front-right block, so that it bumped up and down with each right leg pedal stroke. It did have a red LED, however, and this gave speed, time, and calorie count. The **EMPEROR EN551** looked entirely unused, and had a serious layer of dust covering it.

The green LED clock on the gym wall registered 1507 hours as I sat gingerly on the upward-sloping seat. My trainers just managed to squeeze into the black rubber pedal straps, which were on the last notch and unable to open any wider. I turned the tension knob on the wheel resistance to close to its fullest and put my Sony MP3 playlist on shuffle. *Freak Scene* by Dinosaur Jr. with its clanging opening guitar chords was first on and, immediately energised by its garage/surf fusion, I began to step on the pedals. *Freak Scene* is a great song, and an ideal entree for going hard on the bike, even though the band's musicians look like a collective study in torpor. The LED speedometer looked outrageously inferior, but I saw that it sprang into life as soon as I began pedalling. Straight away I was doing what was for me the unusually impressive speed of 43kmph – and rising – without trying too much. The next song on shuffle was *Gut of the Quantifier* by The Fall. This has a rising tempo that I was matching with my pedal strokes and making me go faster still as the song progressed. Over 50kmph, now. I decided that the LED must be calibrated wrongly (or probably not at all). But it felt good to be tearing along at a professional racer's speed with Mark E. Smith's frenzied and cracking voice piercing my ear drums. With his voice ringing plaintively, I thought of the time I saw Smith calling the classified football results on the BBC in 2006, and wondered idly if he'd lost some of his mid-1990s mojo by agreeing to do that. I wondered also if he was still a Manchester City fan after they'd been bought by Gulf oil potentates; this blatancy would once have gone against his Mancunian grain.

Next up was *Neat Neat Neat* by The Damned, an even faster and even more manic cacophony of early punk. I was now sweating like a racehorse for the first time in what seemed like a long time, what with the Melbourne winter being long and cold and me having to wrap up against the wind and rain when on my bike. Endorphins were flowing freely, too. Sweat was running down my nose and fingertips and constant droplets had already made little puddles on the rubber floor around me. No one was there to be impressed by this display of toughness. The Damned never recorded anything longer than a couple of minutes, so I put this wonderful song on constant repeat and synchronised my pedal strokes to the beat, which took the speedometer up to a Mark Cavendish-like 72kmph. It was clearly not working properly. But the flowing endorphins and the repeating song put me into what had become a practiced reverie.

MÉMOIRE VOLONTAIRE 6

The Damned's song has a history with me. It was my gateway drug into punk. It was mid-1978 and I was in my second year of apprenticeship at Lanarkshire Welding. Work finished around 4 pm each day, including Saturdays, and I'd walk the 500 yards from that inhuman device, the green metal punchclock at the end of the factory building, to my house. Then I'd usually gaze dully at the television until Mum had dinner ready around five o'clock. This was youth time on television scheduling, and so ITV and BBC competed for the demographic's eyes with music shows of various types, all of which were consistently bad. Bad enough that you felt compelled to watch all of them, all the time, to contrast and compare with your friends, and so also to be attuned for any upturn or further regress in quality. At the time, *The Bay City Rollers Show* was new but already the excruciating nadir on ITV; and the BBC hadn't yet hit the mark with anything good until the much more happening *Something Else* began with, incredibly excitingly, The Clash as opener. I was still attired in flared Levi's, listening to Led Zeppelin, Hawkwind, etc., but had also made some tentative steps toward soul music and R&B, with my romantic side being stirred by the glass-cracking soprano of Deniece Williams. I was eighteen and in-between identities and not liking it much.

Anyway, on this particular Saturday, I had no option but to watch ITV's *Supersonic*, a show that had not much impressed before, but as dinner wasn't ready yet, I moved the aerial to the ITV point in the room, which was a sweet spot under the windowsill and behind the curtain and began watching. The TV cowboy detective McCloud, played by Dennis Weaver, was the guest presenter on this day. He was wearing a white ten-gallon hat and one of those string neckties. This wasn't promising, I thought. Then I had to sit through Mary MacGregor's hi-concentrate saccharine *Torn Between Two Lovers*. When the warbling eventually melted away, Weaver materialised from the studio shadows to introduce the next act. He must have seen them off camera beforehand, and I noticed that he seemed rather nonplussed and was looking around uneasily for the producer to guide him. I'd never heard of The Damned. I'd heard of punk, of course, but the BBC tended to ban everything interesting then and so I only knew the genre through tantalising hearsay, and through the daily tabloid paroxysms of outrage and condemnation. Anyway, Weaver retreated back into the murk, leaving the producer, sounding like a train departure announcer, to cue the band.

Television cameras swung around to the set where four men stood on separate little platforms, like The Beatles circa 1964. That's where the similarities ended. They were miming, but that didn't matter because they were making a joke of the artifice, which was then an edgy thing to do. Best of all was the music and how they moved to it. I couldn't believe what I was seeing. It was like a jolt of electricity had flashed out of our old Bush TV set and filled the room. *Neat Neat Neat* was thumping drums and chugging guitar played badly and as fast as possible. Can you do this on television? I thought to myself. The bassist, Captain Sensible, was miming in such freestyle in his child-sized sailor suit that he fell off his platform and sprawled flat on the floor, accompanied by a clearly audible high-pitched shriek of glee from the teenage studio audience. The frontman, Dave Vanian, made-up like a Bela Lugosi Dracula – only cooler, with the collar-up motorcycle jacket – blew away every other performance I'd ever seen in my life. The song finished and the cameras veered again to Weaver, who must have been forced back out into the spotlight by the producer, and was videoed shaking his head in disbelief, in the way that parents have done for generations when kids do their own thing. His paternalistic reaction was the perfect ending to a phase of my musical life up to that point – and the raucous herald of a new one.

After gorging my fish fingers, chips and peas, and half a sliced white loaf, all in a daze, with my mind racing about what I'd just witnessed, I went straight up to my music appreciation friend Wullie McPhee's mum's house and knocked on the door. Wullie opened it and we just looked at each other for fully five seconds, our eyes slowly widening and jaws likewise dropping, no words necessary, until he said: 'what did ye think?' You can see the revered moments on YouTube. Some dear and unknown kindred spirit, with perhaps kindred memories, managed to find a grainy VHS or Betamax recording and uploaded it.

This was my one and only hour on the *Rossini*'s cheap-bought stationary bike. A good deal of the perspiration running off the end of my nose and chin had found its way onto the speedometer. Some of it must have seeped into its substandard casing, thereby causing it to go haywire. The upward-tilting seat was also too much to bear over the course of an hour, and to drive home the political economy point of planned obsolescence built into every commodity, particularly the cheaper ones, the rubber pedal strap on my right foot pedal had developed a tear from the eyehole to the edge, making it useless. It wouldn't stay tight and flapped on the upstroke and dragged between pedal and floor on the downstroke.

At 2 pm the next day, I found the speedometer completely incapable of showing any sign of life, the seat still pointing rigidly upwards and the rubber pedal strap, ripped, limp and forever useless. Seeing Salva Cruz at dinner the night before, there flickered in me a faint hope that he, or someone else, would come during the night and fix it all, as in the story of the Elves and the Shoemaker. But no. Yesterday's pools of sweat had dried to form little salt pans on the floor around the base of the bike, and the handtowel was where I'd left it by mistake on the handlebars. No one had been there since me, twenty-four hours before.

I looked away from this sorry representation of corporate care for staff wellbeing and reluctantly toward the treadmill, a Life Fitness-branded contraption. This was rather more impressive, but its many buttons were unresponsive and its banks of LED display were dark, with its electronic circuitry just visible beneath the arrayed dark-plastic screen. It needed power. And this contraption seemed unused, also. In fact, the electrical cable and plug were wrapped and stored in a little alcove at the bottom of the front of the unit and looked like they had never been touched since the person who assembled the treadmill in the factory deposited them there. I spooled the cable out and plugged it into the wall. It lit up like Las Vegas.

I'd been on treadmills before but could never really say I enjoyed them. Maybe it's physiological or psychological, but I've thought of myself as someone who, in addition to hardly being able to swim at all, can't seem to run for more than a few minutes. I've often ridden upwards of 250 kilometres before lunchtime, but I tire after ten minutes of jogging. Here on the *Rossini*, however, it was either the treadmill or solo table football. The technology was fairly straightforward. Programs ranged from a brisk walk for as long as you liked, to a galloping run to the point where the running belt would hurl the insufficiently-kinetic off the back of the unit. There was no one to compete with, and not even a wall mirror to goad me along. And anyway, I was here precisely to get away from all that. So, I flipped the MP3 player to a selection of podcasts that I'd downloaded in Melbourne and selected a poetry discussion podcast from *The New Yorker*, about Seamus Heaney's *In the Attic*. It lasted for thirty-two minutes, which seemed like a good enough start on the treadmill alternative. Talking is good for walking, so I settled into an easy pace, looked out the port-hole towards a calmish blue sea and listened to the soft Irish tones of

Paul Muldoon introduce the American poet Tom Sleigh, who read Heaney. Coincidentally, *In the Attic* is about getting old, memory and the sea, with its final canto reading:

As I age and blank on names,
As my uncertainty on stairs
Is more and more the light-headedness

Of a cabin boy's first time on the rigging,
As the memorable bottoms out
Into the irretrievable,

It's not that I can't imagine still
That slight untoward rupture and world-tilt
As a wind freshened and the anchor weighed.

A beautiful poem that I hadn't heard before. Muldoon commented in the podcast that the poem, inspired by the novel *Treasure Island*, also had parallels with Heaney's collection, *Seeing Things*, where the concept of memory is a feature throughout. My mind wandered to that collection, as I paced on the treadmill and felt the prickly heat of physical effort just where the neck meets the base of the skull. Scratching and walking, I tried to recall something solid from *Seeing Things* but couldn't. It was too long ago when I read it. I thought instead about memory and how it can gather past and present and future into one, in the objective time and space of the present moment. Where was I? What was I doing? My place in space and time at this moment seemed rather absurd, in a humorous way – walking to nowhere on a treadmill, and measuring the space-time dimensions of the process: how far can you walk in an hour? It was almost five kilometres on that first walk, somewhere in the Indian Ocean.

Just as for the person holding a hammer for whom everything begins to look like a nail, the lights and buttons and numbers on the control panel of the treadmill demanded they be used. The discussion about Heaney had finished and when the hour ran down a bit later, an LED message scrolled across the screen: great workout!! It wasn't, really. I knew it and so did the treadmill. I was sweating mildly, and the heart rate monitor was reading only 70bpm. I was calibrated to the mid-range, but the buttons and lights were signalling to me that there was a great deal more perspiration to be wrung. Mid-range. I'd always been mid-range at school, in both academic achievement and alphabetical order in class registers. Mid-range also in height, and mid-range in looks. Whenever I was reminded of this mid-rangedness, I always sought to raise the barrier, step up as they say, and push myself. A press of the upward-pointing button takes the effort up an increment. I was ten on a twenty-point scale on the speed levels. There was also an incline function which literally raised the running belt at an angle. This was on a ten-point scale, and I was currently on zero. Every day, I said to myself, I'll up the ante between myself and Life Fitness and see where we would get to. Would I win? Or maintain my mid-range?

There is a song by the Aussie band The Church called *Life Speeds Up*. They have it right, I think. Life accelerates incrementally in the time of the world. It creeps up unawares, and stresses us out because we can't figure out the sources of acceleration. But here on the *Rossini*'s treadmill I was programming increasing acceleration, day by day, and feeling better for it. For the hour between 2 pm and 3 pm, my usual mode of *vita contemplativa*, switched to a more energised *vita attiva*. There came a point, around the fifteen mark on the scale, where the walking pace was forced into a jog, and as each day passed the jog gradually became a run, and when up to the twenty mark, a week or so later, I was running at almost full pelt for the whole time. I'd abandoned the incline function, as it was too hard, and when the ship was rolling, the effect was like running on an out-of-control see-saw. This would play havoc with the sense of balance; as the incline of the machine went up and down, outside the port-hole, the sea would either sink from view and only sky would be visible, or as the ship pitched the other way, the sea would rise back into sight and the sky would be pushed upward to the top of the port-hole and disappear completely.

The contemplation-inducing podcasts were abandoned also because I could no longer concentrate on what was being said. I was back on the music and being driven along by *The Best of Joy Division*, a collection that takes about an hour. I'd found them in 1979, when *Something Else* eventually got going on the BBC, and punk was already post-punk. Singer Ian Curtis's austere vocal register, recounting troubled stories for troubled times, has never gotten me down. In fact, I have always found the collection uplifting. The track *Transmission* is where Curtis is at his best and yet most fraught. Who would have thought that someone singing about listening and dancing to the radio could move you? Partly it's Curtis's voice, a mixture of anguish and power; he 'barks in his own monotone,' as music critic Greil Marcus phrased it.

Marcus devoted a whole chapter to this song in his book *The History of Rock 'n' Roll in Ten Songs*. He wrote: '"Transmission" is not an argument. It's a dramatization of the realization that the act of listening to the radio is a suicidal gesture. It will kill your mind. It will rob your soul.' I wouldn't go that far, but I know what he means. It's a scary song. You fear not for yourself, but for Ian Curtis, who we know will kill himself a short while after he recorded the song. The tempo of *Transmission* ramps up at the end, as the frantic precision drumming of Stephen Morris mixes with the strangled and eye-popping cries for help from Curtis. As I say, it's scary, but I found myself moving with its power on this stupid treadmill – a contraption that's almost a metaphor for what provoked Joy Division's introspective rage, a kind of anaemic gothic – running as fast as I could. It felt like I was trying to run away from the song as it reached its manic climax, only to flick it on again once it had finished. I'd struggle to run and at the same time focus on the screen of the MP3 player so as to get my thumb on the right spot to start it up again, so as to chase it once more in its *andante* beginning, to meet it and synchronise with its drum-dominated middle, and then try and fail to outpace its crazed *molto crescendo*. Look at Curtis's goggle-eyed *Something Else* performance on YouTube: 'you can see the suffering in his face' was a below-the-line comment from 'Hangdeath' in 2017. You can.

Measured time becomes a fixation here on the treadmill. I fixate on the speed of the music. I fixate also on the LED clock that quantifies the hour, and the heart rate monitor that counts the bursts of blood pulsing from my pulmonary artery in search of oxygen from my lungs. At the point when my rising heart rate became too worrisome to look at, I would switch off its functionality and keep my eyes on the seconds making minutes and the minutes stretching out to what felt like a never-coming number sixty. By running to nowhere on the persistent treadmill, I felt in an odd way that I was standing up to it, fighting with it, denying it total control over me, determined to exert some control of my own over the limits I myself set. I'd do this by exceeding them, and by exceeding them I'd be beating the clock, not in a race against someone else, but against myself and against the Life Fitness machine that had no life except that which I gave it when I switched it on for the first time in its machine life. So, it only knew me, and in all probability would know no one else, until one day when the *Rossini* would be sold or scrapped and Life Fitness would find itself at a fork in the road: one leading to the Alang beaches scrap heap, and the other to, perhaps, another life in another gym on another CMA CGM ship, and with a lazy or overworked crew set to ignore it, and for the kind of dust that accumulates at sea to settle and accumulate on it anew.

On my last day in the gym, a couple of weeks hence, I ran to nowhere for fifteen kilometres in under an hour. I stopped when the distance was up, noted that the time was 59:29, before vomiting into my sweat-soaked towel.

Later, after showering, then resting, I borrowed Salva Cruz's room trolley, which he usually parked in a corner on the port side of B Deck and walked to the bike and began to clean the salt stains that still lay around it. The cheap speedometer was still dead. Forever dead. I scrubbed the much worse-looking sweat stains on the running belt of the Life Fitness treadmill, and on the surrounding rubber floor. With a can of Pledge, I made the control panel and the aluminium handrails and the black plastic panelling of the entire base glisten like new. Lastly, I unplugged the machine, ran the electrical cable through a cotton rag in the palm of my hand, rolled it up tightly and put it back in its alcove.

The Sunda Strait, Enzo told me, unnecessarily, at that night's spell on the navigation deck, connects the Indian Ocean to the Java Sea. I'd been thinking about it for days and recalling the website warnings about pirates I'd goggled at in Melbourne just before I left.

7

THINGS AROUND YOU

DOES TIME, AS the saying goes, actually go faster when you are having a good time? Well, as another saying goes, it depends – it depends on context. So, what is the context? The first thing is that I've been aboard the *Rossini* now for twenty-two days. To prove it, I have a twenty-two-day beard, with the razor last touching my cheek when I was in cold and dark Melbourne, just before the taxi took me to the gates of the docks on Footscray Road. Such hirsuteness is new for me and, as I brush my teeth every morning, I surprise myself whilst scrutinising my visage in the too-large, too-bright and too-magnified cabin mirror. Is that really you? I think. Looking closer, I see a half-inch-long coating of grey and black whiskers flatten and then bounce back as I run the fingers of each hand slowly down each cheek. Seeing the signature motley pattern of grey, black and white on the cheeks, the chin, and around the mouth clearly for the first time in my life, I realise that it is familiar; many other middle-aged men in the general Anglo-Saxon population have the same. It must be genetic – a dormant gene that is switched on by some kind of internal timer to remind you of time and duration and inevitable old age and general entropy. Should I keep it? Do I look older? Wiser?

Bedraggled? Or maybe even, from a practised angle, like that guy who advertises Nespresso? Itchiness was a problem. Increasingly, I'd feel like a flea-invaded dog that claws at its ear or muzzle, and too often I'd find myself digging my fingernails into the grey-black fuzz and scraping around to try to find the always-mysterious source of irritation on my skin. A discovery: when you apply Nivea Men Crème to the bearded face to soothe the occluded skin, the whole beard becomes an absolute and brilliant white (for a couple of minutes) until the skin begins to itch again.

And so, I look a bit different, physically. Like the returning astronaut who has been on a space station for some months, people who know me would need to look twice. More importantly, and less visibly, I feel different, too. I think I've lost weight. Though always pretty skinny anyway, I feel even lighter. There are no scales on board, however, and so no way of knowing. It's probably an illusion: I've been 69-70 kilograms since I was eighteen, and I'm sure it's not going to change now (or I won't become lighter, anyway). Maybe the feeling comes from the psychology of digital detox. I've forgotten all about my phone and laptop and have not missed them at all, which is a little surprising, given the dopamine loop that I had been swimming around in for several years. But as I said before, maybe letting go of the proverbial digital albatross puts a spring into the step. Who knows? The main thing for me is that both feelings of difference feel good.

The second thing, context-wise, is that, as I look out my cabin windows, it feels like we have left the orbit of Australia's continental gravitational pull at last. We're cruising in proper international waters now. Australia is no longer somewhere over the horizon to the starboard side, lurking and close, but is far behind us, and getting 40 kilometres more distant with each hour that passes. We passed Christmas Island on our starboard side a day and a half ago, an Australian-claimed lump of nitrate 1500 kilometres from the nearest part of the continent that now shamelessly functions as a detention centre for Iranian, Pakistani, Afghan, Sri Lankan and other refugees. I was, to my dishonour, rather glad not to have seen it, so I did not have to consider the miseries inflicted in my name by the Australian government on the people in desperate need of a new life in a welcoming country. For them, no such luck in the Lucky Country. They did not even get close.

Up here beyond the north Indian Ocean, the weather is searing as opposed to warm, with the ship's outside walls and checker plate floor hot to the touch. Looking out my windows, hundreds of steel containers seem to wobble in the heat-shimmering air. While out walking the decks, the smell of blistering paint hangs in corners and alcoves where the sea breezes can't penetrate. And when the sun is highest in the sky, my little seat at the prow of the ship could now fry a sausage as well as an egg. And so, I stand on it instead and just look ahead, like the carved figurehead, or lean over as much as I dare to watch the bulbous orange and blue bow rise up and crash down through the waves.

We entered the Sunda Strait this morning. When I visited the navigation deck just after lunch, I overheard Jesse mention it to Jason Dela Torre, a compatriot of his and another *Rossini* navigation officer. Jesse still hasn't deigned to speak to me properly. Happily, Jason is a bit more relaxed. He was standing over the map table and pencilling in some coordinates at the point where we were heading: through the Strait and into the Java Sea. 'Excuse me, Jason, where are we right now?' I asked with the friendly, passive and wide-eyed smile of the interested tyro speaking to the professional. On a map, the Sunda Strait looks roughly like a human head in profile, one turned to the left. It's narrow at the neck where we enter, then bulges out to a rounded chin and nose on the port-side, or to the east, which is the island of Java. The left side of this head shape looks like long hair flowing in

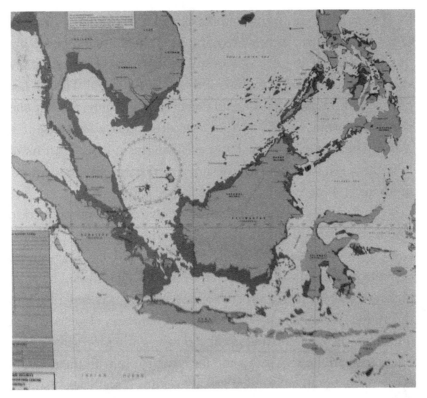

Rossini chart showing the Sunda Strait that opens the way to Java, Sumatra,

Kalimantan and Singapore.

the monsoonal wind, creating a jagged profile forming the eastern shores of the island of Sumatra.

Java, Sumatra: land masses positioned in the middle latitudes where it's always warm. These island names are, to me, as exotic-sounding as you can think of. Light years from the roughcast and pebble-dashed semis in Craigneuk, and light years from Newport's streets of white and grey detached clapboards, in contrast they seem to be an ecological Eden of tigers, fox-bats, orangutans, sun bears, pygmy elephants, human-eating pythons – not to mention, it's the land where ancient remains of the little 'hobbit' people who lived 95,000 years ago have been found. All this fauna competes in my mind's eye with less exotic aspects of Java and Sumatra: clearfell logging and burning crops for palm oil. Estimates of the size of forest that are cut or charred by fire vary, but they are all immense and almost all illegal. For the last day or so, I thought that I could detect smoke tinging the hot and salty air blowing east from Sumatra, although I wasn't sure if it was my imagination – but I suspect that Australians (even natu-ralised ones) have a nose for the smell of distant bushfires drifting in on the summer wind.

With the soft-looking hand of an adolescent, Jason pointed to the ear region of the head shape my mind had projected onto the contours on the map. 'We are here, now,' he said, his bitten stump of nail picking out a little cluster of islands. 'This one,' he said, picking up a blue plastic protractor and pressing a corner of it into the middle of the bunch, 'is Krakatoa. We are very close to it – just out there,' he said, looking up and pointing the protractor to the open door on the left. It was too far away to see with the unaided eye, but the thought of Krakatoa was exciting, nonetheless. I smiled at Jason once again and, taking a bold liberty with Jesse's sensibil-ity, picked up the binoculars that Jesse had placed on the window ledge not five minutes before and walked out to the starboard side.

To be so close to the scene of the volcanic detonations of 26 August 1883 – supposedly 13,000 times more powerful than the atomic bomb that wiped out much of Hiroshima or Nagasaki – was quite fascinating, in the way that the scene of a recent traffic accident can be, with the trace of danger still hanging somewhere in the air. The feeling was compounded by the realisation that the colossal tsunami triggered by the four explosions would have lifted up the waters of the very area through which we were now sailing. The percussion din from the Krakatoa blasts, which oblit-erated the island, was so loud that it was heard in Perth, Western Australia. The smoke from burning sulphur that erupted into the upper atmosphere jet stream, was carried along at over a hundred kilometres per hour, to reach New York in December of that same year, as a strange and unknown light that filled the daytime skies in a kind of nuclear winter. People in New York read about the explosion in the *New York Times* only a few hours after it happened; telegraph stations already linked a good part of the planet, and electronic media was shrinking the world in an informational sense. But the sulphur that darkened the skies a few months later was carried by a rhythm of nature. Human time is shaped by technology – as we can see in this little comparison – but a point of the digital detox was to see what happens when media technology is taken out of the equation as much as possible.

This brings me back to the question of whether time has sped up or not: the twenty-two-day time span actually seems quite unreal to me. I can't recall any other phase in my life that has been so focused upon a particular thing (that is, being cut off from communication with the world) for such an extended period. Yet, in one way, it has been like no time at all. That's not to say that time has flown – that doesn't capture it. Neither does it seem like time has stopped still, as if anchored, and I've gotten bored and wished the whole stupid experiment was finished – that's not even close. Fast and slow (or even normal) don't fit as temporal descriptors for the new context. This is time as I've never experienced it before. I can only describe it as I feel it. So, let me try.

A term that I think kind of describes it, or comes nearest to it, is undistracted consciousness. What is this? There's something like it that exists in Buddhist philosophy, and is achieved through meditation. The word *Vipassana*, meaning insight, describes a meditation practice where a tranquil or still state of consciousness is achieved through wholly focusing your attention on objects. You practise this focus by observing a chosen object closely, examining it in the greatest of detail using both sensory and mental awareness, to the point where you become detached from this activity. The object and you become one, as it were. But in this state of the highest concentration you are outside of this process, suspended in a timeless and spaceless meditative domain, where no distraction is possible because you have stepped out of the realm of distraction – out of the world of things – and are in a purely mental, meditative state. You are no longer the person observing the object, but are detached from it, from its materiality and worldliness.

This example is useful because it's quite the opposite of what I'm trying to convey. More than anything, Buddhism is oriented toward the inner life and inner mental world – whereas, after twenty-odd days without the distractions of the connected digital world, it was my conscious awareness of the outer world of things and objects that, for me, made that world and my life synchronise, or come together in a tactile and physical and conscious world of duration. Through the willed attitude that I wrote about in the earlier chapters, the things around me – things usually ignored or invisible in normal daily life – became objects of interest, and often revealed worlds in and of themselves. I began to realise that it was never an aim, conscious or otherwise, to detach myself from this experience of concentrated observation and reflection, but to be as much a part of the object as I could. I realised that timelessness and spacelessness was not what I wanted or had even considered. Instead, I wanted to be a part of time and space in the most natural and material way possible: through a sensory and mental awareness focused upon the flow of time in the here and now. Buddhism, like other major religions, sees the ultimate source of reality as something extracorporeal, where you ultimately leave the earthly body behind to attain Nirvana or heaven or some other sublime state. In this admittedly constructed state of being on the *Rossini*, which detached me from the time of the world and its digital distractions, I was nonetheless able to become part of the world in a way I'd never done before, through a concentrated focus on certain aspects of the world around me. For example, I could walk down the corridor from my cabin (let's say to the starboard side), push up the door handle and step out on to the checker plate platform. There was so much to see; you only had to notice it.

The sea and the sky, for instance, are constantly changing colour and shape. Waves spill onto waves and disappear into each other; the silver mirror-glint of a fish, or a shoal of fishes, are often spied, then to quickly disappear. Sea birds, often alone and hundreds of miles from land, circle the ship, swoop down to have a look at me – usually because I'm the only human around – and then dive into the water, having seen a more interesting and edible target (likely an unlucky flying fish picked out whilst swimming with its group just beneath a smooth patch of water). Organic matter, such as seaweed, clustering microorganisms and phytoplankton, floats everywhere here in the Strait, on and just under the surface of the water. It drifts like green and black spaghetti on small, tangling cross currents that are the endings of the larger, established sea currents that have been rendered beautifully in blues and creams on the *Rossini*'s charts. Overhead, cloud formations of every sort also drift. But unlike clouds over land, they – especially the tiny cumuli, some no bigger than distant hot-air balloons – are more accurately 'wandering lonely', to employ William Wordsworth, because nobody sees them. Their shape and consistency are like Melbourne clouds on a hot summer day: billowing, brilliantly white and rainless. Yet here in the Java Sea, their base is flat, paralleling the surface of the water over which they hang low in what seems to be some atmospheric interaction, which perhaps some scientist understands. Moreover, these cumuli are formed by tropical water from tropical seas, and this makes them qualitatively different, and therefore special and local, never to be found anywhere else. And all around me the *Rossini* expands and flexes and twists in the heat as it surges through the cool waters, scattering everything before it. Mapping, absorbing, considering things around me, even this small selection of them, extended (or slowed) my perception of time here on the hot checker plate, and I was able to test this for myself.

Was this fast or slow time? Stefan Klein, in his book *The Secret Pulse of Time*, wrote that 'in moments of happiness ... senses and memory become highly receptive, and every impression they absorb, slows down the time we are experiencing.' Here he describes time's subjective psychological centre becoming salient, just when the time is right. But happiness is perhaps a subjective state too vague to measure. It's possible to go a little further than that, I think. For example, those psychologists and neuroscientists who study time perception believe that they know why time seems to slow down in the context of more measurable emotions, such as the stress experienced when involved in a car accident, when people often report afterwards that 'everything seemed to be unfolding in slow motion.' In such moments of extreme trauma, the subconscious mind reverts to an instinctual survival mode and flips into automatic overdrive. Through the senses, the mind maps (or absorbs, as Klein puts it) as much of the situation as possible; it tries to read as much of the environment as it can in the desperate attempt to somehow control it. And so, as the car spins or rolls or careens out of control, the mind frantically assesses the situation from every possible angle: What's happening? Am I going to die? Is this how it ends? Simultaneously, it also works to throw up memories – thoughts of family, of loved ones – producing the my-entire-life-flashed-before-my-eyes phenomenon that is frequently reported in such situations. In other words, the mental effort of the mind functioning at the primal level seems to expand time, but also focuses on the most important things for the individual such that the perception of time is that it has slowed down.

On the *Rossini*, mapping and absorbing the things around me was not, of course, an emergency situation. But the willed effort of connecting with my immediate world did, for me, actually change the flow of time.

Usually, I can tell what the clock time is with a margin of error of a couple of minutes. I've been good at this since I was a kid. On my way back to my cabin one afternoon, it was my guess that I'd been on the navigation deck for maybe three-and-a-half or four hours. I didn't take a watch with me on the detox, so I was interested to know if my clock time sense was still as sharp. Once inside the cabin, however, the ship's green-painted clock on the wall told me that just over an hour had passed – one hour and seven minutes, to be precise. This was a mini-revelation: the distance between estimated and actual time had never been so wildly off-target for me. For the first time in my life, I was experiencing time differently and more authentically. I was having a good time, but time did not flash past. It was slow and constituted a much more human and natural form of duration that I could control and savour. Through the isolation from clock and network, I was thrown back onto my own latent temporal resources, and I was a different person (for now, at least).

However, the thing about all this time travel is that it is mentally tiring. Out on the checker plate platform, I've found that just looking, in the way I've described, takes effort. In the normal state of affairs, when there are few external constraints or distractions, the urge is to let your mind wander and to daydream, or to worry about something, or to have all kinds of mental distraction crowd in, uninvited. These are not in themselves necessarily bad – but this is what we all do in the modern world, and the *Rossini* trip is supposed to be an experiment. But, like close reading or any kind of concentration, absorbing the things around me exercised parts of my brain that were not used to being exercised. And so being happy in a new kind of time meant, also, that I was tired more, sleeping more, and sleeping differently.

The quotidian phrase 'did you sleep well?' poses a modern question for modern people living in modern societies. To utter it would not have occurred to the pre-industrial peasant or lord. In pre-modern societies, people slept and people woke and people did their work in patterns that conformed to ancient rhythms based more upon the interaction of the natural environment and human biology. At the beginning of this book, I wrote about the manufactured nature of the time of the world. Time is manufactured because it was, and is, required in the service of manufacturing. The needs of capitalism were those of predictability and coordination in the work process. Sometime over the course of the eighteenth and nineteenth centuries, work became the salient reason for living for the majority of people, and so an historically unprecedented phenomenon occurred in the affairs of men and women: the rigid work day was instituted. Later, as literate labour was needed in addition to predictable labour, the school day was also established. We began to move in time with the work day and school day, with no account taken of the temporal rhythms of millennia being crushed or sublimated.

Paul Lafargue, son-in-law of Karl Marx and a troubled soul who would die in a suicide pact with Marx's daughter Laura, was tortured by the thought of what machines and industry were doing to us and our sovereign time. In his 1883 essay, *The Right to Be Lazy*, written from his prison cell where he was imprisoned for his political work, Lafargue howled in despair:

> But what do we see? In proportion as the machine is improved and performs man's work with an ever-increasing rapidity and exactness, the labourer, instead of prolonging his former rest times, redoubles his ardour, as if he wished to rival the machine.

O, absurd and murderous competition!

A generation or so later, the poet Basil Bunting (another jail-bird, imprisoned for his World War I pacifism) noted that things hadn't gotten any better for industrial man and woman. He expressed this in his elegy to the continuing drabness of industrial life in his 1931 poem *Attis, or: Something Missing*:

> In the morning
> clean streets welcomed light's renewal,
> patient, passive to the weight of buses
> thundering like cabinet ministers
> over a lethargic populace.
> Streets buffeted thin soles at midday,
> streets full of beggars.
> Battered, filthily unfortunate streets
> perish, their ghosts are wretched
> in the mockery of lamps.

The question 'did you sleep well?' has always been coloured with an edge of concern, an ancient remnant of the limbic system of our brain where emotions are held and generated. This part of the brain realises, even if our conscious mind doesn't, that something is missing, something is wrong: we are being systematically deprived of precious sleep every single work day and school day.

In our post-industrial society, where clock and network extend our waking hours, perhaps billions of people go through their whole life in what the neurologist and sleep study expert Matthew Walker calls an underslept state. In Walker's terms, this is anything less than the absolute minimum of seven hours of sleep per night. In the zero-sum equation, modernity takes this sleeping time from us and does not give it back. Not only that, modernity has transformed the manner of sleep, too. We are drilled into sleeping in a single phase, where we go to bed at night and then get up for work or school in the morning. However, the exigencies of the work and school day flatten out the natural variation in human chronotypes (the genetic predisposition for people to be 'larks' or 'owls') and the variations in biorhythms or circadian rhythms (how your sleep patterns naturally shift during your life-cycle). In other words, we are denied the natural sleep patterns that we have evolved with, which takes away from the little we are allowed to have.

From what little reference there is to sleep in the 1000 years of written history before the Western industrial revolution, historians know that people did not sleep in a single, insufficient block of time as we do nowadays. They slept in two phases, known as biphasic sleep, where they went to bed, got up naturally at some point in the middle of the night (roughly between one and two o'clock), ate or read or conversed or had sex or pottered about for an hour or so, then went to bed again and would sleep through until morning. These phases were contemporaneously called the 'first sleep' and the 'second sleep'. An example of this can be found in Geoffrey Chaucer's *Canterbury Tales*, written in the late fourteenth century. In The Squire's Tale, he mentions matter-of-factly that Canacee, daughter of Genghis Khan, soon after darkness fell, 'slepte hire firste sleepe, and thanne awook.' When we wake in the middle of the night today, it's a mini-crisis because we know we have to be up and awake and switched on for a whole sleepless day ahead at work. So, we lie there and fret; we turn left and right, count sheep, and think morosely of our mortality or the meaninglessness of life or the dread of the job and the inexorably approaching work day. Today, no one wakes at 3.19 am and hums a happy tune.

I had already decided that sleep was an important element of my experiment, because it's a temporal question and because so much depends upon warding off sleep deprivation in normal daily life. My mother had a saying, one I've not heard anywhere else, which is 'sleep's meat'. She would say this if we kids were sick with some minor ailment, and it means go to bed and sleep and you will get better. It's not a pretty aphorism, which might explain its lack of commonality, but it's clear and simple in a bucolic sort of way: meat is nourishing, and so is sleep. This is of course true; we all know it intuitively. But Matthew Walker has seen the evidence of the effects of not getting eight hours' sleep, and it's a scary indictment of the modernity that holds us all in its grip:

> Once you know that after just one night of only four or five
> hours' sleep, your natural killer cells – the ones that attack the
> cancer cells that appear in your body every day – drop by 70%,
> or that a lack of sleep is linked to cancer of the bowel, prostate
> and breast, or even just that the World Health Organisation
> has classed any form of night-time shift work as a probable
> carcinogen, how could you do anything else?

The *Rossini* was my chance to see how much sleep my body wanted and in what pattern. And so, I can report that after maybe five or six days on board, my sleep habits changed quite radically. By consciously seeking to fall into a natural pattern, I discovered that the single overnight phase soon divided into two, just like our pre-industrial ancestors. But I also slept in the afternoon, partaking in a blissful siesta that could last up to an hour. So, in the context of almost complete freedom, my body opted not simply for the biphasic routine, but for the rather more indulgent tri-phasic package.

I take back the word indulgent. Given what Walker's and others' research tells us, we sleep because the mind and body need it. In fact, an important little lesson that I learned was that we all need to be much less guilty about how and when and for how long we sleep. What Max Weber called the Protestant work ethic has a lot to answer for, even for lapsed Catholics like me. The modern cultural principles of working hard, being regular and dependable with time, and saving as much money as possible are Biblical and Christian in origin, as Weber shows, and come applied to the modern context with a spadesful of personal guilt. Think of the politicians who excoriate the 'work-shy' or 'skivers' when any mention of the inadequacy of unemployment benefits is raised. UK Chancellor George Osborne fired up the delegates at the 2012 Tory party conference, when he repeated an old mantra directed at those with not enough of the Protestant ethic on display: 'Where is the fairness, we ask, for the shift-worker, leaving home in the dark hours of the early morning, who looks up at the closed blinds of their next-door neighbour sleeping off a life on benefits?'

But what is the guilt? Partly, it's borne of a fear in us of not being able to keep up, echoing Lafargue's 'O, absurd and murderous competition!' But it's also the social opprobrium attached to the thought of being personally lazy, or being seen to be so. Lafargue's ironic use of the term in the title of his essay was lost on many (if not most) who thought he was advocating the right to put one's feet up and smoke a pipe, whilst other right-thinking people toiled all day. But, in fact, he wrote politically of the right to be free from the slavery of a machine-industry that used people as appendages and deprived them of sufficient rest. We need to remember Lafargue and see sleep as a political issue, and recognise the proper length of sleep as being a human right: a necessary refuge, a realm or sphere where the individual can rest and repair and be as free as is possible in the context of modernity. And to be guilt-free when doing so.

Anyway, my triphasic routine soon became an actual routine, with my body and mind fitting into this ancient rhythm, into the salvaged tempo buried somewhere deep inside me, remarkably quickly. In this Protestant ethic-free zone, my siesta need came, as it probably does for many, just after lunchtime. I'd walk up the five flights of stairs from the mess room to my cabin, clean my teeth, kick off my flip-flops, pick up my book and lie on the bed. Usually a page of text at most was lightly scanned before unconsciousness swept over me like a soothing shadow. The duration of the sleep was maybe from twenty minutes to an hour – never any longer than that. In the first few days of succumbing to the need to sleep, I felt groggy when waking up. But the more I went with it, the more the sleep became more than a snooze: it was a dreamless blackout. And then I'd suddenly find myself awake and feeling really energised, jump straight to my feet, have a pee and get ready for the visit to the gym.

At night, after dinner, I'd either go to the navigation deck to see what's what, or, more often, go back to the cabin and read. Three weeks in, though, I was running out of things to read, so I would write up my notes and try to stretch out the dwindling number of pages of my last book, *Gray's Anatomy*, by John Gray. I'm up to the last couple of short chapters and am treasuring his essay titled Sweet Mortality which is, in part, about the poet Edward Thomas, who was killed in France in January 1917. I'd never heard of Thomas before. But for him, sleep and death became synonymous longings for a writer 'prone to melancholy', as Gray gently phrases it. Both were a kind of freedom for a suffering spirit. Gray reproduces a very long quote from Thomas's 1913 book *The Icknield Way*, a journal of his walks around the countryside in Essex. These passages are from day nine of a ten-day journey and record his descriptions of lying in bed, listening to the rain and contemplating the nature of death. With time to read it and savour it, I see that Thomas's words are extraordinarily beautiful. I make a note to read the book when I can, and write down these latter paragraphs of the words quoted by Gray, the more to etch them into my memory:

> I have been lying dreaming until now, and now I have awakened, and there is still nothing but the rain. I am alone. There is no room for anything else in the world but the rain. It alone is great and strong. It alone knows joy. It chants monotonous praise or the order of nature, which I have disobeyed or slipped out of … Lie still. Stretch out yourself like foam on a wave, and think no more of good or evil. There was no good and no evil. There was life and there was death, and you chose. Now there is neither life nor death, but only the rain. Sleep as all things, past present and future, lie still and sleep, except the rain, the heavy black rain falling straight through the air that once was a sea of life. That was a dream only. The truth is that the rain falls for ever and I am melting into it. Black and monotonously sounding is the midnight and solitude of the rain. In a little while or an age – for it is all one – I shall know the full truth of the words I used to love, I knew not why, in my days of nature, in the days before the rain: 'Blessed and the dead that the rain rains on'.

Wow. I'm lying in bed reading, not yet sleeping, and it hadn't rained in these parts for a long time – but 'the rain falls forever and I am melting into it' is as beautiful a notion (for life as well as death) that I've come across in print. Rationing my pages, I read Thomas's words again and again, slowly. I imagine the poet in a lonely country hut in 1913 Essex, at the very end of *la belle époque*, somehow having premonitions of the catastrophe that was soon to upend the whole of Europe. Gray conjectures that Thomas enlisted in the British Army in order to find peace in the permanent sleep of death amid the general killing by the living. We will never know, I suppose. What I do know is that there are interesting parallels between this excerpt and James Joyce's 'The Dead'. Joyce's short story ends similarly, with his snow replacing Thomas's rain. Again, it's something we'll probably never know, but I wonder if Thomas had read Joyce's equally beautiful lines:

> Yes, the newspapers were right: snow was general all over Ireland. It was falling softly upon the Bog of Allen and, further westwards, softly falling into the dark mutinous Shannon waves. It was falling too upon every part of the lonely churchyard where Michael Furey lay buried. It lay thickly drifted on the crooked crosses and headstones, on the spears of the little gate, on the barren thorns. His soul swooned slowly as he heard the snow falling faintly through the universe and faintly falling, like the descent of their last end, upon all the living and the dead.

Both excerpts are about time and about death and about sleep: the sleep of the dead and of the living. From this conjuncture, my now-wandering mind wandered its final wandering of the day, to a scene in the British comedy *Father Ted*, where Ted Crilly paraphrases Joyce in a eulogy at the funeral of Father Jack before he faints at the sight of Father Jack waking from the dead and screaming at him to 'shut the feck up!'

It gets darker a lot sooner around the equator, and so – prompted by having no television, or laptop or smartphone video, and only a low candle-power bedside lamp – my body was being signalled for sleep as soon as I got back from dinner around seven-thirty. With few other options available, I immersed myself in reading and writing as soon I'd showered, had a cup of green tea, and brushed my teeth. As many would attest, treasuring printed words on paper by reading slowly and closely is an idyllic way to prepare for sleep. And in my unpressured sleep patterns on the *Rossini*, I would succumb to sleep rather early, between nine-thirty and ten o'clock. Once I'd become aware of my routine of first and second sleep, it was oddly reassuring to know that I'd be awake in the middle of the night. I knew it would be a peaceful waking, with no need to worry about having to get back to sleep, and with maybe a dream to reflect upon as opposed to banishing it from my thoughts in order to get back to sleep. There is also a release of tension in feeling that you don't have to pray for eight hours of uninterrupted sleep. In fact, I could happily anticipate two sets of dreams, which I could compare and contrast once the sun was up, if I felt like it. Even if there was someone to ask me, the question 'did you sleep well?' would have been superfluous, as it would be for all of us, if the clock and work and modernity did not dictate and make spartan our sleep patterns.

When I awoke from what I now recognised as the first sleep, I got into the habit of getting up and out of bed straightaway. To just lie there, I found, was to doze in the dark. So, I would switch on the little bedhead lamp and jump on to the couch and kneel to look out the open windows. Tonight, as always, the air is warm, and the little red light twinkles at the prow. The luminous hands on the Hanil cabin clock show 2.33 am and it's a clear sky, as it is nearly every night. The cliché of the swirling abundance of stars in these unpolluted skies applies. Peering out, I see that almost the whole of the sky is a silvered brilliance, so closely do the stars cluster and shine. I have no idea of the organisation of the con-stellations and am happy to content myself with just gawping at them. We seem to be sailing with a three-quarter moon, hovering at about ten o'clock in a blacker part of the night sky. Maybe it seems blacker there because the moon just outshines the billions of stars that surround it in space.

The stacked and lashed containers crack and snap in the dark as they do in the light. It doesn't matter that we are in smooth seas; the constant vibration of the ship means that the containers continually try to shake themselves loose from their manacles. As the *Rossini* ploughs on, thousands of screws turn imperceptibly counter-clockwise. During the day, I sometimes see a worker going around with a big spanner, giving the lashing rods a clockwise turn to keep the containers fast and in line. Tonight, as on most nights, the containers around me appear as black silhouettes against the light-glow of the stars and moon: like a short and chunky Manhattan skyline but without the Manhattan lights, like the photos you can see of the great New York blackout of 1977.

At the very end stack of containers on my left, at the furthest point out to sea toward the prow and the little red light, I can see another silhouette in the moonlight: that of a large seabird, genus unknown. It's perched right at the very corner of the container on the extreme right of the stack, almost on the vertex of the side, like a high diver with their toes curled over the end of the platform. It's not making any sound that I can hear. But it's moving. It hops from left to right and back again, and ruffles its feathers every now and then. It lifts one wing and then another and nuzzles its beak into the undersides. Then it raises both wings simultaneously and gives a few half-hearted flaps, then seems to settle. After a few seconds, it begins to hop from side to side once more. What's it doing? Maybe it's injured and unable to fly, or lost and exhausted.

With half a mind to see if I could get closer to the seabird, I got dressed, opened the door, tip-toed down the darkened corridor to the left, trod an especially light step past Captain Calment's room (there was no light coming from under his door), squeezed up the lever of the steel bulkhead door and stepped out onto the still-warm checker plate, in my bare feet. Looking up to the navigation deck, just a few steps up to the next level, I could see through the window in the door to the desk lamp and computer glow that was thrown up onto the ceiling tiles. I wondered whether I should go up and pay a visit. I quickly decided not to: I'd be disappointed if I found it unmanned, but I wouldn't want to give anyone who was there a heart attack, either. Instead, I sat halfway up the stairway to get a better view of the shadowy seabird.

I couldn't. In fact, I couldn't see the bird at all; maybe it had hopped out of sight, or fell off its container perch and into the sea, or took off in a night-flight to somewhere. There were islands all around, so perhaps one of these was its home and it had recognised the silhouette, and I had witnessed its pre-flight preparation. My thoughts of the seabird caused me to think about the islands we were drifting past amidst the atmospheric moonlight and starlight, at a speed that seemed to be a good deal less than the 40kmph that the *Rossini* could churn out when it wanted to. I had a fair idea of where we were and I was quite pleased that, as a lubber, I was able to work it out for myself. I had noticed on Jason's map, as he was pointing out Krakatoa, that he had plotted a course into the Java Sea proper with pencil, dividers and ruler. To the right of his pencil line was a group of islands, at the point where the Sunda Strait merged into the Java Sea itself. I had asked him what these were, as they looked very small and I thought they were perhaps reefs. Another piece of exotic information from Jason was that this cluster of map specks was called Thousand Islands. There weren't a thousand of them, in point of fact, but a rather more modest 108, which extend north, deeper into the Java Sea, starting from the mouth of west Jakarta Bay. I moved back down to the checker plate platform to stand at the railings at the highest point in the ship, except for the navigation deck, to see if the shadowed islands might be clearer. The natural light of the middle of the night gave the aspect of the islands an evocative chiaroscuro effect. The nearest that I could see was perhaps three or four kilometres away. The New York blackout analogy works here too, except that there were no straight lines or flat summits. Rising up from the black-blue sea, against a backdrop of dark silver sky, were tiny islands, some of them no more than atolls, covered entirely by trees. In some of them I could make out the classic sea stack shape, the plinth-like column of sheer rock that is so spectacular in pictures but always seen in the daytime. Here, in the middle of the night, they appeared like spectral giants, standing guard over something important – a bit like some of the early modern depictions of the Colossus of Rhodes.

Here and there were lights that suggested habitation by humans. They were small, yellow, low-powered lights that reminded me of porch lights that you sometimes see in the Australian countryside – twinkling evidence of a homestead high up in the dark hills of Mount Macedon, north of Melbourne. But these were isolated porchlights on isolated islands in the middle of the Java Sea. Who would live there? Maybe someone on a more natural biphasic sleep pattern would be looking out from one of them now, looking out at us: a slowly passing ship, its own lights dimmed and yellow, with perhaps no one on duty to look back, guided instead by computer programs through well-travelled sea lanes.

The interlude of the mysterious seabird and islands between sleeps had been like a dream – a dream between dreams where the body and mind synchronise with ancient and lost rhythms of sleep and rest and wakefulness and mindfulness. It was still dark and luminous and warm out on the checker plate. I could see my own shadow, thrown by the moon onto the door of the deck corridor, as I made my way back to my cabin. I'd been outside for maybe an hour and I was now ready for bed once more. I looked up again at the navigation deck in the hope of seeing the vigilant head of a vigilant navigation officer steering us safely through the dark and the Thousand Islands.

8

TIME FOR WORK

WAKE UP naturally now, between about 7.15 and 7.30 am. And factoring in the siesta, the triphasic pattern is delivering me maybe ten hours of sleep a day. I've never felt better. I feel rested, happy, fit and psychologically like a new person. And yet, something is missing. Something rather large. But what? I'm not sure.

After lunch I step outside and the air outside is stifling. It's strange to think of heat way out here in the middle of the Java Sea. You can understand the radiant heat that comes up from roads and fields and valleys and hills to make your day feel hot, but when you are floating atop relatively cold waters, logic suggests that it should be cooler. But it's not. I stop just a few steps after leaving the mess room and lean over the gunwale, with the expectation of some cooling air blowing up onto my face. But there's no air coming up. Indeed, there's hardly any sound from the sea or from round about me. It's as if the heat has stifled it, as if we're becalmed. But we're not. I'm looking at where the sea meets the ship down below at the waterline. From where I stand the *Rossini*'s dark blue hull seems to run over the sea like a slow, hot iron over a damp sky-blue towel. If there was a sound to describe this, it would be a kind of soft, barely audible hissing sound. The hot air seemed to be hissing all around me. Maybe the sound was real, and was coming from the ship somewhere, or maybe I'd just had too much Beaujolais at lunch. Anyway, deciding that it might be cooler and airier up at the prow, I begin to walk.

A high sun was burning my unshaded forehead and my flip-flops were sticking slightly to the checker plate with each lifted step. I thought about going back to the cabin and sleeping it off, but I knew I would wake up and feel hungover if I did that. Better to skip the siesta today. As I got to amidships the hot air suddenly seemed to ripple with the rat-a-tat sound of an air-powered chipping hammer being applied, I surmised, to some rusty checker plate up ahead. I knew this eardrum-shredding sound well from my days as a welder. Walking up to the source, I could see that the passageway had been ineffectually blocked off with sagging, ragged fluoro-yellow barrier tape. On the other side of it there were four fully suited and helmeted workers, wearing earmuffs, dust-masks and sunglasses, all kneeling to drive the chisel-point of the hammer into the brown patches of rust on the checker plate floor. I couldn't make out Yunus, but I put up a hand of greeting to one of the men who must have spied me in his peripheral vision, and to my embarrassment he prodded the others into stopping and standing up to greet me in return. I waved them back down again, and when they resumed I looked out to my right over the gunwale at nothing in particular; it was clear that this was as far as I could go in my walk today.

I looked back at them again and saw they were all sweating through the backs of their faded blue overalls. I looked at them some more and wondered if the reason they were all actually working was that the Bosun, Jean-Claude, was lurking somewhere, or was expected to swoop at any time. A Cockatoo Island welder's cynicism. As I watched them shatter the fragile rust metal with the pneumatic hammer and then use the air blower function to carry it all into the sea, I wondered vaguely about pollution and the health of any fish that were around, before it occurred to me what had been missing from my time on the ship: it was *work*. I had been weeks on the *Rossini* with no physical work to do, beyond washing my tea cup in the bathroom sink and straightening the sheet on my bed. The daily physical activity of the gym was a different thing; that was more intellectual in a way, a time to think and concentrate and be in my head even more than normal. No, it was the absence of opportunity to do things with my hands: to cook, chop vegetables, do the washing up, or any kind of housework or repairs, or tinker with my bike with it hooked up on the stand, and me dismantling parts of it and then reassembling it with a new part or repaired part. That's what was missing. Working with my hands. Immanuel Kant is credited as saying that 'the hand is the window onto the mind'. I'm not completely sure what this means, but it does suggest that a symbiosis between hand and mind is needed in some kind of healthy balance. And that sounds right. My job is mostly intellectual labour, but much of its character, much of what grounds it, comes from time spent working with my hands in the sort of tasks I've just listed. I need to be doing both these things – to scrub the burnt bits from the bottom of a pot, as well as read and think and write. It didn't occur to me that in my detox experiment I would be idle as far as being able to work with my hands, and it didn't occur to me, either, that this would be an issue.

The problem of increasingly unoccupied or untrained hands is not confined to me on the *Rossini*, of course. It's something generalised and is connected to modernity and computing and the rendering of our hands as little more than extensions of keyboards or touchpads. Rust will still have to be chipped off ships by guys like Yunus, for the foreseeable future, but automation is changing what work is and who does what. For instance, the *Rossini*'s management lets their navigators plot elegant pencil lines on beautiful charts, because they were trained to do this and because they all love to do it. But there is no real need for it. Computer systems can guide the ship to within an inch of its intended destination through GPS. And so one day, sooner rather than later, in a Marseille office overlooking the sky-blue Mediterranean, a middle-management layer at CMA CGM will decide after consulting their Excel spreadsheets that this duplication is a needless waste of money; and when they do, another step toward captainless ships, like driverless cars, will have been taken. More widely, the scope of what is automatable is fast climbing up the vocational ladder. The robots are coming for me and they're coming for you. No longer is the tyranny of the algorithm confined to repeatable and wearying tasks in factories and offices, but it also applies to forms of work done with the brain as well as the hand, that were once seen as too complex (too human and clever) for dumb androids. Lawyers, doctors, journalists, lecturers, even novelists now have to worry about their skills being diluted by intelligent machines. And all this has the time factor at the centre of the process. Automation has only two objectives: to replace the human (who is too slow, expensive and mistake prone) and to produce things at a *faster* rate (quicker is cheaper).

Computer automation is presented to us as both progress and something unavoidable – the sugar with the pill. But we are not paying enough attention to what Google cars, or home-care robots or dark factories – dark because robots don't need light to work in (just think about that!) – actually mean. The destruction of many jobs, and job classifications, is just one thing, the headline issue is that automation will doubtless mean upheaval, uncertainty, job-lessness and the scrap heap for millions of older-age workers – and it will also mean a perpetual requirement for retraining, upskilling, as well as constant upheaval and uncertainty for every new gener-ation of workers to come. That's bad enough, but it goes deeper than that. It's also what philosophy terms an *ontological issue*: that is to say, it concerns the nature of being, or who you are, or what you will become, when something so fundamental, like the character of work, is changed in your life, in all our lives.

Making and creating is what defines us as homo sapiens. This propensity eventually got us out of the grip of the bare life and early death that was the lot of thousands of generations of ancestors and enabled the species to thrive like no other. But it was Marx who declared that the specific social relation of capitalism and factory production created a form of alienation, a process where the worker is separated from the thing that he or she makes (or makes a small part of) in their daily wage-earning jobs. This is a thing or a service that is actually a commodity for sale in an abstract marketplace, and can be anything from making pizzas to selling insurance. What Marx recognised was that most of us now have no real connection with making and creating in this way, beyond earning money to pay the bills. In this industrial model, the time at work becomes a time of clock-watching and wishing you were somewhere else. But, by way of recompense, eventually the worker goes home and rests and repairs and has a life formally separate from the life of work, and he or she has relationships with people and the physical world in core human ways that have not changed for hundreds of years. Since the time of the industrial revolution, we have sort of internalised this trade-off, and accepted its terms, because what were the alternatives? And if born into this world, then it just seems natural anyway. For early thinkers of the dangers of automation, such as Herbert Marcuse, writing in the 1960s, this free time was when we were tranquillised by the consumer society, so much so that, in echoes of Paul Lafargue, we would even fight for the right to work in jobs that we do not really want, to buy things that we do not really need.

In the post-industrial networked world, the realms of work and not-work have become blurred. And this is new. Transformative even. And this upends all our previous (positive or negative) assumptions about work. The computer revolution that brought us the robots and automation will ensure that most of the new jobs that are created will be information-based jobs in services. Working with your hands will mean typing on keyboards to operate machines or to process information. We are creating a world where we interact with its physical dimension even less, and so our innate propensity to work, to make with our hands in the myriad ways that humans have done for thousands of years, is beginning to attenuate. Our alienation, not just from work but also our environment, can be seen all around every day, with the sight of people going to a job in front of a screen, who have already been in front of a smartphone or a tablet since they got out of bed. This divorce from our physical surroundings was brought home starkly when I read recently that something like three quarters of kids under twelve in the UK spend less time out of doors than do jail inmates. One out of three kids, according to another survey in the UK, have never climbed a tree in their lives. Playtime now means smartphone/social media time.

Nonetheless, the propensity to make and create is biological, even genetic, and if you look you can see counter trends to what I've just described. They're everywhere, with people expressing this need by pushing against the logic of mass automation of things and the mass standardised consumption of things. For example, and not a little ironically, the internet, or YouTube anyway, overflows with DIY videos from DIY men and women who will give you a tutorial on fixing or making just about anything, as opposed to simply replacing it, which we tend to do. These vloggers often do it just for the sake of it, with no money or sponsorship involved, and regularly have thousands upon thousands of viewers trying to learn

DIY skills from them. I've watched many a vlog on the trickier elements of bike repair, and when they work, the feeling of a small triumph over the reflex action of taking it to a shop is so satisfying that it's almost primal. We see the pushback, too, in the growing artisanal culture and the search for authenticity that is permeating much of Western society. Beer, bread, hipsterism, veganism, grow your own, repairing, recycling, farmers' markets, coffee culture, cooking from scratch, ethical tourism, etc. all emphasise the need to become involved more in the local, physical environment in ways that by their very nature de-emphasise automation, virtuality, acceleration and globalisation.

Sociologist Richard Sennett sees that we are becoming alienated from the essential human trait of working and making and creating with our hands. His specific point is that we are losing the skills acquired through training and apprenticeships and long-term dedication to the craft element of a work process. We can't all be (or want to be) craftspeople, but I think the general point of working in fulfilling and non-alienating ways is a good one. Doing things for yourself, or for their own sake, or because they are needing doing in your life (like housework or repairs) help create and sustain that hand and mind balance that we all need. I find Sennett's emphasis upon time compelling, too. Think about it: if we are working with our hands for the sake of something, for ourselves, to learn and to experience, for its intrinsic subjective meaning, or for fun, it is unlikely that we would seek to speed up the process. The need for speed comes from the outside, from the world of business, of profit, of faster is cheaper. We would not cheapen the experience for ourselves were we not compelled to do so by the time of the world and its demands.

All this also suggests that the actual object of making and creating with our hands is not the key element of my general argument. The thing itself could be anything, from needlepoint to building a wall with bricks; from peeling potatoes to making a billy cart for your kids. We are all different and can have different paths to fulfilment in working with our hands. I'm reminded here, in this respect, of the artist and environmentalist Andy Goldsworthy, who works in nature and with nature, using ephemeral forms such as ice that has formed overnight and will melt when the sun comes up. Goldsworthy works with the ice in that temporal window of opportunity, whereby if he sculpts it at dawn, and sets it at a particular angle to the rising sun, then the morning rays will illuminate it dazzlingly, if it all comes together. What he aims for, in the dawn with his frozen hands, is an ephemeral moment of sparkling illumination. You can see Goldsworthy create his short-lived creations on YouTube in a film called *Rivers and Tides*. What I'm saying is that it's about engagement with the things and the world around you, to engage with materials in a physical world that may or may not be useful or permanent; an engagement that is diametrically set against, say, scrolling absentmindedly through Instagram with your index finger as soon as you open your eyes in the morning.

•

As I walked back to the cabin, I thought of speaking to Salva Cruz to ask if he needed a hand to do something, but then I thought this would seem a bit weird and undermining of him and his job. I also thought about trying to fix the bike in the gym but this, too, seemed like something that's not my business. In fact, on the *Rossini*, as a paying passenger, nothing is any of my business. This was more or less spelled out in the 'Partir en Cargo: Special Conditions' that CMA CGM emailed to me, and which I signed, before I departed. This is a working ship, not a pleasure ship, and so the cabin is my chief domain. That is what I agreed, I suppose, and I am really ok with that. But still.

Back in the cabin, I looked around to see what I could do beyond cup washing and sheet straightening. I noticed part of the curtain had come off its runner, and so I stood up on the couch and put it back, and clipped the end of the runner, which must have micro-shaken itself off after some unknowable length of time. This took about ten or fifteen seconds. To my left, the glass face on the light-green coloured Hanil brand ship clock opened like a door, and the clip on this had been loosened too, perhaps with the constant vibration also. I stood on the bed, reached up and closed it. One second. What else? There was nothing.

The cabin was nice enough, but it never had any aspirations beyond being a functionally designed, industrially constructed, impersonal accommodation space. Apart from the nearly self-sufficient plants above the fridge, which, incidentally, seemed to enliven greatly in the tropical air, everything was fixed, either to the wall or to the floor. Partly, of course, this was to stop furniture and fittings shifting about with the movement of the waves and the shaking by the engines. But partly, too, it was an element of boring functionality. The navigator, the captain, welders like Yunus (even the owner which this cabin is named for) are expected to only sleep and shower here. The bolted-to-the-floor couch and coffee table and framed posters are there, not to encourage any sort of home life, but to make the room seem less like a prison cell. A cheap psychological adornment. The writing desk was similarly conceived, I think, and most of the writing and reading I've done has been done on the blue-painted chair at the prow, or on the bed. This leaves only the black office chair, which has been tucked under the desk for most of the trip, secured by the red plastic cable.

The *chair*. I looked at it more closely for the first time and pressed my thumb into the back-rest fabric that rose up beyond its black plastic back. It didn't look or feel all that cheap – quite comfortable and professional-looking, in fact. But it was ugly, nonetheless. I unhooked the red plastic cable and let the chair roll with the ship's listing force of gravity toward the coffee table, where it clipped it at just the right speed and angle to tip it over onto the floor, with its back hitting the carpet and sliding for about a foot, and its five castor wheels spinning in the air like a crashed skateboard. Damn. There didn't seem to be any damage done either to the chair or the coffee table. Whilst watching to see which wheel would stop spinning last, I remembered the Victorinox Swiss Army Knife 40-in-1 that I packed in Melbourne as an afterthought. I sat down cross-legged on the floor in front of the wheels, spun them each again, and, as they thrummed silently, wondered if I could take the whole chair apart and rebuild it.

What would be the point of that? It was a question I never asked myself. It struck me that to dismantle and rebuild that chair would not only give me something manual to do, but it would also fulfil an element of work, of creating and recreating, in a way that recovers something that industrial 'time is money' work has nullified in most of our lives. I jumped up and pulled out the black sports bag that had lain undisturbed in one of the built-in cupboards and retrieved the Victorinox from one of the side pockets. It was still in its little soft-leather pouch, which it had come with, and I realised that I'd never properly looked at it, much less used it. It looked a bit crazy, when each of its (yes, there are 40) tools are pulled out. I slid the chair, still on its back, to the middle of the cabin floor and looked again to see if it could be taken apart, and if so to what degree. As far as I could see, the thing was held together in three main ways that were dismountable: with the normal screw, the Phillips screw, and Allen Key hex bolts. The seat column seemed to screw off from a fixture in the bottom of the seat and at the top of the five-legged base that held the castors. Plastic mouldings were snapped into grooves and holes and corners on the arms, the seat, the back, the seat column and on the tilt mechanism underneath the seat. What could not be disassembled, again as far as I could see, was the plush seat and back that were both stitched and glued, fabric onto spongy foam, which covered a wooden or metal core, probably plywood. I looked again at the Victorinox and could see a normal screwdriver, a Phillips screwdriver and an Allen Key. Would they fit? The first two, I knew from a glance, would be ok. What about the Allen Key? There were hex bolts under the arm rests, on the plastic mouldings that covered the five castors, and there were probably more under the various mouldings. This was a tense little moment. I would have to abandon the task before I'd even begun if the Allen Key was too big or small. Yes, it fit, exactly. Standardisation sometimes has its advantages.

I did all this preliminary stuff slowly and with my MP3 player turned up high and emitting the soulful voice of Anohni on Antony and the Johnsons' album *I Am a Bird Now*. The album has ten songs and takes all of thirty-six minutes to complete; I finished looking at the chair from as many angles as possible by the time the album was repeating its fourth song on the list 'Man is the Baby'. The song is beautiful, but its title got me thinking as to why I was doing this, and feeling (weirdly) excited by it, and by the chance to put two main ideas to the test. First is something that informed part of what I tried to convey in chapter five, 'To See'. There I quoted David Abram's notion that the alphabet can get in the way of direct perception of something, meaning that doing and seeing is much better than reading about it, because reading is always at least one degree of remove; writing is always the mediated experience or imagination of the author. Writing can provide so much, but only so much. I want to bring Abram and his wonderful book *The Spell of the Sensuous* in again in order to think about something he says about looking at and contemplating and living with an object. He calls it 'the event of perception as we ourselves experience and live it'. I am going to excerpt a fairly lengthy couple of passages from his book. This is partly because I agree and partly disagree with what he imagines to be the limitations of the process of perception and experience – in this case, a simple clay bowl. Stick with it, because it's at least an exquisite example of what the alphabet can do to suggest the power of seeing and being with an object:

> The clay bowl resting on the table in front of me meets my eyes with its curved and grainy surface. Yet, I can only see one side of that surface – the other side of the bowl is invisible, hidden by the side that faces me. In order to view that other side, I must pick up the bowl and turn it around in my hands, or else walk around the wooden table. Yet, having done so, I can no longer see the first side of the bowl. Surely I know that it still exists; I can even feel the presence of that aspect which the bowl now presents to the lamp on the far side of the table. Yet, I myself am simply unable to see the whole of this bowl all at once.
>
> Moreover, while examining its outer surface, I have caught only a glimpse of the smooth and finely glazed inside of the bowl. When I stand up to look down into that interior, which gleams with curved reflections from the skylight overhead, I can no longer see the sunglazed outer surface. This earthen vessel thus reveals aspects of its presence to me only by withholding other aspects of itself for further exploration. There can be no question of ever totally exhausting the presence of the bowl with my perception; its very existence as a bowl ensures that there are dimensions wholly inaccessible to me – most obviously the patterns hidden between its glazed and unglazed surface, the interior density of its clay body. If I break it into pieces, in hopes of discovering these interior patterns or the delicate structure of its molecular dimensions, I will have destroyed its integrity as a

bowl; far from coming to know it completely, I will simply have wrecked any possibility of coming to know it further, having traded the relation between myself and the bowl for a relation to a collection of fragments.

As I say, beautiful. An evocative example of how the ordinary thing, and this can be almost anything, can open up like a flower to reveal itself, or aspects of itself, and what this means to the sensuous touch and gaze and contemplative intellect. Abram tells us that it is possible, through the willed attitude and willed effort, to interact and live with the object at the level of consciousness and physical reality that we normally overlook, or are blind to, in the everyday time of the world. And time is a vital aspect here, too. As Abram goes on to write, '… like myself, the bowl is a temporal being, an entity shifting and changing in time, although the rhythm of its changes may be far slower than my own'. We live our lives too fast, and feel we cannot devote the time to the slower pace, a pace that will allow us to at least perceive and experience the object in a different way, in a way that draws us closer to it as a thing to know more deeply, but to never know fully, because our time and our rhythms can never be the time and rhythms of an inorganic thing such as a clay bowl.

I want to question the limitation Abram places at the point of 'breaking [the bowl] to pieces' and where its integrity is destroyed and there being no further possibility to know it as it once was. Yes, I agree as far as the idea and example of the bowl goes. Its integrity is clearly gone once shattered, and its wholeness disintegrates, and it becomes a different thing. Moreover, its temporality is no longer intact, and it has become, in an instant, a 'collection of fragments'. One could respond that the bowl could be painstakingly remade, fragment by fragment, but anyone who has done this with a bowl, or cup, or teapot will know that it is no longer the same thing. In terms of simple market value, it is much diminished. And in terms of any intrinsic value – its meaning as an heirloom, or as being significant of a special time or person – it borders on ruin. The relationship to it has been made fragile and tenuous and likely emptied of whatever meaning it once contained.

But we need to think beyond Abram's bowl. It works well as an example, because it makes possible an understanding of the potential power of things in our lives. The bowl, however, is a specific technology. It's one of the earliest technologies that humans developed and is (or was for thousands of years) endowed with special qualities that modern technologies lack. For instance, the clay and water that comprised the ancient bowl came directly from nature, from what was local and near-to-hand; it was formed by those hands, and as an object lived to serve deep and vital human needs. Today, machines (not hands) make much of what surrounds us, and these objects fulfil all manner of deep as well as superfluous human needs. However, the machines that make the things we need separate us from the object itself and from nature. They separate us from the link with nature that the bowl gave us and would still give us, even if we were not its maker. For many centuries, and across many societies, the simple bowl was a profoundly social and cultural object, which is why our ancestors almost always tried to mark or colour or design them in some unique way in order to increase the power of their meaning. But beginning in the seventeenth century, modern machines started the process of separating or alienating us from the increasingly standardised products that began to fill our lives. Capitalism industrialised and socialised and intensified that process of separation. Today, computer automation is rapidly completing that process.

In a small way, in a personal and hopefully meaning-filled way, to dismantle and rebuild this black industrial office chair would be to subvert the modern logic of machines and automation and insert something human into it. It's fundamentally about meaning, as I see it. By taking the chair apart and putting the bits back together again, I would be transforming it into something different, another chair with new meaning, a different thing in the cabin. Does that sound crazy? I don't think it is. Sitting here on the floor of my industrial cabin, on an industrial ship, on an industrial mission, it seems to me to be perfectly sensible to undermine, or reverse, everything that that innocent-looking black office chair represents. Let me try to illustrate this with the closest thing I can think of, which I'll call the IKEA logic. IKEA straddles the world. It colonises cultures, and occupies the homes and offices of millions, with an industrial sameness. IKEA says something about our world, and something about what we have become in our relationship to things and to work. The machine-made flat-pack parts of say, a HEMNES chest of drawers, which looked beautiful and a little bit French Provincial in the equally beautiful-looking IKEA catalogue, comes to you and me with perhaps a human hand never having touched it. Computerised machines cut the parts, pack them together and plastic-wrap them in a factory in China, and these are shipped in a ship like the *Rossini* to all parts of the planet. Craft or love or care or individuality or quality or quirkiness or carelessness are absent inside the bleak plastic wrapping. The flat-pack unit is a dead thing; a purely functional, meaningless thing. Dragged from the back of the car, and heaved into the house, the HEMNES lies like an unfulfilled dream on the bedroom floor, because it still has to be assembled, and brought into some kind of life. By you. A non-craftsperson, who will, with a cheap throwaway tool, put the HEMNES together inexpertly and badly, for it to last a few fleeting years before its cheap materials betray its catalogue promise, and its plastic paint coating peels, its drawers stick, and their bottoms split from their sides. And you will break it apart and throw it all into the bin, there to be interred until delivered to the local landfill.

The IKEA object comes to you unbuilt, and you build it according to an infantilising step-by-step diagram. It is an industrial and alien thing, from the time of its birth in China until its inevitably early death within an unloving household. The black office chair that I'm looking at now has come to me industrially built, and it too would someday meet its end in that same unloved and unlived state unless I save it by transforming it. To dismantle the chair is to dismantle the machine logic that brought it into its present state of non-being – and to rebuild it is to insert the hands of a human and insert a little life and meaning into it in the process. There is hardly any need to assert the power of meaning: we all know it and we all experience it in many ways and in many forms in our lives. Meaning is personal and fungible, but it is also able to be made general. Let me nonetheless indulge in an example.

In a glass case in a room somewhere in the British Museum, there is an exhibit, a cross made of wood, which is called *The Lampedusa Cross*. It is a simple Christian cross (383mm high and 280mm across) and is fashioned from two pieces of boat timber, one coloured blue, the other yellow. Its colours have been washed out and faded from long exposure to the sea and the sun. It was made in 2015 by an Italian carpenter named Francesco Tuccio, a resident of the island of Lampedusa, which is Italy's southernmost territory and is situated only 130 kilometres from Tunisia. Why is it in the British Museum – a roughly-hewn cross that is only a few years old? It's there because every atom and millimetre of it is filled with meaning. It came from a dangerous and ill-fated boat that sunk off Lampedusa on 11 October 2013, drowning 366 Eritreans seeking another life in Europe. Tuccio collected the reef-smashed fragments of the boat from his Lampedusa beach. For him, these bits of broken timber made him think of holy relics, and they smelled, for him, of 'salt, sea and suffering'. You could say that the cross that he made, and which was collected by the British Museum, contained these elements in the form of meaning. If the same fragments had been left to the time and tides of the beach on Lampedusa, then any meaning would have very soon been lost and forgotten with them. But for Tuccio, human and craftsman, to fashion them into an object, into a relic, and for it to be put it in a glass case in London creates and preserves meaning and the memory of those who drowned. The meanings of 'salt, sea and suffering' – as well as those of tragedy and inhumanity, and greed and desperation, hope and anger, and whatever else the future millions who will now look upon it choose to imbue it with for themselves – are now imperishable, because of what human hands did with the fragments and what human consciousness and the willed attitude impressed upon them.

The black office chair on its back in front of me does not compare with the *Lampedusa Cross*. The *Cross* represents the cosmic-level drama of the human condition and its deep-rooted tragedy throughout the ages. But the process of meaning, and the process of transformation through rebuilding that which has been destroyed or taken apart, is the same. Whereas the *Cross* sits on the metaphysical continuum of space and time and human history, the overturned office chair sits at the level of me, in a container ship, somewhere in the Java Sea. Slightly bored and looking for something to do.

Which brings me, somewhat belatedly, to the second of my two main ideas that I wanted to test and was reminded of by Antony and the Johnsons' song, *Man is the Baby*. The opening line of the song, 'Yearning for more than a blue day' is sad. But I'm not sad today. The song title, however, implicitly critiques the contrast between man and child, and says something significant for me about life and the artificial construction of the idea that man and child are almost two separate species, especially in the modern world. Adults work and children learn and (sometimes) have fun and play. Fun and play are for children and work is for adults. This is clearly the case where using your hands to create is concerned. Children play and have fun but play and fun in our world are a means to an end, and the end is to be a productive adult. Play and fun transmute, in adulthood, into making and into working, and for the great majority of us, making and working is done for money. For the adult, play and fun are squeezed out, day by day, year by year. And childhood purposelessness in play soon becomes adulthood purpose in work.

The division between man and child, and between work and play are socially created. And like so many other un-reflected upon aspects of our modern life – such as the way we think of time – it doesn't have to be that way. The early twentieth-century psychologist, educator and reformer John Dewey understood this. In his 1944 book *Democracy and Education*, he makes an important (and now largely forgotten) point about the relationship between work and play:

> It is important not to confuse the psychological distinction
> between play and work … Psychologically, the defining
> characteristic of play is not amusement nor aimlessness. It
> is the fact that the aim is thought of as more activity in the
> same line, without defining continuity of action in reference to
> results produced. Activities as they grow more complicated gain
> added meaning by greater attention to specific results achieved.
> Thus they pass gradually into work. Both are equally free and
> intrinsically motivated, apart from false economic conditions
> which tend to make play into idle excitement for the well to
> do, and work into uncongenial labor for the poor. Work is
> psychologically simply an activity which consciously included

regard for consequences as a part of itself; it becomes constrained labor when the consequences are outside of the activity as an end to which activity is merely a means. Work which remains permeated with the play attitude is art – in quality, if not in conventional designation.

This is amazing, is it not? Take away the economic imperative, the means-to-an-end context, and suddenly work and play are, or can be, the same, on a par, and mutually constituting. They become *art* – and I love this ('in quality, if not in conventional designation'). The ancient maker of the bowl and the Lampedusan carpenter are both craftspeople and artists, and their work and play meld into one in the process. The key point is that work and play are *unconstrained*: the ancient bowl being expressive of a physical human need (as well as a cultural need); and the *Cross* being expressive of human empathy – a fundamental psychological emotion – for the maker, as well as those who will see it in its glass-covered plinth in the British Museum, there to reflect upon it and its meanings (for them). And so, in another possible world that is not modern or post-modern and is absent of robots to do the tedious stuff, play is freedom to create, and work is merely the technical process that accompanies that freed-up creative process.

Again, I'm dealing only with a black office chair on the cabin floor. But the willed attitude I take toward the object and toward work and play are the same. The willed attitude is unconstrained toward the process of deconstructing and reconstructing the object. The cash-nexus is not present, and I have the free time to do this and the psychological posture to make it meaningful. I thought about the consequences of me breaking the chair somehow, by putting it together badly, like an **IKEA** project, and rendering it uncomfortable or useless for the next paying passenger. I thought also about Salva Cruz coming in on his daily cleaning visits, and seeing an exploded chair on the cabin floor, and wondering what the hell I'm doing. That would take a bit of explaining – to him, and possibly to Captain Calment as well. But I would be careful. I have the time and would take the time to do it logically and properly. And after all, the *Rossini* would be gaining a new chair, handmade and authentic, a unique and meaning-filled one at that. It's just that no one will ever know about it except me, and for the purposes of this little experiment, that's enough. A proof of concept, you might say.

I reached to the coffee table for the Victorinox and flicked out the Allen Key. I sat cross-legged in front of the chair and put the tool into the nearest hex bolt I could see, which was the middle one of three which held each of the chair arms in place at the base of the arm itself. I placed the Allen Key head firmly into the bolt head, making sure it was at a proper 90-degree angle, and turned the tool anti-clockwise. Nothing. It wouldn't move. Maybe it's the other way? Apply the torque. No movement in that direction, either. Experience with the bike told me that if you force it, or have the tool at the wrong angle, the torque will likely distort the hex shape in the bolt, and then there's nothing to be done. I pulled the Victorinox out and placed it on the floor, then stood up and stretched my neck muscles and shook my shoulders and arms, like a swimmer about to start a race, and then picked up the tool and made sure the Allen Key was fully extended from the handle and that the angle was right. I blew on the Allen Key head and rubbed it on the sheet at the end of the bed – I did this without thinking about it. I don't know what I was trying to achieve. Anyway, I looked at the Allen Key head closely for dust or oil or anything that might cause it to slip and wreck the bolt. It was clean, solid and well-made. Breathing in and then holding my breath, I placed the Allen Key into the bolt, checked the angle and turned it firmly, but not aggressively, anti-clockwise again. A tiny bit of movement. Did I just tighten it then? Relax the torque. Breathe out, then in. Apply the torque once again, slowly building up the pressure. Suddenly the hex bolt gave a sharp metallic squeak and then proffered no further resistance.

I put the chair back under the writing desk and hooked the red plastic cable around it. I held the hex bolt to the sunlight, under the windows. It was painted black on top, but the screw thread was shiny, new bare steel, with a faint sheen of oil on its length. Who screwed it in? Was it a male or female? Power-drilling these hex bolts on each arm rest before moving it along to another worker who would then do his or her little assembly-line task seemed like alienating work. Or 'uncongenial labour', as Dewey put it. Much of humanity works this way, and for a reason. Adam Smith, the Glasgow University moral philosopher and writer of the world-changing *The Wealth of Nations*, in 1776, had, back then, sussed out why. As part of the research for his book, a treatise upon why Britain – or a class of Britons – was becoming so rich, so quickly, he went to one of those new-fangled establishments called manufactories to see what was going on. He described the astonishing productivity he discovered in a hat-pin-making factory, through another new-fangled thing called the division of labour, a way of working, which as Alexis de Tocqueville lamented around a half-century later, that deprives work of 'the faintest trace of mind'. The division we see between man and child is institutionalised and industrialised in this division of labour. One person, Smith observed, if making a pin from beginning to end, might make no more than twenty per day. However, if the process was divided into many sub-tasks where, say, ten workers perform up to eighteen separate tasks in the making of a pin (and there were that many in Smith's day), then the productivity shot up from twenty per day to 'upwards of forty-eight thousand pins in a day'. This astounding leap in productivity was what was transforming eighteenth-century Britain. A question that Smith the moral philosopher did not ask was: what did those first industrial workers in the history of humankind think about as they applied themselves to this strange new way of working? And the person who screwed in this hex bolt I'm holding now under an equatorial sun – what is he or she doing now? For sure that person would not be thinking about this little screw in between my thumb and forefinger and wondering where *it* is now.

The lunchtime Beaujolais had completely worn off as the afternoon wore on, and my temples throbbed in the way that they sometimes do on hot days. And the cabin, with its windows wide open to the Java Sea air, was hot. Feeling a bit like an obsessive compulsive disorder sufferer, I placed the hex bolt upright on the writing desk top, with a view to lining them all up once I'd unscrewed them – hex bolts, screws and anything else that is small – so as to keep them together, and be able to put them back in a kind of reverse process, where the last bolt or screw goes back first on to the last part to come off, parts which I thought I'd lay all out on the floor. I thought of Salva Cruz again, and of him thinking that I'd gone crazy in the heat or something, if he walked in mid-way. I'd deal with it later. I drank half a litre of Zilia from the fridge and then stood under a coldish shower for fifteen minutes to get my body temperature down a bit. I got dried, knelt on the couch to look out the windows and immediately got hot again. I lay on the bed and looked up at the cream and yellow false ceiling and idly wondered what it concealed. The track 'What can I do?' from the Johnsons' album came on, and I realised for the first time that the words were sung by Rufus Wainwright III. How come I'd missed that after years of listening to it? It was another example of the routinely overlooked backdrop of my life – a song I'd listened to perhaps hundreds of times suddenly becoming apparent to me, because when staring at the ceiling I gave it my time. The song lasts for one minute and forty-one seconds, but I never got to the end of it. Sleep came with the speed of a blanket being thrown over a birdcage, and I slept for an hour, a late siesta, which was a sticky blackout.

Dinner, 7.27pm. This is the latest I've ever turned up for the evening feed. Usually, I'm among the first to arrive and to leave. Tonight, all the tables are full, some with faces I've never seen before. How come I've not seen this person on the table next to me? He's about forty-ish, with faded blue overalls, like those Yunus and his friends wear, but he's French, and at the captain's table, and he's chatting and laughing and holding court (Calment is not there) like he runs the place. He can only be from the engine room, that vast and incredibly noisy submarine space that I spent an hour touring with Enzo, about midway through this trip. I'll try to arrange my impressions of that experience another time. The name on his overalls, a patch above his heart, is PRENTOUT. I presume that's his name, anyway. More importantly for me is that he is eating what is unmistakably pesto rigatoni with proper par-mesan, and not the stuff that comes in a cardboard drum shaker, but from a pungent mound in an open bowl, with a fancy-looking spoon spiking it. And from the evidence of wrappers lying on their table, there's also a Magnum ice cream on offer. Not bad tonight, considering. Salva Cruz brought me a replenished carafe which I immediately stretched for after he turned back to the galley with-out a word or glance in my direction. My headache lingered, and it was evening, so what the hell. Salva Cruz came back, looking slightly flustered, with a large bowl of pasta and the Magnum, unwrapped and placed in a glass, stick up. It was already melting. I thought better than to ask him about the reason for this, but tried to lighten his evident state of agitation. 'Excuse me,' I said, when catching his eye. 'Yes, sir?' said he, only half smiling. 'I was thinking about your coming to my cabin every day to tidy up, and so on, but really, there's hardly ever anything for you to do. Why don't we leave it to, say, once a week?' 'Yes, of course, sir,' he said. 'Why don't you leave your sheets and towels outside your door, in the little basket in the cupboard, and I'll replace them with fresh ones?' 'Done,' I said. No more not knowing when he'd knock on the door. I should have done it weeks ago. I like Salva Cruz, but this did feel like a little bit of a relief. Another glass of Beaujolais went well with the pasta. But the bread and the fruit had gone, or anyway was not offered. The cupboard really must be almost bare. I left the Magnum untouched and drowning slowly in its own melting chocolate.

Working at it for two or three hours a day, it took three and a half days to dismantle and reconstruct the chair. To begin I had to use brute strength, contorting the hands, feet, legs and torso like a yogi, to unscrew the aluminium seat column. This first task almost thwarted me. It took a patient morning of thinking and experimenting with ways to loosen the machine-tightened tube. After that, I knew it would be easier. I had to use the knife from the Victorinox to prise out the various mouldings. But for everything else, the screwdriver, the Phillips head and the Allen Key were the means to free the chair from its industrial and machine-born existence. Over the next day, and for another afternoon, the chair became no longer the sum of its parts. It was in bits. Not 'wrecked' like Abram's bowl, but a 'collection of fragments', albeit fragments or parts that were industrially designed to go together. Anyway, the room no longer had a chair, and I hoped that Salva Cruz, or Enzo, or Captain Calment would not come in unexpectedly. But they hadn't before, so they would be unlikely to now. I hoped. If they did, what would they see? On the writing desk, there were ninety-seven screws and bolts lined up. Standing them up wasn't going to work, what with the rolling of the ship, so I had lain them down according to their category and the stage at which they had been dismantled. There were also twenty-four white plastic plugs that held together a seat plate and a part inside the arm rests. And next to forty-four assorted screws and bolts, there were also the accompanying washers: sixteen of them painted black, and the rest bare metal.

The freed-up parts of the chair took up almost the whole of the available cabin floor: black plastic, black painted metal and black coloured plush. These too were laid out as they came apart. Fifty-four bits of plastic, metal and plush of various sizes and shapes. As I surveyed the exploded chair taking up much of the cabin, I felt oddly satisfied that it had 'worked', but also a little anxious should someone come to the door; how would you explain this?

Surprisingly, putting it all back together was much easier. I'd sneaked a few cotton cleaning rags from Salva Cruz's trolley, which I saw parked at the end of the corridor. I used these to give each part a spit and a wipe before assembling it. The sputum was a little beyond the call, I grant you, but it did personalise the rebuild that bit more, and painters do this sort of thing and more in the privacy of their studios, I justified to myself. The five feet on the base were in fact too filthy to be cleaned by spittle, so I put them under the shower and watched with a slight horror at the amount of black shimmering grime that slithered down the drain. They looked like new when dried in the hot air and sun at the windows. I brought with me on the trip a large orange tin of Murrays Pomade, which I had hardly used in my new dishevelled mode. Its waxy consistency made an excellent lubricant for the screws and bolts. Before re-inserting, I'd dip the screw or bolt into the pomade and then wipe the excess off with the rag. This process was particularly satisfying, as there would be no squeaking or sticking in the fastening-down, just a beautiful, smooth, and silent turning of the screw. And in the final turn, a little excess pomade would squeeze out from the tiny gap between screw and bolt head and the body of the part it was securing. Wiping that off each time began to give the chair a sheen that made it look fresh and almost new. Also, the coconut smell of the pomade began to give the chair a tropical scent as the build progressed.

The chair is now whole again. It looks very much like the chair it was before. But it's not the same; how could it be? For one, it's no longer an industrially made thing. That thing fragmented forever into nothingness when it was dismantled by my hands and by the tool I brought with me as an afterthought. The machine torque energy that fixed its bolts and screws in a factory some-where was released into the world by muscle-generated power and then recreated with muscle power. With that release and dis-mantlement of the chair's energy, the abstracted and repressed meaning and instrumental integrity of the chair, the logic of the whole industrial age, dissipated with it into the air of the cabin, and there to drift out through the windows, over the containers, out over the back of the ship, to swoop and touch the waters of the churning wake, and then to dissolve over the Java Sea. It's no longer an industrial thing but, as I said before, it's now some-thing unique, at least something hand-built, if not necessarily handcrafted. What this chair does now contain is the trace of hand and mind that the assembly-line process had no need for. So, it is a new whole, a different whole. But what kind of whole does it constitute? Given that it was created freely in the spirit of work and play combined, it is now tucked neatly away back under the writing desk and secured by the red plastic cable, a work of art (if not in conventional designation). The no-longer-industrial office chair has every atom and millimetre of its reconstituted self filled with meaning, just as much or as little as Marcel Duchamp's mass-produced *Fountain* did, which he bought from a hardware store. Duchamp's 1917 artwork lives on, and appropriately in several iterations, in collections around the world, and continues to provoke both acclaim and anger over its meanings. What is indisputable is that its meanings live on, one hundred years later.

What about my anonymous work of art? What will happen to it? To its meanings? To think like this is to project into the future and to things existing there at points in that river of time that can't be predicted. But I can speculate. Like the stuff in the gym, the fittings of the *Rossini* will most likely be removed either at different points in time, or en masse, on that day, if it ever comes, when the vessel makes its last voyage to the wrecking beaches of Alang, in Gujarat. Either way its end will doubtless be ignominious, like the end awaiting the identical chairs that were made in the same factory, day after day. When this chair is broken up, or when it becomes landfill, or when (preferably) it will be dismantled for recycling, then its shattered integrity will be akin to that of Abram's fragmented bowl; it will be lost forever. As I was creating the artwork-chair, I thought about the recycling worker, a person who is perhaps alive now, and at this moment is sleeping, or eating, or laughing with his or her children and who will see it at that unpredictable time in the future only as an old chair, with parts to be smelted, or reused, or thrown away. As the chair approaches its final moments in the hands of that future worker, the smell of coconut from the pomade might still be intact and be released by it being broken apart. Who knows – waxy substances can last a long time. However, even if the worker were suddenly to catch a whiff of long-ago deposited, coconut-scented pomade from a strange process of deconstruction and reconstruction, there is no chance that it would be recognised as such, and very little chance that it would conjure a madeleine-like moment of involuntary memory in him or her.

Thinking about this probable dénouement for my ready-made artwork, I thought I would add another secret to its secret life, to give it another chance of life and meaning at some unknowable point in the future. For maybe ten years, from about 1990 until about the turn of the century, I kept a diary. One day I simply decided to do it and bought the first of a collection of little dark-blue hardback notebooks, which I scratched my thoughts upon daily, more or less, for all those years. They are scattered around on bookshelves at home, in the university office, and in old boxes here and there – testimony to a lack of organisation or real devotion to this particular habit. One of them, I think from 1992, was given to a time-capsule project in Melbourne and chosen by the project's organisers because it was the year-long diary of an unemployed person (me). I'd forgotten the details of the capsule, where it is or when it will be opened; I'd never really thought about it since the time I donated it. I did take the opportunity, when packing to come on this trip, to take an old diary, at random, from the shelf at home, with a view to reading it, to see whether it would trigger any thoughts or memories whilst here on the *Rossini*. It has lain in the black sports bag the whole time; I'd completely forgotten about it until now. So, I pulled it out and looked at its first page, written in 1997. It was from when I was travelling a bit in Asia, and it reminds me of the time when I was stuck in Kuala Lumpur, waiting to get a re-entry visa for Australia. My visa had expired when I was in Thailand, and I had to get documents sent from Melbourne to KL to update it.

Before I screwed the seat column of the chair back on, I placed inside it a rolled-up random page from the 1997 diary, which I'd copied into my notebook. A bit like a message in a bottle. There's a slight chance someone might read it one day, in the Alang break-ers yard, or maybe a recycling worker in a place where CMA CGM contracts such things. Whichever, lodged in an office chair aluminium seat column, it might give the reader some kind of message from someone's past. The page is dated 14th April, a

Monday, and to read it now brings back a memory which had been locked away from that day until now. In (as always) HB pencil, it reads:

Monday, 14th April:

An hour at least in the Embassy today. A Malaysian woman called Amy, I think, was nice enough but no one cares, really. Walking around before and afterwards, looking for places to eat that are cheap. The hostel is vile. A terrible room, like a cell, with mosquitoes everywhere, buzzing in the air, and squashed onto the walls. Noisy Irish tourists singing and talking shite through the walls. I'm writing this with earphones on and listening to a local radio station, a talk show in English. People are calling up to talk about local stuff, relationships, the best gift to give a girl. One guy has just called to say that a 'honourable lady' would only want something simple, like flowers ... aaargh.

The weather here is mad. It is steamy and hot all day, and then at five o'clock more or less exactly, a tremendous storm breaks and the rain is so heavy the droplets bounce about two feet up off the roads. Everyone knows it's coming and gets out of the way. Tonight, I was heading for a shopping centre near to here when the first thunder clap hit. It's like the sky is in a terrible rage, it's so loud, and not like it's God shifting his furniture around upstairs, as we used to tell each other as kids, when the pathetic low growl of a summer storm in Scotland got going. As I crossed the road I began to choke and gasp for breath, with my airway blocked again. The doctor says it will always clear, but when it hits all you can do is stop yourself from panicking. I thought I was going to die on the street. I was trying to get air into my lungs and wheezing like a crazy person. I was thinking in my panic, fuck, what a stupid way to die – here of all places, with no visa too. How would they ship me back to Australia? I must have looked funny to one guy who was laughing at me! Fucking bastard. I wish I could see him again. Why would you think that someone who looks like he's about to expire is funny?

Hot and hungry.

If I'd had the wherewithal at the time, I would have added to the space left of the page, a stanza from a poem by D.H. Lawrence. It would have connected this diary entry to the chair and what I tried to do with it, and perhaps give the reader a clue. The poem is titled *Whatever Man Makes*, and reads:

Whatever man makes and makes it live
lives because of the life put into it.
A yard of India muslin is alive with Hindu life.
And a Navajo woman, weaving her rug in the pattern of her dream
must run the pattern out in a little break at the end
so that her soul can come out, back to her.

Maybe one day we can think of work like this. Not just for artists and craftspeople in their spare time, but for all of us. Ironically, automation may be the answer, if only we can control robots and democratically organise them. An obscure book, written by a friend of a friend of mine points the way. He calls it a 'postwork future', a future where automated machines do almost everything, and where all new innovations are oriented toward abolishing those paid jobs that are left, creating a world without jobs. In other words, what robots provide is the possibility, the thinkability for the first time since the beginning of the industrial revolution, that our collective aim should not be for full employment but no employment. Work would eventually dissolve as a problem for society, and we could replace it with unconstrained labour that is both playful and creative. I think I had a little taste of what it might be like in my *Rossini*-bubble; and the office chair, the secret artwork, the message to the future that is vibrating away under the writing desk and secured by the red plastic cable, has a little bit of that future life contained in it.

9

THE *ZIIING* OF THE MOULDMASTER®

NLY FOUR DAYS to Singapore and to the end of the detox experiment. I know from experience that the city-state is internet central, with high-speed Wi-Fi pinging into every nook and cranny, bringing network connection and network time and space to millions of fingertips. Will I revert immediately to my pre-detox habits? I hope not.

Singapore. I've not given it any consideration so far. I remember reading somewhere, probably Wikipedia, that the lowest recorded temperature there was 19 °C. And in another Wikipedia date-based happenstance, the Singaporean mercury plunged to its historical nadir on 14 February 1989 – my birthday. This was also the day that Ayatollah Khomeini issued a fatwa against Salman Rushdie for adjudged blasphemy in the pages of a book the old tyrant had not read. And in a politically tumultuous 1989, the final chapter of the Cold War was played out, too. But with the temperature being permanently tropical, the stones and walls and roads and rooftops across Singapore never become cold. Odd to think that many Singaporeans' only experience of not hot would be in their shopping malls.

The lunchtime menu today announced Sautéed Green Beans with Ground Beef and Rice (Filipino-style Ginisang Baguio Beans) followed by Sweet Rice with Mango and finishing with French Cheese Platter. A double helping of rice, one plain and one sweet. Ho-hum. The beans, when they arrived via Salva Cruz, were at an early stage of entropy, and the black spots of decomposition could not be totally obscured by the cook slicing them into ten-millimetre wedges. Still, I reasoned, they're not poisonous and with soy sauce and rice, it was ok, I suppose. Salty, though. The dessert ingredients, judging by their glistening appearance on the officers' plates, have come from syrup-filled tins, and their sugared taste is presumably serving as a counterpoint to the soy-saltiness of the main course. Was this the chef's idea of balance or just his way of finishing off the food stocks? Brie and crackers are to provide a bland finale to the midday offering.

I unwrapped the cork napkin and poured a full glass of Beaujolais after deciding the two-litre bottle of Zilia could offer no proper accompaniment to such a meal, nor consolation for its eater. When slightly guiltily savouring my first mouthful from the glass at this early hour, I noticed an addendum to the menu. It was just three lines underneath today's menu embellishment: a jpeg photo of a topless woman on a beach, lying under a palm tree. The words announced, in capitals: PLEASE NOTE THAT BEGINNING 1100 TOMORROW (THURSDAY) THE PASSAGEWAY DOORS ON THE LOWER DECK WILL BE LOCKED. PIRATE ACTIVE AREA MEANS THAT OUTSIDE ACCESS WILL ONLY BE ON LEVEL D UPWARDS UNTIL FURTHER NOTICE.

Putting down my glass to read the words again provoked one of those little tests that come your way sometimes; a moment when the Western bourgeois life of a Western bourgeois man with his Western bourgeois assumptions is suddenly called into question, a moment when the future and its possibilities push nearer to you in a way that forces you to confront it. The kind of moment when the personal comfort zone, and the myriad beliefs that sustain it begin to evaporate. Well, sort of. I did experience a slight tightening in my chest, for a second, a bit like the car accident experience of time slowing down, which I wrote about earlier, where your mind switches to survival mode and maps its surroundings, looking for ways to understand what's happening. My own survival mode reaction wasn't so dramatic, though. A five-second experience of mind mapping registered just one single fact – that I was trapped on a ship in the western end of the Java Sea, with no one to look to but myself. I would need to deal with it. And as I thought on, I asked myself: 'How will you cope, Robert, if we are boarded by armed crazies?' I thought also about my pre-departure research on the Java Sea as a contemporary pirate hot-spot. Again, remembered sequences from stressful scenes starring the highly convincing pirate actors in *Captain Phillips* flashed across my brain like a fleeting electrical storm. What was it the Somali pirate leader said, standing in the navigation deck and pointing his AK-47 at the helpless and petrified captain and his navigation officer? Holding a finger to each of his Khat-fuelled, bloodshot eyes, he said: 'Look at me! Look at me! I am the captain now!' and snarled a terrifying snarl.

I grasped the glass and had another drink. As I swallowed, I furtively looked around the mess room, scrutinising for fear or concern in the eyes and countenances of the officers. But they looked like they always do. Normal. Captain Calment, who was also already onto his dessert, was discoursing in French about something seemingly amusing. He looked like he was telling a joke, and his table mates were all goggling at him expectantly, as if waiting for the punchline. If it was a joke, it must have been a poor one, or his timing was out, because no one laughed when he ended his monologue. The most he got was a smile and a nod from two or three of them, whilst another two immediately struck up a conversation between themselves, evidently eager to disengage with whatever it was Calment was talking about. This is a normal, if slightly awkward, conversation, I surmised. Although awkward is normal at Calment's table. But still, no one looked remotely worried.

I looked again at the menu-borne warning. The bold type and capitals were irritating. What was the point? If the situation was so important, then surely the senior officers should speak to people individually. That seemed the responsible thing to do. Putting it on a menu? In screaming capitals? If it was related to me verbally, by anyone at all, then that would be fine. The upshot was that I didn't know if this was something to worry about or not. Placing a warning on a throwaway menu seemed to suggest that an armed boarding by ransom-seeking and drug-addled pirates wasn't a clear and present danger, and the French officers' behaviour seemed to reinforce that reasoning. I decided that I wasn't going to ask anyone about it. So where did that leave me? I wasn't sure. I read the notice once more to see if there was anything else to be gleaned from it. I then drained the Beaujolais, refilled the glass, flipped open my notebook and wrote the three lines down, in capitals, for the record. Then I wrote underneath: To hell with it. I'm not going to worry about this. If it happens, I'll deal with it. Then in capitals again, to counter the menu capitals, I wrote: BE A MAN! Feeling as if I'd committed a minor gender crime with these words, I closed the notebook and smiled at a morose-looking Salva Cruz, who was busy clearing away plates and provided only a half smile in return. Maybe he knows something?

The only thing that was certain from the little bulletin was that the downstairs doors were soon to be locked, presumably to stop any pirates from gaining access to the vital areas of the ship. But locking those doors would make little difference. It would be easy enough for someone to clamber up to the next level from the outside. Then they'd be in. One person with an AK-47 slung over his back could do it in thirty seconds. All he'd have to do is swing his assault rifle around to the front, walk down the stairs, finger on the trigger, past the framed poster of a CMA CGM container ship proclaiming TOUR DU MONDE, gun down anyone who stood in his way, open the door from the inside, and let all his associates in. Voila. Then they could make their way upstairs to the navigation deck, sure in the knowledge that the crew (and I) would all be scuttling like mice for hiding places. I quickly discounted that particular scenario; this is not the movies. It was the consequence of the locked doors that I was thinking about, now that I'd gotten over the mild panic. It meant that my daily wanderings around the deck of the ship, to the prow and stern and back again, were now, or soon would be, *interdit*. That meant also that I'd need to make the most of the lower deck today, whilst it was still open to me.

It was a hazy and hot midday. I'd take the Zilia and go for what might be the last chance to roam the decks unimpeded. Unable to face the sweet rice and even sweeter tinned mango, and with the brie having not materialised, I put my dishes into collectable order, and made for the door. Salva Cruz must have been hovering behind me because as I started to walk, I felt his hand on my right arm and his voice saying, 'Sir, can I have a quick word?' My thoughts went straight to the office chair and that he'd perhaps come upon it in its exploded state when I was out walking or at the gym. As I was trying quickly to think of a plausible answer, he followed up: 'Jesse's father in the Philippines died last night. He had been very ill for some weeks. We are collecting money for his family. Would you like to offer something?' 'Sure,' I said, with a deep-down feeling of selfish relief that it wasn't about me or pirates, and wondered pointlessly if the Filipino-themed lunch was in honour of Jesse's dad. Jesse would be disembarking at Singapore, not going on to Tilbury in London as he would normally have done. I wondered, more pertinently for Jesse, if his pay would be docked for leaving early. But that's not the sort of question one could ask – and his dad dying did put his general moroseness in a different light.

I left the mess room and went out into a sun that struggled to burn through the haze. In my rotating routine, today was the day to go to the stern first. There's also a bit of shade there at this time of the day, with D Deck above providing cover for a largish open space with a checker plate deck that is fairly clear of ship stuff. There is a basketball backboard with a hoop attached to the end bulkhead at what might even be the regulation height. There were no welders around. Unusually, I didn't see a single soul on my way to the stern. When I got there, it was also empty of people. It was beautifully cool in the expanse of shade, with a seaweed-smelling wind blowing up from the south. Putting my Zilia in a dark corner, I went over to the *tricolore* and unfurled it. I watched it flap at its full length and thought of Marseille and if this particular flag – or even this particular ship – had ever visited the place where its owners have their offices and plan their world routes and staff rosters and count the euros earned from paying passengers. And again, I wondered whether the bean-counters in Marseille would cut Jesse's wages. I looked down into the churning wake and then up the length of its trace as it hissed and bubbled and drifted toward the horizon. Mysterious, small green islands still dotted the seascape, here and there, right and left, and we passed them pretty quickly.

Reflecting, as I do a lot these days, upon how I am outside of the loops of dopamine and distraction and the times of the clock and network, I try to understand what it is, this difference, that I feel in so many ways. The deconstruction and reconstruction of the office chair was a process of discovery. It was not so exotic or spiritual an experience as Abram had with his bowl, but it compares and even exceeds, I think, in the capacity I found to make the chair live 'because of the life put into it', as D.H. Lawrence explained. And that 'life' in the reconstructed chair was not the captured life and time of the original worker, but the free life and time that I created through the willed attitude and willed effort that enabled ordinary experience to become a little extraordinary.

The fact that I could do this, it seemed to me, was evidence that I had acquired some kind of new resource on the *Rossini* – a capacity that I either did not possess before, or have been able to tap into at some deeper level. Resource is a good word for it. It conjures up an image of a large, dark pool: still and waiting and deep and peaceful. And full of latent power. It's a form of energy. Moreover, it's energy I can feel within my torso, arms and legs, giving me an overall sensation of lightness – that's the only word that comes close to describing this feeling. It's a physical energy, yes, but it's also an energy that shapes my thinking and attitude. That's not to say that my mind is rioting with brilliant ideas and amazing thoughts – just that I know that I can draw upon this energy and make it work in ways I wasn't able to (or hadn't thought of) before. The ordinary world of the *Rossini* and its pre-planned routes and automated warnings of pirates, or heavy seas, or rocky shoals, or ships coming the other way, didn't matter to me. What did matter was the detox experiment and the engagement with subjective forms of time, and to see how far I could go beyond the everyday and find what else the willed attitude to subjective experience might throw up. The context of the ship was, in a sense, an unreality, an inflated bubble that could not be sustained. But that was fine. This is an experiment, a proof of concept in the laboratory of the container ship. And it works. Here and now, the clock and the network are gone, fallen from me like weights that I've been able to drop. And I now feel like I could float. My brain works more freely. It's largely been cleared of clutter and this enables me to be more tuned in to my surroundings, an environment where everything looks potentially interesting and is so simply because I have had the time to explore and map and reflect upon it.

I turned from the *tricolore* and the sea wake and looked over to the basketball hoop. Directly below it, there's an orange basketball – caught between two strengthening brackets welded to the bulkhead – and it was rolling to and fro, animated by the gentle pitching of the ship. The welders must have left it there. Basketball was not something that was ever on my horizon, at school or in Catholic working-class culture. It was football or nothing at all, and so the basketball had always looked like a football to me. I stepped out of the flip-flops and walked over to the ball. Flicking it up with the toes of my left foot, I bounced it onto my chest and then allowed it to drop to my rising right knee in an example of muscle memory that saw me keep the ball in the air: knee, head, knee, head, knee, head for an impressive (for me) six moves. Feeling cocky, I tried it again but managed only one. Another try, and again only one. A reminder that I wasn't a barefoot Brazilian. Picking up the basketball, I bounced it hard onto the checker plate. Instantly, I was transported in time. The ball made a particular sound I remembered from school, when we had thick plastic Mitre Mouldmaster footballs to play with that, with a hard bounce on a concrete or wooden floor, emitted a squeaky sound from the pressurised air inside. *Ziiing, ziiing, ziiing, ziiing.* The sound is hard to describe, but there it was again as I bounced the ball on the checker plate, a sound and a memory from long ago in primary school. This *ziiing* sound was accompanied in that deep memory by another sound, which I also retrieved – the metallic *clack, clack, clack* of aluminium screw-in studs on football boots walking across a wooden or concrete floor as we made our way in a line from the dressing-room to the red ash playing field, bouncing the Mouldmasters as we walked.

With the ball now held within ten outstretched fingers, I rolled onto the balls of my feet. Stretching my calves and concentrating on the hoop, I flicked the basketball up towards the hoop in an arc that seemed quite hopeful in its trajectory – but which then thumped onto the backboard and bounced off it at a 90-degree angle and back towards my waiting hands to catch. I'll get it soon, I thought. Changing my stance to one of feet flat on the checker plate, set wider apart, I adjusted the angle of the flip and pushed the basketball harder as it came off my middle finger. Straightaway, I knew it was going to be a bad shot. With too much force behind it, the basketball smacked the rim of the hoop almost square. It came straight back towards me at speed, but was curving upwards and high above my head, looping over and behind me to come down and bounce hard on the checker plate, and then up again with a final Doppler-effect *ziiing* to fly past the flagpole and then to disappear over the gunwale and into the sea. *Merde.*

Peering out over the end of the *Rossini*, I scanned the churning seawater for any sign of an orange globe. Not seeing it immediately, I imagined that the huge propellers had dragged the ball down to the depths, to mangle and tear its fragile plastic skin to bits. And then its pieces would sink down or float up, according to the weight and size of the shredded fragments. My thoughts went to the welders. I hoped that they had a spare ball to play with and wondered whether or not to come clean with them at the next opportunity. Just as I was deciding to take the coward's way out and say nothing, I spied the basketball popping up out of the white foam, and then making its way to the side of the wake to bob and roll in the flat water to the right. There was no way to get it back, of course.

Free of the wake, the doomed basketball floated and rolled on towards the east and began to merge with other forms of plastic detritus that I hadn't really taken much notice of previously. Watching the ball drift to become part of the suddenly noticeable debris, the scale of the floating plastic problem became apparent to me. Varieties of the stuff had accumulated everywhere around the basketball, everywhere around the ship, and everywhere as far as the eye could see. Jesus. I'd never seen anything like this up close before. In what seemed like all of a sudden but probably wasn't, the vessel was in the middle of a vast covering of plastic. How hadn't I noticed this before? I recall in previous days seeing the odd thing float past and this put me in mind of childhood days walking the North Sea beach at Anstruther and marveling at a washed-up plastic dishwashing liquid container, with a funny-looking Dutch name and a 1970s-style drawing of a happy housewife with her rubber gloves on. This was on a vastly different scale. I wanted to see what this actually consisted of. Time to go up to the prow and watch the plastic as it approaches.

On the way to the prow, I slipped into my cabin to exchange the warm Zilia for a cold one and get my National-Geographic-brand birdwatching binoculars. I was standing on the blue seat five minutes later, with the cold Zilia tucked under the back of my shirt to give me a few minutes of cool respite. Looking over the very point of the ship, I could see that the rising and sinking bulbous bow had lost some of its paint since I last looked closely at it. It showed a black undercoat, now, in parts where it had once been white.

Besides the plastic, the immediately striking thing was that the whole area in front of the ship was full of flying fish, to the left and the right, diving and skimming the water in discrete shoals, and at a speed that must be at least as fast as the ship. It's not clear what they were doing, they seemed to be in a frenzy, maybe feeding, maybe freaked out by all the plastic. Just as I was conjuring these thoughts, a large seabird zoomed past my right ear and dive-bombed into a cluster of flying fish that were parallel to the bow. It selected one, surfaced, flapped and arced out to my left, leaving a contrail of sea water behind, all in a single, smooth three-second action. It flapped at maximum effort for a further three seconds to get the height and then, as it found a thermal, wheeled higher and higher behind me to land just at the spot where I'd seen the dark shadow of a bird hop and flap the night before last. I could see clearly through the binoculars that it was a sooty tern and was making short work of its prize by swallowing it in two effortless gulps. Without delay, it jumped up into the air again and began to circle the whole length of the *Rossini* looking for more prey, and was soon diving into another shoal, this time to my left and further out from the ship. When it returned to its spot on the foremost container, it seemed to rest for a bit, doubtless digesting its lunch and marveling to itself about its luck and the lack of competition. So, this is the mysterious bird from the other night. It was not lost, or injured, or dying, but thriving in a clever hunting adaptation, where the fish come to it, by way of a free ride on a container ship. The only work it had to do, it seemed to me, was to distinguish between the fish and the horrendous and thickening shoals of floating plastic that the *Rossini* was cutting through like an icebreaker.

I have mentioned Allan Sekula and Noël Burch's documentary, *The Forgotten Space*, which explores the space of container ship travel. In 2017, Australian journalist Christopher Allen wrote about the film's evocation of this out-of-sight world, which is so central to sustaining the way we live today, and how the way we live today is not sustainable at all. Allen observes that the documentary powerfully depicts:

> The vastness of the ocean, which has been, so to speak,
> denatured in this relentless pursuit of trade. [The film] too evokes

a transgression of the order of the natural world ... We used to think that the ocean was too big to suffer serious damage from human activities, but we now find that we were wrong: apart from the dangers of overfishing and other forms of pollution, the scourge of plastic fragments is beginning to be understood.

Understood by too few people, still. Certainly, I was one who appreciated only dimly the scale and quality of the concealed catastrophe of plastic pollution. The oceans are not only forgotten spaces, but also invisible ones, with one aspect reinforcing the other in a negative dialect that will be very difficult to break in a global system and culture addicted to the use of plastic for just about everything. The basketball, now well out of sight, had joined, via my clumsy hand, an estimated twelve million metric tonnes of plastic that enters the world's seas every year. I'm standing on the prow and the ship is slicing through it, its bow parting the plastic canopy with a speed and violence that makes it seem like it's revealing the sea's terrible secret. Plastics of every shape and size and consistency mix and tangle with organic matter to resemble the post-tsunami scenes I remember from the 2011 TV reports in Japan, where every inch of water was taken up with floating plastic debris. I knew that there was serious pollution at sea. But looking at it now, I could hardly believe that it is so impossibly bad. The surface of this part of the Java Sea is almost completely carpeted by plastic. The *Rossini* seems close to full speed, so small patches of clear sea, which give relief to the eye for a short time, are quickly followed by kilometres of thickly packed drifting junk. After taking this in, I turned around to look at the navigation deck with a kind of expectation that Captain Calment, or anyone, could help me do something about it. But the navigation deck windows were opaque, as they always are in the daytime, and we sailed on. I felt guilty as hell about the basketball.

I looked around again with the naked eye and saw a grey canopy of plastic atop the water, horizon to horizon. Here and there, primary coloured plastic, probably the more recently deposited stuff, stands out amid the sun-bleached mass of millions of bags in various stages of degradation, mixing with shampoo bottles, plastic rope, polystyrene chunks, bottles of cleaning fluid, dishwashing liquid and fishing net. I continue to scan with the binoculars and still see no end to it. Individual bits of stuff loom up in terrible detail. A bright blue smudge, about 250 metres away, catches my eye and this time I train the binoculars onto it. It is a polyethylene cooler box, the kind you take on picnics, floating accusingly high in the water, with the lid still on and its handle up. It looks like it joined the flotilla only five minutes ago, so vivid is its blue colour. The sticker on its side is still there and, through the binoculars, I can see that it is an IGLOO brand item. The cooler comes up fast and is past me in a matter of seconds. How did that get there? Who would do such a thing? And then I remembered the basketball that I've just added to this hellish mess.

Does our pollution, our throwaway stuff, say anything about us as a species, as a culture? I don't know, but I wanted to get a better sense of what this oil-based gloop was made up of. Sitting up cross-legged on the space at the very point of the ship, I looped my belt around a pad eye, which is a kind of eye bolt to thread ropes or cables through, and which was welded about a foot from the edge of the prow, and then fastened the belt around my right leg. My bare feet were dangling over the prow, but it was more-or-less safe. With the binoculars around my neck and my notebook in my lap, I could look around me and list the stand-out bits as the general accumulation went past.

The flying fish have disappeared, and the sooty tern looks like it's asleep on its perch atop the front container. It doesn't feel like we're at sea anymore. It's like I'm in a post-tsunami water city, somewhere horrible and denatured, a transgressed and violated place. It's as if the rubbish of an entire city has been gathered up by an immense wave and sucked back out to sea to assemble in a vast mass, to float aimlessly and forever with the tropical currents. What do the fish below make of this environment? Are there any fish below?

Something catches my eye and I take up the binoculars. Rubbing up against the hull, way down at the waterline, I see one of those plastic children's books, the fat, little five-page ones for two-year-olds. It is semi-bleached and all I can make out is the face of Hello Kitty and the word SMILE! in red. Single-use water bottles, their translucent bodies turning brown, are floating in clustered groups of ten or fifteen, dotted all around the book as if guarding or following it. These bottles are particularly pernicious. Our newly acquired habit of carrying around bottles of fresh water is horrendously wasteful; something like five million single-use plastic bottles are sold every second. These compete for space around the *Rossini* with rubber or plastic soles from hundreds of shoes in a crazy procession, items never to walk the earth again.

A large pink bottle of Emeron shampoo glides past, with a raven-headed woman on the label smiling up at me. I catch a suggestive pout and glossy hair cascading over one eye before the bottle spins and the picture disappears to reveal its list of chemical ingredients. A short, dark brown bit of wood with a nail sticking out of it has snagged a decomposing faux leather, and doubtlessly faux branded, Louis Vuitton tote bag. Bits of broken toys. A yellow washing-up glove. The hood of a stroller. A single brown, adult-sized Croc shoe. A giant glass Kikkoman soy sauce bottle, its screw top not yet rusted and so seaworthy for some time yet. Fishing nets of green, white, yellow, orange, clear – all different lengths and thicknesses and all tangled up in vast agglomerations that must have taken the time and tides of ages to form. What looks like a broken plastic chopstick. Five plastic picnic plates that have somehow managed to stay together. The left leg of a doll. Four red plastic tulips tied together. A two-litre Lipton's Ice Green Tea bottle. Water-resistant Styrofoam takeaway containers, the type they sell in burger shops, floating easily in countless numbers. An infant's nappies with Eeyore and Winnie the Pooh only just visible. A welder's black face-mask. A large part of a once orange but now faded grey laundry basket. Bottle caps. Bottle caps. Bottle caps. Six-pack rings, many of them, seemingly impervious to breaking up or breaking down; they are always intact, in their six. What at first seemed to be a dead dog turns out to be a decomposing parka jacket, identifiable by the fur around the hood. Millions of smaller unidentifiable things, of every colour, but all fading from the sun and the sea, forming the macro parts of the larger soup all held together by a stringy web of millions of plastic bags.

All this stuff belonged to people, individuals who wore it, or ate from it, or drank from it, or used it, or cared for it, or didn't. People who once bought it, new, with money, which sealed the deal of production and consumption. It once was owned and placed in a cupboard or on a shelf, on someone's foot or back or dinner table, or bought as a single-use item in a shop or vending machine somewhere in the world. The plastic matter that floats past me now is dead labour, dead profit, and dead consumption, and in its uneconomic state, makes way (literally, by floating in the Java Sea) for more plastic, new plastic, plastic for money that will replace it, for a time.

'Bonjour,' said Enzo, who was making rounds of some sort, checking this dial and that fitting and ticking them off a list on his clipboard. His white safety hat and orange Hi-Viz jacket seemed, in my present state of shock, to be just more potential pollution. 'Bonjour,' said I, deciding not to mention the surprise he gave me, creeping up like that. I loosened the belt from the pad and jumped down to the checker plate and put my binoculars into my pocket.

'Have you seen all the plastic rubbish in the sea?' I said, with an air of genuine shock that he must have missed. 'It's all around us, as far as you can see,' I continued. I was going to reach for my binoculars to offer them to him to prove that the catastrophe was real. But Enzo looked up from putting his initials, with a marker pen, on a laminated sheet of paper that was affixed to the wall and said simply, and smilingly, 'Yes!' He said it with the patronising look that a primary school teacher would give a pupil who has just worked out how to subtract two from five. It was the sort of look and way of saying 'yes' that would not have been out of place if accompanied by a pat on the head. Yet, I was old enough to be his father.

I decided to leave the binoculars in my pocket. I thought I'd better play it cool, as he was obviously aware of the plastic-covered Java Sea but clearly not interested either in its scale, its provenance(s), its effects, or its multiple meanings. 'I didn't think it would be as bad as this,' I said, thus conveying the neutral attitude which said that of course I knew about this hidden pollution but was just a little surprised at its extent. Enzo didn't answer, he just walked to something else that jutted from the inside plate of the gunwale and made ready to check it and tick it off his list. Switching his marker pen for a blue biro in the breast pocket of his overalls, he knelt down to properly read the mysterious instrument, and said to me, looking over his left shoulder and wafting the biro in small circles above his head, 'There's a book about all this environmental stuff in the library. But it's in French.' 'The *library*?' I said. Thoughts of plastic receded quickly from my consciousness and an onrushing tide of books, glorious books, and their multitudinous possibilities began to fill the vacuum. 'Where's the library?' I cut in with a probably impolite and too rapid demand. I had finished my last book a few days ago and had been on another cold-turkey detox, from print, since then. 'It's across from your cabin. Or, rather, just across from Captain Calment's.'

I know the room, but whenever I pass the captain's cabin, which is right at the door that leads outside at the port side of the fifth-floor deck, and where I often go out to sit, I always tip-toe past it quickly, not wishing to disturb or bump into him. I'd never given it a second thought. 'Can I go in there?' I said. 'Sure, but I think all the books are in French, and they are pretty old and boring.' I grabbed my now-warm bottle of Zilia, said goodbye to Enzo, and made my way to the soon-to-be-locked lower deck door. En route, and looking out to the choking sea once more, I spied a large, bright blue container with white Arabic writing on it, which possibly once held body-building powder – it looked like that kind of thing, anyway. It was now behind us, drifting to certain oblivion, by the time I got to the deck door. Once inside, I caught a glimpse of Captain Calment ambling solo down D Deck corridor, with his hands in his pockets and giving off an unworried-looking ambience that made me feel better about pirates. I was pleased that I wouldn't need to confront him either coming out of his cabin or worse, sitting reading in the library.

I slipped into my own cabin on the way, splashed my face with water from the sink and swapped warm water for cold from the fridge. Twenty seconds later I was flip-flopping towards the library. However, when I got there I could see that the captain's door was open, wide open, and with no one around, I had to take a look inside. The corridor was empty, and the lift was lifeless (Calment never took the stairs; in fact, none of the crew did). Not daring to go right on in, I stood with my toes at the very threshold of the door and with my left hand touching the door frame, I craned my neck to look around inside. It was twice the size of my cabin. Space was needed, perhaps, for all the communication devices it contained. A NASA-sized flat-screen TV was on a wall across from the end of his bed. Next to the TV was an open door that led into a bathroom, which had a bathtub inside! It looked like one of those short and deep Japanese affairs. Did he use it? It was a thought I didn't want to visualise. He had a large desk in the middle of the room, CEO-style, with a big, modern desktop computer, fitted with a large flat-screen monitor. What did he watch on TV? What did he do on the computer? The bed was a double. I heard a distant clatter coming from the other end of the corridor and so, without thinking about it, I spun on my heels, took two long strides, and pushed open the door of the library. I feigned an insouciance, ready for anyone who might be in there.

No one. In any case, there seemed to be room for only one or two persons at a time, with a small, red plush tub chair and a laminex coffee table purporting to be made of either English oak or Malaysian hardwood. The wall facing the door had a bookcase, which took up half of the space. It contained the books, three shelves of them, totalling maybe a hundred or so volumes. The other half of the wall had a port-hole, through which, I noticed, an unbroken tide of plastic was still drifting past. The other three walls had three ancient and identical flower prints in screwed-on metal frames. Bizarre, that someone would do that. Again, I thought of the nondescript buyer in the Marseille office clicking X 3 in a box on the same day he was ordering stuff for the gym. The wall to my right had a red couch fixed to it, like the one in my cabin. And at the door wall, also to my right, there was a sideboard running along its length with an electric kettle and the tea, coffee, sugar, and milk-sachet accompaniments that for some reason hotels all over the world consider a nice touch.

The books. I walked straight up to them. Eye level first. They seemed to be in an order of some sort. I thought of Salva Cruz. Would they get him to do this kind of thing? Mass-market paperbacks, old ones with cracked spines and all from the same publisher, Le Livre de Poche, were arrayed and gave an air of never having been disturbed. I disturbed one at random, *La Planète des Singes* by

Pierre Boulle, a 1973 edition. There was no need to try to translate. The front cover was a still from the 1969 movie, *Planet of the Apes*, the Charlton Heston one. In it, he's naked and caged like a dangerous hominid human, whilst civilised and clothed hominid apes look on like they are discussing his fate. I slid it back into its place. I dragged my forefinger across the spines and hooked it on the top of the very last book on the right. It was *Le Troisième Homme* by Graham Greene, with a 1960s vintage-coloured drawing of a worried-looking young woman in a yellow raincoat and hat. She's also wearing a red scarf and holding a green clutch bag. There's a shadowy figure of a man in the distance behind her, watching her. I had seen the Orson Welles film but couldn't recall the story. I would have read it if it wasn't in French. For the sake of symmetry, I went to the very first book on the left of the row and found *Le Rempart des Béguines* by Françoise Mallet-Joris, published in 1975. Not easy for me to translate. There is a cool 1940s jazz tune called 'Begin the Beguine' by Artie Shaw, I think, but I never bothered to find out what that meant. The cover looked interesting though, with again the kind of artwork from the sixties or seventies. This one is of a young woman, smouldering in a swirl of charcoal browns and blacks that emanate trippily from her head. She has a 1960s bob haircut and wears a green cocktail dress with a shoulder strap slipping down on her right side. Must be about sex – a bit Lolita looking. Nothing for me at this level.

The shelf below. Like the top shelf, someone had arranged them by their publisher. These were mostly orange-spined paperbacks and seemed to be of the same cheap 1970s vintage as the ones in the Le Livre de Poche row. They seemed all to be in French again, and were from the very French-sounding imprint, Librairie des Champs-Élysées. Scanning across the spines, and with not much hope of finding anything in English, I spied the name Agatha Christie. I've never been a fan of crime fiction but in my print-starved state, I would read anything by anyone. I was even thinking about borrowing the technical books that were gathering dust in the navigation deck, but that was the last resort. Maybe she's ok, I thought. Millions of buyers can't all be wrong, and maybe I'll learn something. I pulled on its spine. Drat. The title, *Le Train de 16 h 50*, smirked back at me. Sorry buster, should have paid more attention in French class at school, when Mr Smith tried to interest us in the language through fables about him meeting Eddy Merckx in an early 1970s Tour de France, or giving us a content analysis of the Guinness adverts doing the rounds on TV in the mid-1970s. One I recall him liking especially was where two French tourists are in England in the summertime, and baffle the barmaid in the pub with their gallic pronunciations of the black stuff, which sounded like 'gwans' or 'gwince'. Why do such inconsequential things stick in the memory? And yes, it's there to see on YouTube, as a good deal of my unmediated youth seems to be. Was this book a version of *Murder on the Orient Express*? It hardly mattered.

Three books along, there was another name I recognised – Val McDermid, a Scottish crime writer. I hoped that she was too obscure to be translated into French. But no. The daughter of Kirkcaldy's book was titled *Le Dernier Soupir* and, apart from the generics of crime and murder, I couldn't even guess what that was about. Maybe I could try: isn't a *dernier* one of those odd little motorbikes that pace cyclists around the velodrome? The plain yellow cover didn't offer any clues, but I doubted it would be about murder at the bike races.

Onto the bottom shelf. This looked a bit more hopeful – a sub-set comprising of a mixture of thin and thick, hardcover and paperback, and, as evidenced from the variegated spines, from a range of different publishers. There was a theme though, that I quickly discerned as I slid them out for a preliminary check, which was French modern history. Drat, again. Nothing against French modern history, and I would have loved to have read some, but it was all in the local lingo once more. However, as I looked along the top edge of the books I could see that many had pictures (plates) in them. That might be interesting. Something to look at – to engage with at least. I took six or seven of the thickest looking books, all with picture-plates in the middle, and put them on the coffee table. I made myself an English Breakfast tea, without the milk powder, and before I sat down to read (or look) at them I stood at the port-hole with the tea and was pleased to see that the plastic was beginning to thin out.

Flicking through these books (through the plates in the middle, anyway), I was struck by how intensely local and national history still is, and how all of us must carry around in our heads quite different appreciations of what constitutes history – and whom it is constituted by. In book after book, there were pictures (and stories) of French war resisters I'd never heard of before. Jean Moulin and Albert Camus were internationally celebrated Nazi resisters whom I know of and had read, or read about. But these black-and-white 1940s photos of the subjects of these books were people unknown to me. They were mainly women, some of whose names I noted, such as Yvonne Pagniez, Charlotte Delbo and Simone Segouin.

I've read a lot of history since my induction to the discipline on Cockatoo Island Dockyard, with some French history thrown in, but this was often, or possibly exclusively, written by Anglophone historians. For example, I was in Paris in August 2014 and there was a good deal in the French and international media about the 70th anniversary of the Liberation of Paris in August 1944. One day, I found myself in the Shakespeare and Company Bookstore on Rue de la Bûcherie. It has mostly English titles (that's why I was there), and there was a promotion on that day for the book

Eleven Days in August by Matthew Cobb, which dealt with the events surrounding the freeing of the city from German occupation. I looked at the plates in the middle and saw that there had been a good deal of shooting between the local resistance and a garrison of nervy Germans around where I was staying near the Place de la Concorde. I bought the book, walked back to a café near my hotel and bought a small carafe of white wine, sat myself down, and looked forward to savouring this nice little moment of historical and geographical convergence.

Cobb's book is a good one, and deals, Antony Beevor style, with the lives of ordinary people and their moments of courage or treachery during those days of high anxiety and broiling summer humidity. Cobb, however, says nothing about Yvonne Pagniez, Charlotte Delbo or Simone Segouin, the resistance heroes that the French read about in their own publications. There is an interesting little twist here, though. In Cobb's book there is a goodly selection of plates that show various aspects of the eleven days being played out: ordinary Parisians at the barricades, liberating troops marching in columns into the city, dramatic photos of people diving for cover in the Place de la Concorde, just metres from where I held the book at the outdoor café table.

There's a picture of eighteen-year-old Simone Segouin. She's named in the photo caption, but Cobb says nothing about her in the text. Why is she there, and why does the author not tell her story? Admittedly, the photo of her looks dramatic, and it has become somewhat iconic in the Francosphere. She's standing side-on against a wall and is behind a soldier wearing what looks like hastily put together pre-war army fatigues. They both look like they are hugging the wall to take cover from the shooting that's going on nearby. Maybe they are about to counterattack. The photo seems to have captured a finely balanced moment of tension. Anyway, the makeshift soldier is carrying an antique-looking rifle and is similar in appearance to many other *résistants* during those days – quite dashing but also homogeneously scruffy. Segouin, however, is startlingly different. She is wielding a captured German submachine gun, an MP 40, a *Maschinenpistole 40*, that looks rather more handsome and deadly than my dad's borrowed Lanchester from the year before in Italy. A product of excellent German design, or *vorsprung durch technik*, as the Audi ads tell it. But there's something else. Seguoin is wearing what only can be described as hot pants, along with her polka-dot summer shirt, a forage cap set at an angle, a classic 1940s hairdo (think Rita Hayworth) and white rolled-down socks in boots. She looks like something dreamed up in the mind of a Hollywood hack screenwriter. The French have a little historical subculture around Simone Segouin, but in English language books she seems only to be a sexy adornment, something typically French and part of what Laura Mulvey in the 1970s called the 'male gaze'.

Whilst I was putting the books back, I noticed that, in the gaps that the borrowed ones had opened up, a book had fallen over onto its side, allowing me to read its cover. My god. It was in English. Its title was large black typeface on a black background, but the words, THE BLACK BOOK were clear enough. It was by Ian Rankin, another Scottish crime novelist. In fiery yellow, running down the right side of the cover was the clinching evidence of its English-languageness: 'An Inspector Rebus Novel'. Yes! I grabbed it with an unexpected haste, a brutality almost, like someone in a scrum at a Black Friday sale. It was a hardcover, with that plastic contact sheet that goes cloudy with age. A first edition by the looks of it, Orion, 1993. It also looked well thumbed. I thought of a previous paying passenger either finding it here and thanking god, like me, or leaving it here as a present to someone in the future, someone like me who had nothing more to read and who would be so grateful for it. Nearly three hundred pages. I wished it was twice the length, and I hadn't read a line of it yet. I was thankful for hundred, nonetheless. I restored the shelf, minus the Rankin novel, and slipped back to my cabin like a thief, as if I'd found a wallet on a train seat and jumped off at the next station before someone could say something.

In the cabin, I tossed the book onto the bed and went to kneel at the window and noticed that we were in a field of plastic that had again become more packed and expansive. Staring at the pollution, I wondered why I had acted like a shoplifter with the book just then – grabbing the book and needing to get it out and away from where others might see it. It was no big deal, really, in and of itself, but to reflect on little actions like that sometimes gives insight into how one might act in more serious situations, and how we can realise that we are able to act in ways that don't necessarily accord with our self-perception. It's a serious question. For instance, political scientists and experienced politicians in developing countries know that bread riots, when they occur, can be the portent of something very bad in terms of the political status quo. When there is little or no bread left in the shops, two things can happen: First, political authority loses its legitimacy in the eyes of the hungry citizen or worker, and with that, a terrible uncertainty can fill the vacuum, wherein anything can happen and usually something bad does. Second, the knowledge that you or your family are or will be hungry causes something primal, buried deep inside under layers of culture and education, to become salient, and you feel yourself capable of doing whatever it takes to get that last loaf from the grasp of others, those who are also on the brink. Traditional morality can evaporate, in other words. Primo Levi, in his book *Survival in Auschwitz*, writes of his first-hand experience of this, where extreme situations can upset the moral compass. He writes, 'Survival without renunciation of any part of one's moral world ... was conceded only to a few superior individuals, made of the stuff of martyrs and saints.'

At the risk of making too much of this, and also noting that Levi's circumstances were utterly on another plane of human experience, I think that this is something to think about, in terms of moral action, of my grabbing greedily at that book and taking it to my room quickly, and making sure that no one else could get to it. Moreover, the opportunity – in time and space – to think about our moral conduct is just as important a consideration. We have these little moral lapses in our lives all the time, thinking of ourselves first and automatically in encounters at home, at work, in life more generally. But in our distracted and busy lives, it is too easy to be unreflective about many of the ways that we act, and so they pass, and pass, also, any personal moral scrutiny. The point is that we forget, or don't realise, that we can quickly become some-one else, morally speaking. We can become a different person, and not necessarily one that we would like.

•

Back on my bed and flicking through the pages of THE BLACK BOOK, I reflected that I had undergone a metamorphosis of sorts on the detox experiment. Here on the *Rossini*, and leaving the moral issue to one side, I was able to experience and reflect upon how I had become someone else – for a time, anyway. And this is more than subjective musing on my part. Science, or neuroscience to be more accurate, is now uncovering facts about how we read and how we can be transformed neurally by the means through which we read text. One of the books I brought along with me is Maryanne Wolf's *Proust and the Squid*. In it, Wolf argues that the invention of the technology of writing was a major turning point for our species. We know that writing has been a key invention, and has enabled us to become who we are, but new insights are emerging.

Writing emerged independently, and almost simultaneously (how, we don't fully know), in different parts of the world – the Middle

East, China, South America – around three and a half thousand years ago. This caused the relations between people to change, and the world began to change as a result. The rate of change was relatively slow, but writing made possible religion, philosophy, history and the centrality of narrative in human culture. Knowledge could be recorded and reproduced. It could be shared and could act as the basis for further knowledge accumulation. The invention of moveable type by Johannes Gutenberg in the fifteenth century ramped up that pace of change to the point where, barely a century later, the bases for industrialisation and modernisation were in place.

Reading changed us. As the media philosopher Walter Ong put it, 'Writing is a technology that restructures thought', and with the development of writing and literacy, the technology of the written mark 'takes possession of [human] consciousness.' Wolf sees this revolution as being responsible for the transformation of the ancient brain into the modern 'reading brain' – or to be more precise, the printed word brain. Today, MRI scans show that the reading brain is architectured in a certain way because of the reading of printed words on paper. We know this because these scans can be compared with those of someone who mainly reads text on a screen, with the latter displaying what Wolf terms the 'digital brain'. What does this mean? The reading brain, sculpted by print on paper, is characterised by the development of stronger synapses – these are the junctions that allow neurons to pass chemical signals to each other. These synaptic connections are what constitute the capacity for deep memory and prolonged concentration. In other words, reading print on paper improves and encourages memory concentration. The digital screen interface, by contrast, promotes the very opposite of long-term and concentrated reading. Reading predominantly from a screen actually weakens the synaptic connections and renders the brain as less developed in memory and concentration capacity. The digital brain is thus *shallower* than the reading brain and less able to hold to any subject of great depth or length. Bad news in so many ways. The good thing, though, is that experiments have shown that the weakening of the synaptic connections through screen reading can be reversed. That is to say, if someone who reads mainly screen-based text switches to reading print instead, then the synaptic connections, and with them the capacities of memory and concentration, can swiftly strengthen and improve.

It is clear to me now, after reading Wolf, and after some weeks of concentrated reading and writing, that my digital brain has atrophied and my reading brain has become much stronger, with the synaptic connections more powerful and the memory enhancement more palpable each day. I have no scientific proof of this. Just a feeling, or set of feelings and capacities, that I have not had before.

With a differently engineered brain, I have become a differently thinking person – someone who *has* changed, someone *who is* someone else if the brain and its consciousness have anything to do with self-identity. This feeling has been building in me since the very first days of detox on the *Rossini*. Disconnection and isolation – being thrown back onto myself, as I phrased it before – have meant that, as my memory strengthens, I begin to uncover things I'd forgotten or did not know were there. An increasingly powerful memory has brought to mind people, things, places, conversations, actions which may (or may not) be true in my experience and in my life. Nonetheless, this deep subjective consciousness is true for me insofar as it comes unbidden and as part of piecing together a personal memory mosaic that has a real centre of past experience. With new capacities of memory, reflection and concentration come new dimensions of phrases, of texture, of light, of faces, of smell, of feeling, of touch, of places, of taste, of sounds, and so on. These become part of a deeper and richer picture of my life that I have in my head in the form of subjective experience and which I've tried to articulate in writing this book.

To remember and to write about remembering is, as Richard Macksey wrote of Marcel Proust's work, a process of '*restoration through involuntary memory.*' Macksey wrote this in his introduction to a book called *On Reading Ruskin*. In that same book about the Victorian art critic, which is a translation by Proust of two of Ruskin's books, *La Bible d'Amiens* (1900) and *Sésame et les Lys* (1906), Proust provides a long introduction to each. Writing in *Sésame et les Lys* about the process of reading, Proust notes that 'reading, in its original essence, is that fruitful miracle of a communication in the midst of solitude.' This is almost a throwaway line from one of Proust's millions of printed words. But, like much of his writing, it is pregnant with insight and profundity regarding the everyday and the subjective. Let me try to deconstruct his views on the act of reading: the 'original essence' of reading, as I see it in Proust's words, is the engagement of consciousness that has been 'taken possession' of, as Walter Ong put it – engagement meaning to *be as one* with the words, with as little distraction or distance as can be willed or brought to the process. Reading is a solitary practice, but the 'fruitful miracle' that Proust speaks of is to be able to communicate in that solitary state with a consciousness that is fully immersed in the world within the book. The book itself is the flipside of the human who holds it, with consciousness being the mysterious connective link. The actual genre of the book is not so important.

The way I feel now, I could have immersed myself in the technical books that sit orphaned up on the navigation deck. As it is, I've scored an English-language novel, a story classed as crime fiction, from among the unreadable *librairies* 'de poche' and 'Champs-Élysées'. I've never been a regular novel reader. I'm not sure why. Maybe it's a simple preference for nonfiction. Whenever

I do read a novel, I almost always enjoy it, but I suspect that this essential lack of passion for the genre has something to do with my lack of imagination. However, imagination is a capacity that you can let yourself have, if you allow yourself to be immersed in the author's explorations of situations in time and across space. I don't think that this would be so easy for me, ordinarily, in the time of the world, where distraction and preoccupation rule, but I do feel that I've been conditioned for it in these last few weeks of detox and especially these last few days of not having read anything at all.

I propped the pillows up on the bed and sat cross-legged with **THE BLACK BOOK** resting on my thighs, the sharp corners of the plastic cover sticking me like tiny needles, prodding me to open it up. I turned the cover, immediately relieving the discomfort and, not wishing to rush or skip, read the front flap. Exquisite: part hackneyed contrast, part tantalising. Next page. The copyright statement confirms that this is indeed a first edition. The Edinburgh connection made me think of J.K. Rowling (I wasn't immersed yet) and of the Harry Potter series phenomenon, and the fact that a first edition of her first book, published when she called herself Joanne Rowling, can fetch £40,000 these days. There is a TV series of the Rebus novels, but Rankin is not in the same league in terms of collectability. I closed the book, wanting to prolong the bliss, and put on the kettle for a cup of green tea.

I read the entire book twice over two and a half days.

On the early evening of my last night aboard the *Rossini*, and after a supper of scrambled eggs and rice and a final glass of Beaujolais, I stood outside on the navigation deck checker plate watching the multitude of ships, hundreds of them, that were now all around as we crawled closer to the terminal at the Port of Singapore. Plastic pollution was sparse here, with only the odd cluster of bottles or polystyrene. Earlier, just before it darkened, I watched the sooty tern through the binoculars as it leapt from its perch for one last time and flew the few hundred metres to a Hong Kong-registered container ship called MOL *Belief*, which was heading the other way. It came to rest on the container roughly corresponding to the one that had been its eyrie on the *Rossini*. The seabird seemed to know what it was doing, and that the flying fish are back east, in that area where all the plastic floats. No pirates had shown up, so the doors were unlocked this morning whilst I was into my second reading of the Inspector Rebus novel. At 5.18 am the next morning, we berthed at Singapore. I had been up for about an hour, packing my bag, and so could see that the red container cranes were waiting for us as the *Rossini* manoeuvred into position. They got immediately to work outside my windows as soon as the ropes had been secured. It was overcast and sultry when the sun rose from the Java Sea behind us.

At breakfast, Salva Cruz said goodbye and Enzo asked me to sign some kind of indemnity for CMA CGM, stating that I had survived and wouldn't be suing. We said *au revoir* in what was a rather formal scene, sadly. Captain Calment noticed the interaction from his table and ordered Salva Cruz to go to my cabin after breakfast and take my bag to a van that would be waiting onshore to take me to customs. And that was it. Just as quickly as I had been inducted in Melbourne, my time on the *Rossini* was brought to its end. In my cabin after breakfast, Salva Cruz took my bag and we said goodbye again. Not knowing what to do next, I knelt on the couch and watched the frenetic crane work outside. They seemed even faster at unloading than the Melbourne workers did at their loading. A few minutes later, in what seemed like a change of plan or a visa problem for me, two customs men rapped on my open door and stepped inside. One checked my passport whilst the other was scrolling on his mobile. Fifteen seconds later, both smiled in unison and then the passport-checker said: 'Welcome to Singapore. You are free to leave.' They turned and made for the lift.

With some thought of closure or book-ending in my head, I made a final check for anything left behind and then summoned the lift, too. I'd never used it since that cold August night in Melbourne. All of a sudden I wanted to be away, so the lift seemed to take ages to come up and then even longer to get back down to D Deck. When the doors finally creaked open, I stepped out and looked into the operations room across the corridor. There was no one around. I walked on towards the exit door and stepped out to where an aluminium stair was fastened to the ship and which led the way down onshore to where I could see a parked white van with its orange top lights flashing. The sounds of bunkering and unloading were deafening, and this was obviously what all the crew were preoccupied with. There was no one around out here either and the little gate to the aluminium stairs was open.

•

When I was aged about nine or ten, semi-mythical sounding stories used to periodically circulate about a place called the Silk Factory, which was a bus ride away in a nearby village called Forgewood. The Silk Factory made football shirts. This was a time when the only people who wore football shirts were proper football players and kids who were football obsessives. It was fabled among my schoolmates that on a Thursday, at morning tea-time, you could go to a certain window at the Silk Factory, knock on it, and if you asked politely, 'have you got any baddies?', a kindly woman would delve into a big, waist-high bag of rejects and throw you a random shirt.

One Thursday, Brian Meechan – like me, a keen but untalented footballer, and who, also like me, psychologically compensated for this lack of ability by wearing football shirts in informal games – and

I skipped school to see if the legend was true or not. I did not dare to dream for a Celtic shirt, and anyway, it was also rumoured that the Silk Factory was owned and operated by Protestants – Rangers supporters and likely freemasons, too – who would refuse on principle to produce this symbol of Catholic and Irish defilement of Christianity. On the Number 4 blue single-decker bus to Forgewood, we asked the driver if he knew where the Silk Factory was and where we should get off and then, following our noses, soon found the red-brick Victorian factory, and also, around the back, what looked like a candidate for the special window. Soon after ten, I knocked and a woman with curly blonde hair and wearing a blue nylon work coat appeared as she pushed up the window. I spoke the words and she said nothing. She spun around, stopped for two seconds with her back facing me, and then appeared front on again with a shirt in her hand, which she tossed through the six-inch gap in the window. I grabbed it with a 'thanks missus!' and moved aside for Brian, and the performance was repeated. He got a one-sleeved shirt bearing the black and white stripes of Newcastle United, and I got one with the claret and blue of West Ham, which looked fine apart from needing the blue collar at the back stitched. Almost perfect. My mum would do this and then West Ham would become my English team.

•

West Ham are down 1–3 and there's only fifteen minutes to go. The live transmission from London, of their game with West Brom, brings me back into the time of the world. But I feel only a vague interest in my reconnection to the global village and the global game. I'm jotting in my notebook instead. The local Tsingtao beer, my first in weeks, tastes good, and allows me to linger. I'm sitting alone in one of the many bars in the Singapore Raffles Hotel, with a late-night flight to catch back to Melbourne.

I'm looking at a young couple speaking Arabic, who are gazing into each other's eyes, talking softly, and comporting themselves like honeymooners. They sit side-by-side on enormous, wing-backed white wicker chairs, which flare out behind them like peacocks. Each looks dazzlingly well-dressed, and they radiate like movie stars. Maybe they are; maybe they're pretending to be. He is wearing a tailored slim-fit linen suit with a thin, grey pinstripe, a linen shirt of sky-blue, a dark red tie and matching cufflinks, pale pink socks, and dark red velvet loafers, each with a bright silver buckle. His watch is an Omega Seamaster, I think, and is attached to a chunky and loose shark mesh silver bracelet. The ensemble all looks so new. He's holding a cocktail of some kind. She has the same drink but hasn't touched it yet. It sits on the small, round, yellow marble-topped table between them. She wears a short, round-necked jacket, also linen, loosely stitched together in inch-sized squares of muted pinks and creams and yellows, each with traditional-looking and understated Arabic patterns set in little red stones that glitter in the light from the West Ham game. Underneath, she's wearing a bottle-green linen maxi dress with a high, round neck and a stitched, dark red rose motif that is repeated in a line down the front. She wears cream Jimmy Choo-looking shoes that have a kind of necklace arrangement of clear diamante jewels that fit around the ankles and run down in a V shape to the strap just above the open toe. Her toenails are painted the same colour as the rose motif. She reaches for her drink and they clink glasses.

I get up and go past them towards the bar for another Tsingtao and catch the trace of an expensive fragrance from one or both of them, something I've smelled before, but can't think where or when. As the barman slowly and theatrically pours the beer into a long, narrow glass, I find myself slightly annoyed that I had to repeat the order twice, breaking it up rather rudely the second time: sing-tao. I'm annoyed only with myself and my accent. His English, by contrast, is flawless. On the mirror behind him, I see that West Ham have pulled one back, and it is now 2–3, with four minutes to go, plus any stoppage time. Walking back with the beer, I wonder whether to continue people watching or close the notebook and turn my chair to the big screen.

vi: **Intellectual effort, when conducted without books...** Cited in Anka Muhlstein's 'Time Regained', New York Review of Books, 18 December 2018, pp.15–18.

PROLOGUE

3: **One of his last diary entries reads...** Jon Krakauer (2013) 'How Chris McCandless Died', New Yorker, 12 September. https://www.newyorker.com/books/page-turner/how-chris-mccandless-died

4: **The joy of life...** Cited in Goodreads from John Krakauer's *Into the Wild*, New York: Villard. Goodreads link for the quote is at: https://www.goodreads.com/quotes/472392-the-joy-of-life-comes-from-our-encounters-with-new

5: **Facebook would be blamed for just about everything...** Jaron Lanier (2018) *Ten Arguments for Deleting Your Social Media Accounts Right Now*, London: The Bodley Head.

6-7: **A part of this, he says, is to...** Mark Boyle (2018) 'My advice after a year without tech: rewild yourself', The Guardian, 19 March. https://www.theguardian.com/commentisfree/2018/mar/19/a-year-without-tech-debt-gadgets-reconnect-nature.html

11: **As Theodor Adorno put it in his Minima Moralia...** Theodor Adorno (2005) *Minima Moralia*, London: Verso, p.222.

1 ZERO-SUM TIME

14: **Apparently a majority of mobile phone users even sleep with their devices.** Alexandra Ma (2015) 'A Sad Number Of Americans Sleep With Their Smartphone In Their Hand', Huffpost, 30 June. https://www.huffingtonpost.com.au/2015/06/29/smartphone-behavior-2015_n_7690448.html

14: **Many eighteen to thirty-five-year-olds say...** Tyler Kincade (2013) 'Millennials Would Rather Ditch Car Than Smartphone Or Computer: Zipcar Survey', Huffpost, 2 March. https://www.huffingtonpost.au/2013/03/01/millennials-car-ownership_n_2789454.html

16: **A recent Pew Research Center survey...** Pew Research Center (2017) 'More people will be connected and more will withdraw or refuse to participate', Internet and Technology, 6 June. http://www.pewinternet.org/2017/06/06/theme-4-more-people-will-be-connected-and-more-will-withdraw-or-refuse-to-participate/

16: **The stickiness and value of a connected life...**ibid.

17: **Facebook's former president Sean Parker said...** Mike Allen (2017) 'Sean Parker unloads on Facebook: "God only knows what it's doing to our children's brains"', Axios, 9 November. https://www.axios.com/sean-parker-unloads-on-facebook--god-only-knows-what-its-doing-to-our-childrens-brains-1513306792-f855e7b4-4e99-4d60-8d51-2775559c2671.html

17: **How do we consume as much of your time and attention as possible?** ibid.

18-19: **Max Stossel slam poem.** Max Stossel (2016) 'The panda is dancing'. http://www.maxstossel.com/#/this-panda-is-dancing-time-well-spent/

22: **Introduction to Savages' song 'Shut Up'.** Savages (2013) 'Shut Up'. https://www.youtube.com/watch?viiFuIB8HEmnoY

22: **Elsewhere I've compared the vicious circle...** See my *Age of Distraction*, New York: Transaction Publishers (2012).

28: **The United States Weather Bureau released a report...** Wikipedia entry for 14 February, 1959. https://en.wikipedia.org/wiki/February_1959#cite_note-23

32: **George Orwell observation on Depression-era generation.** George Orwell (1957) *Inside the Whale and Other Stories*, London: Penguin.

33: **Roger Fenton's Crimean War photographs...** Roger Fenton Crimea War Photographs, 1855. http://www.allworldwars.com/Crimean-War-Photographs-by-Roger-Fenton-1855.html

33: **Susan Sontag wrote...** Susan Sontag (1973) *On Photography*, New York: Farrar, Straus & Giroux, p.6.

38: **Quote from Proust describing tasting the madeleine cake...** Marcel Proust (2002) *Swann's Way*, (trans. Scott Moncrieff) New York: Dover Publications, p.39.

38: **Extract from Proust describing how the madeleine cake triggers a memory.** ibid.

39: **Bachelard's descriptions of 'his little room at the end of the garret'...** Bachelard, op. cit., p.35.

39: **I alone in my memories...** ibid.

40: **Murakami quoting Henri Bergson.** Haruki Murakami (2006) *Kafka on the Shore*, New York: Vintage Books, p.273.

40: **It is rather to be free as part of the flow of time...** See Fredrick Sontag's (1967) 'Heidegger, Time, and God,' The Journal of Religion, 47(4), pp.279–294.

41: **What, then, is time?** Augustine, of Hippo, Saint, 354-430 (1950) *The Confessions of Saint Augustine*, Mount Vernon: Peter Pauper Press, p.189.

42-43: **The geographer Nigel Thrift called this process 'clock time discipline'.** Nigel Thrift (1997) *Spatial Formations*, London: Sage, pp.193–206.

43: **Indeed by the time Benjamin Franklin coined his famous phrase...** Benjamin Franklin (1748) cited in Houston, A. (2004) *Advice to a Young Tradesman*, Written by an Old One (21 July 1748). In B. Franklin (Author) & A. Houston (Ed.), *Franklin: The Autobiography and Other Writings on Politics, Economics, and Virtue* (Cambridge Texts in the History of Political Thought, pp. 200–202).

44: **In Henri Bergson's much-reported and discussed debates...** Jimena Canales (2015) *The Physicist and the Philosopher: Einstein, Bergson, and the Debate that Changed our Understanding of Time*, Princeton, Conn.: Princeton University Press.

44: **Some, like the anarchist George Woodcock, speak...** George Woodcock (1944) The Tyranny of the Clock, The Anarchist Library. https://archive.org/stream/al_George_Woodcock_The_Tyranny_of_the_Clock_a4/George_Woodcock__The_Tyranny_of_the_Clock_a4#page/n1/mode/2up

45: **...what I've elsewhere called 'network time'...** Robert Hassan (2003) 'Network Time and the New Knowledge Epoch', Time & Society, 12 (2/3), pp. 225–241.

2 DIGITAL LIFE

48: **In Mike Davis' book City of Quartz...** Mike Davis (2006) *City of Quartz*, London: Verso Books.

49: **Karl Marx told us that the daily grind of economic life...** Karl Marx (1976) *Capital*, Volume One, London: Pelican, p.899.

50: **Marx's quote about the subjection of the labourer to the capitalist.** ibid.

50: **For example, British Prime Minister Harold Macmillan ...told the Brits in 1957...** Harold Macmillan (1957). See BBC Home: On This Day. '20 July 1957: Britons 'have never had it so good', https://news.bbc.co.uk/onthisdayhi/dates/stories/july/20/newsid_3728000/3728225.stm

51: **Apple has more debt-free dollars…** In 2017 Apple Corp. had amassed $256 billion in cash reserves, with most of that held outside the US for purposes of tax avoidance. See CNBC Tech News:https://www.cnbc.com/2017/05/02/apples-cash-hoard-swells-to-record-256-8-billion.html

52: **Steve Jobs' quote.** See the 28 September 2014 article in the Huffington Post, by Gregory Ciotti. https://www.huffingtonpost.com/gregory-ciotti/why-steve-jobs-didnt-list_b_5628355.html

52: **Waldorf of the Peninsula is a campus in Silicon Valley, established in 1984.** Mathew Jenkin (2015) 'Tablets out, imagination in: the schools that shun technology', The Guardian Online, 2 December: https://www.theguardian.com/teacher-network/2015/dec/02/schools-that-ban-tablets-traditional-education-silicon-valley-london

53: **Quote from Mathew Jenkin article.** ibid.

53: **…the education authorities in England had axed the teaching of Art History as an A-level subject…** Rachel Pells (2016) 'Art history A-level dropped as government trims creative subjects from curriculum', The Independent online, 13 October. http://www.independent.co.uk/news/education/education-news/art-history-a-level-dropped-creative-subjects-aqa-gove-a7359436.html

54: **In *Understanding Media* (1964), McLuhan argued…** Marshall McLuhan (1966) *Understanding Media: The Extensions of Man*, New York: Signet Books.

56: **Quote from Arthur C. Clarke.** Arthur C. Clarke (1973) *Profiles of the Future*, New York: Harper & Row.

56: **Explanation of the term 'black boxing'.** Bruno Latour (1999) *Pandora's hope: essays on the reality of science studies*, Cambridge, Massachusetts: Harvard University Press p. 304.

56: **Reference to the title of Sherry Turkle's book.** Sherry Turkle (2012) *Alone Together: Why We Expect More from Technology and Less from Each Other*, New York: Basic Books.

56: **…the computers that construct our digital lives act as 'the architects of our intimacies'…** ibid., p.1.

57: **But then internet addiction is a recognised clinical condition nowadays…** Christian Montag and Martin Reuter (2017) 'Internet Addiction: Neuroscientific Approaches and Therapeutical Applications Including Smartphone Addiction', Springer Verlag.

58: **With more phone and social media use…** Susan Weinschenk (2012)

'Why We're All Addicted to Texts, Twitter and Google Dopamine makes you addicted to seeking information in an endless loop', Psychology Today, 11 September. https://www.psychologytoday.com/au/biog/brain-wise/201209/why-were-all-addicted-texts-twitter-and-google

58: **A US survey in 2018 estimated...** John Brandon (2018) 'The Surprising Reason Millennials Check Their Phones 150 Times a Day', Inc.5000. https://www.inc.com/john-brandon/science-says-this-is-the-reason-millennials-check-their-phones-150-times-per-day.html

58: **And scientists tell us that neural activity is higher...** Trevor Haynes (2018) 'Dopamine, Smartphones & You: A battle for your time'. http://sitn.hms.harvard.edu/flash/2018/dopamine-smartphones-battle-time/

60: **Quote from Murukami.** Haruki Murakami (2006) *Kafka on the Shore*, op. cit., p.273.

60: **The problem of distraction...is what the media scholar Clay Shirky called a filter failure.** Matt Asay (2009) 'Shirky: Problem is filter failure, not info overload', CNET, 14 January. https://www.cnet.com/news/shirky-problem-is-filter-failure-not-info-overload/

63: **In Japan, for example, there has been a large-scale 'flight from intimacy'...** Abigail Haworth (2013) 'Why have young people in Japan stopped having sex?', Guardian Online, 20 October. https://www.theguardian.com/world/2013/oct/20/young-people-japan-stopped-having-sex

63: **2010 survey discussing the percentages of Japanese men and women not in romantic relationships.** The Fifteenth Japanese national Fertility Survey in 2015, 'Marriage Process and Fertility of Married Couples Attitude Toward Marriage and Family Among Japanese Singles', National Institute of Population and Social Security Research (2017).

63: **Reference to an interviewee who spent two years obsessed with a virtual game where she acted as manager of a sweet shop.** Abigail Haworth (2013) 'Why have young people in Japan stopped having sex?', Guardian Online, 20 October. https://www.theguardian.com/world/2013/oct/20/young-people-japan-stopped-having-sex

64: **Quote from James Gleick's book.** James Gleick (1999) *Faster: The Acceleration of Just About Everything*, New York: Abacus, p.10.

65: **Quote from Robert McBride's book.** McBride R (1967) *The Automated State: Computer Systems as a New Force in Society*, Philadelphia, PA: Chilton, p.4.

66: **Quote from John Gray's book.** John Gray (2002) *Straw Dogs: Thoughts on Humans and Other Animal*, London: Granta., p.xiii.

3 ANTICIPATE

68: **Quote from Paul Virilio.** Paul Virilio (1995) 'Speed and Information Cyberspace Alarm!' ctheory, 27 August. http://www.ctheory.net/text_file.asp?pick=72

70: **How riding a bicycle helps you learn the contours of a country.** Cited in Matt Seaton's *Two Wheels: Thoughts from the Bike Lane*, London: Random House, p.19.

73: **As I said before...** See Prologue in this book on the film *Into the Wild* and Christopher McCandless.

73: **Reference to notes for film by Allan Sekula and Noël Burch.** Allan Sekula and Noel Burch (2010) 'Notes on The Forgotten Space'. http://www.theforgottenspace.net/static/notes.html

74: **Quoted extract from notes for film by Allan Sekula and Noël Burch.** ibid.

79: **Reference to Philip Zimbardo's 1971 Stanford Prison Experiment.** Haney, C.; Banks, W. C.; Zimbardo, P. G. (1973) 'A study of prisoners and guards in a simulated prison', Naval Research Review. 30: 4–17.

80: **And in this very short timeframe, anticipation had become magnified...** Ben Fountain (2013) 'Soldiers on the Fault Line: War, Rhetoric and Reality', International Journal of the Humanities, p. 3.

84: **Extract from CNBC scare story on piracy.** CNBC.com (2014) 'The World's Most Dangerous Waters'. https://www.cnbc.com/2014/09/15/worlds-most-pirated-waters.html

84: **Extract from an article in The Maritime Executive on piracy and CMA CGM**. The Maritime Executive (2016) 'CMA CGM-Chartered Ship Attacked off Nigeria'. https://www.maritime-executive.com/article/cma-cgm-containership-attacked-off-nigeria

86: **Quote from John Culkin, channeling McLuhan.** John Culkin (1967) 'A Schoolman's Guide to Marshal McLuhan', The Saturday Review. http://www.unz.org/Pub/SaturdayRev-1967mar18-00051

4 WAITING

94: **As I write this on my laptop, a check on the UNHCR website...** The UN Refugee Agency, 'Figures at a Glance'. https://www.unhcr.org.figures-at-a-glance.html

95: **...we can move, as Henri Bergson put it, from 'state to state'...**

Henri Bergson (2001) *Time and Free Will: An Essay on the Immediate Data of Consciousness*, New York: Dover Publications, p.66.

95-96: **Research study on Time Moving and Ego Moving.** Julio Santiago, Juan Lupiañez, Elvira Pérez and María Jesús Funes (2007) 'Time (also) flies from left to right', Psychonomic Bulletin & Review, 14 (3), 512–516.

96: **Bergson wrote that, 'the free act takes place…'** Bergson, op. cit.

97: **Extract from Kia Lindroos.** Kia Lindroos (1998) *Now-time Image-space: Temporalization of Politics in Walter Benjamin's Philosophy of History and Art*, University of Jyvaskyla: SoPhi Publications, p.12.

97: **Quote from Manuel Schneider.** Manuel Schneider (2002) 'Time at High Altitude: Experiencing Time on the Roof of the World', Time & Society, 11(1), p.143.

124: **Since the 1800s, hundreds of vessels have come to their end here or hereabouts…** The Age reported in 2008 that there have been 180 shipwrecks in the Bay (and 50 at the narrow Port Phillip Heads between Point Lonsdale and Point Nepean). https://www.theage.com.au/national/shipwreck-stories-of-the-bay-20080108-ge6108.html

5 TO SEE

132: **It was Theodor Adorno, the German cultural theorist and Jewish refugee, who wrote…** Adorno, op. cit. p. 221.

134: **Extract from essay by Mark Greif.** Mark Greif (2016) *Against Everything*, London: Verso Book, p. 89.

135: **Quote from David Abram.** *The Spell of the Sensuous*, New York: Vintage, p. 273.

136: **Extract from book by Alain Robbe-Grillet.** Alain Robbe-Grillet (1967) *In the Labyrinth*, Richmond: Calder & Boyars.

6 DISSOLVES IN WATER

163: **Christopher Hitchens summarising Mark Lilla.** Christopher Hitchens (2007) 'God's Still Dead', Slate 20 August. https://slate.com/news-and-politics/2007/08/mark-lilla-doesn-t-give-us-enough-credit-for-shaking-off-the-god-myth.html

180: **Reference to vita contemplativa and vita attiva.** Hannah Arendt (1998) *The Human Condition*, Chicago: The University of Chicago Press.

181: **Partly it's Curtis's voice…** Greil Marcus (2014) *The History of Rock 'n' Roll in Ten Songs*, Yale University Press, p. 33.

7 THINGS AROUND YOU

191: **Quote from William Wordsworth.** William Wordsworth 'The Daffodils' from *The Penguin Book of Romantic Poetry*, (2006) Penguin Books, p.385.

192: **Quote from Stefan Klein.** Stefan Klein (2007) *The Secret Pulse of Time*, Melbourne: Scribe, p.186.

194-195: **Extract from essay by Paul Lafargue.** Paul Lafargue's 'The Right to Be Lazy' (1883).

195: **Extract from poem by Basil Bunting.** Basil Bunting (1931) 'Attis: Or, Something Missing', *Complete Poems*, Richard Caddell (ed), Bloodaxe Books, (2000).

195: **Reference to Matthew Walker's 'underslept state'.** Matthew Walker (2018) *Why We Sleep: The New Science of Sleep and Dreams*, Penguin Books Ltd.

196: **Quote from Chaucer's The Squire's Tale.** Geoffrey Chaucer (1400) from *The Canterbury Tales* (2nd Edition) Robert Boenig and Andrew Taylor (eds) (2012), Broadview Press, p. 237.

197: **Matthew Walker on the effects of not getting enough sleep.** Rachel Cooke (2018) '"Sleep should be prescribed": what those late nights out could be costing you', The Guardian, 24 September. https://www.theguard-ian.com/lifeandstyle/2017/sep/24/why-lack-of-sleep-health-worst-enemy-matthew-walker-why-we-sleep

198: **Max Weber on the Protestant work ethic.** Max Weber, *The Protestant Ethic and the Spirit of Capitalism*, Dover Publications (2003).

198: **Quote from George Osborne.** George Osborne (2012) Conservative Party Speech *New Statesman America*, 8 October. https://www.newstatesman.com/blogs/politics/2012/10/george-osbornes-speech-conservative-confer-ence-full-text

199: **Quote from John Gray on Edward Thomas.** John Gray, (2016) *Gray's Anatomy: Selected Writings*, London: Penguin (Chapter 40).

200: **John Gray quoting from Edward Thomas's 1913 book The Icknield Way.** ibid., pp.495–496.

201: **Extract from James Joyce.** James Joyce (2016) *Dubliners*, Centenary Edition, London: Penguin, p.149.

8 TIME FOR WORK

210: **Herbert Marcuse and the consumer society.** Herbert Marcuse

(1964/1991) *One Dimensional Man*, Boston: Beacon Press.

211: **One out of three kids, according to another survey in the UK, have never climbed a tree in their lives.** Arthur Martin (2011) 'Go OUT and play! One in three children has never climbed a tree and half have never made a daisy chain', Daily Mail Online. https://www.dailymail.co.uk/news/article-2012435/1-3-children-climbed-tree-figures-60-watch-TV.html

216-217: **Quote from David Abram on 'the event of perception'.** David Abram, op. cit., p.50.

217-218: **Extract from David Abram.** ibid., p.51.

223-224: **Extract from John Dewey on the relationship between work and play.** John Dewey (1916) *Democracy and Education*, New York: Macmillan Company, p.205–206.

9 THE ZIIING OF THE MOULDMASTER

247-248: **Extract from Christopher Allen writing on the film The Forgotten Space.** Christopher Allen (2017) 'Staying afloat: The Ocean After Nature, Samstag Museum, Adelaide' The Australian, 13 May. https://www.theaustralian.com.au/arts/review/staying-afloat-the-ocean-after-nature-samstag-museum-adelaide/news-story/07e68d3cb1a38a583101937ce3102396

260: **Primo Levi, in his book Survival in Auschwitz...** Primo Levi (1996), *Survival in Auschwitz*, Simon and Schuster, p. 92.

262: **Quote from Walter Ong on writing as technology.** Walter Ong (1982) *Orality and Literacy: The Technologizing of the Word*, London: Methuen & Co, p.77.

264: **Quote from Richard Macksey on Proust's work.** Richard Macksey (1989) *On Reading Ruskin*, New Haven: Yale University Press, p.113.

Robert Hassan is a Professor of Media and Communications in the School of Culture and Communication at the University of Melbourne. He is the author of *Empires of Speed*, *The Information Society*, and *The New Media Reader*. His work has appeared in numerous journals including *Cultural Politics*, *World Futures*, and *Southern Review*.

AUTHOR ACKNOWLEDGEMENTS

What began as an uncontracted writing project was taken up by Mark Davis and Sybil Nolan from Grattan Street Press, both of whom were friendly, constructive and supportive of the ideas and insights I was trying to wring from the digital detox experiment. They got it straight away and had faith in its feasibility. Many thanks to them. Thanks also to Katherine Day who, as editor, went well beyond contractual requirements in getting the text to a much more respectable state. And further thanks to the Masters students in the University of Melbourne Publishing Program who went over the text as a group and gave valuable feedback.

Deepest appreciation and love to my family, Kate, Theo and Camille for supporting me in the venture, and sometimes even seeming to be interested in it.

The book is dedicated to my brother Mark and sister-in-law Josie who both died within a week of each other on opposite sides of the world, just as this was going into the final stage of publication. They met once in Scotland in the mid-1990s. Mark remained his whole life where he was born, in Wishaw, and became a kind of living repository of family memory and lore that was permanently rooted in place and through time. Josie moved to Melbourne from Western Australia to pursue a career in choreography, and bought a house in Williamstown with a magnificent view of the sea. She died at home whilst I was in the air en route back from Mark's funeral. Her bedroom overlooks the sea where all Melbourne's incoming and outgoing ships, including the *Rossini*, would pass, doing their routine work in their routine days. And so in some strange ways the processes and mysteries of time, memory, sea, ships, place, families and people seemed to coalesce in that week to form a poignancy that connected my life with theirs a bit more deeply – and also to resonate with what I have tried to say here.

Semester 1, 2019

Editing and Proofreading:
Larisa Coffey-Wong, Vanessa De Lutiis, Abigail Hough, Coral Huckstep, Hal Langley, Daria Ledovski, Robyn Stern, Leah Winterton

Design and Production:
Hal Langley, Daria Ledovski

Sales and Marketing:
Sally Gearon, Julian Spiller, Hugh Palamountain

Social Media:
Georgia Howard

Submissions Officers:
Ellie Clitheroe, Steph McClelland

Website and Blogs:
Tasabbur Haidar, Kira Hartley, Megan Kerr, Ella Patrick

Academic Staff:
Sybil Nolan, Katherine Day and Mark Davis

Uncontained is the first academic monograph that GSP has published, and we hope it will be the first of many. The project was suggested to us in 2016 by its author, Professor Robert Hassan of the Media and Communications program in the School of Culture and Communication. It has been a great pleasure for us all to work with Robert since he first talked to us about his 'digital detox'. Thanks are due to many people both inside and outside the press who assisted in the book's production. First, to the work's reviewers, Professor Stephen Muecke and Associate Professor Esther Milne; then to the School, and particularly its head, Professor Jennifer Milam, for a publication grant that enabled structural editing, and for funding that assisted with the printing of the book. Thanks particularly to managing editor Katherine Day, who conducted the structural edit over the summer break and then led students in the copy editing, typesetting and proofing: the editorial team did a fine job. Thanks to Julian Spiller for the handsome cover; Jocelyn Hargrave for the index; Alexandra Dane for advice to the sales and marketing and website teams, who worked energetically to promote the book; and Mark Davis for the internal text design. Thanks also to Kerin Forstmanis from the University's legal department, who prepared the author agreement; to Elizabeth Tregoning, who assisted us in relation to our online store; and as usual to our printers, IngramSpark.

Thanks to Max Stossel for the excerpt from his poem 'This Panda is Dancing'; to BMG Records and Jehnny Beth for the introduction to Savages' song 'Shut Up'; Bloodaxe Books for the excerpt from Basil Bunting's 'Attis: Or, Something Missing', *Complete Poems*, (ed. Richard Caddell); and Faber and Faber Ltd., London, for the excerpt from Seamus Heaney's poem 'In the Attic', *Human Chain*.

Sybil Nolan, coordinator and publisher, Grattan Street Press

Grattan Street Press is a publisher based in Melbourne. A start-up press, we aim to publish a range of work, including contemporary literature, trade non-fiction, and children's books, and re-publish culturally valuable works that are out of print. The press is an initiative of the Publishing and Communications program in the School of Culture and Communication at the University of Melbourne, and is staffed by graduate students, who receive hands-on experience of every aspect of the publication process.

The press is a not-for-profit organisation that seeks to build long-term relationships with the Australian literary and publishing community. We also partner with community organisations in Melbourne and beyond to co-publish books that contribute to public knowledge and discussion.

Organisations interested in partnering with us can contact us at coordinator@grattanstreetpress.com. Writers interested in submitting a manuscript to Grattan Street Press can contact us at editorial@grattanstreetpress.com.

Abram, David 135, 216–19
Adorno, Theodor 11, 132
Age of Distraction 76
All Is Lost 159
Alone Together: Why we expect more from technology and less from each other 56, 132
Angels with Dirty Faces 32
affect 11
algorithms, data-collecting 51–2
alienation 210–12
Allen, Christopher 247–8
anticipation 58–60, 80, 87
  digital-based 59
  dopamine-chasing 59, 64, 78–9
  FIC-charged state of 82
  mathematical 85
Antony and the Johnsons 216, 222, 227
Apple 51–2
Aristotle 23, 42
Attis: Or, Something Missing 195
Augustine 40–41, 42, 43
The Automated State 65

Bachelard, Gaston 39
The Beano 32

Bergson, Henri 39, 44, 85, 95, 96, 154
biological time 23
birthday 23, 25–7
THE BLACK BOOK 259, 261, 265
Bourget, Enzo 105, 110, 125, 126, 128, 137, 157, 159, 166, 168, 169, 170–71, 183, 251–2, 265
Boyle, Mark 6–7
brand pressure 48
bread riots 260
British Museum 221, 226
Buddhism 190
Bunting, Basil 195
Burch, Noël 73, 247

Cagney, James 32
calendars 30, 37, 40
Calment, Captain 108, 109, 110, 122, 124–6, 137, 159, 169, 238–9, 252, 265
Chaucer, Geoffrey 196
The Church 180
City of Quartz 48
Clarke, Arthur C. 56
climate change 27–8
clock time 23–4, 37, 40, 42–5, 60, 85, 87, 193

in post-industrial society
195–6

in pre-modern society 43,
44, 45, 194

Cobb, Matthew 258

Cockatoo Island Dockyard
116–17, 257

computer automation 208–
9, 219

computers 47, 53–4, 56,
64–5, 208

speeding up of life 68

Confessions 40–41

constant present 60

connectivity 16, 17, 21, 22

Cruz, Salva 103, 108, 121,
177, 213, 228, 240, 240,
254, 266

Culkin, John 86

Curtis, Ian 181–82

The Damned 174, 175–6

Davis, Mike 48

Dawkins, Richard 163

'The Dead' 200–201

death 201

and living as a Catholic
35–7

Dela Torre, Jason 186, 188,
204

Democracy and Education 223–4

Descartes, René 85

De Tocqueville, Alexis 226

Dewey, John 223

desolation 131

digital

age 46

brain 262–3

dementia 22

design 19

detox(ification) 5–7, 10, 21,
40, 78, 86–7, 130–31, 261,
263

panopticon 19

technology 4, 20

digital life 4, 5, 7, 9–10, 11,
19, 21, 40, 47–66, 133

and computers 56

and economic life 48–50

and peer pressure 48

as forgotten space 74

digital effects of 85

employment in 49

Fantasy Industrial Complex
(FIC) 80, 82

flow of information in 49

psychic toll of 68, 78–9

digital screen interface
and reading 262

displaced people 94

distraction 7, 22, 60–3, 190,
242

and time 21

as anticipation   78
chronic   20, 60, 64
division of labour   226
Dodds, Baby   29
dopamine   58, 242
dopamine-chasing anticipation   59, 64
do's and don'ts (for paying passengers)   110–11
Duchamp, Marcel   231
Dubliners   152

economic gobalisation   73
economic life   48–50
  and cars   48
Ego Moving (state)   95–6
Einstein, Albert   24, 44
elastic time   8, 23
Eleven Days in August   258
Elias, Norbert   172
English time   86
European Marxism   87
everyday life
  patterns in 163–4
  unsustainability of   247–8

Facebook   5, 17, 46, 49
Fantasy Industrial Complex (FIC)   80, 82
Faster: The Acceleration of Just About Everything   64
Father Ted   201

Fenton, Roger   33
filter failure   60
Flaubert, Gutave   134
Fleming, Renée   29
FOMO   23
Footscray Road   70, 71, 75, 102, 184
forgetting   161
The Forgotten Space   73, 247–8
Fountain, Ben   80
Franklin, Benjamin   20, 43
future discounting   79

gig economy   49
Gleick, James   64
Goldsworthy, Andy   213
Google   50
Gray, John   66, 199–200
Greif, Mark   134, 135
Gutenberg, Johannes   162
gyms   171–2, 182

A Handy Tip for the Easily Distracted   63
Harry Potter series   265
Hassan, Frank   32–33
Hassan, William (Bill)   31–7
Heaney, Seamus   178–9
Heidegger, Martin   40
Hitchens, Christopher   163
Hotspur   32

The Ickield Way   199
IKEA logic 220–21
Industrial Revolution   43, 44, 45, 210
information overload   4, 7
internet   4, 12, 16, 40, 46
   addiction   57–8, 64
In the Attic   178–9
In the Labyrinth   135–6
Into the Wild   1
isolation 131–33, 263

Java Sea   191, 204, 205, 206
   and piracy   239–40
   pollution of   248–51
Jesse (Navigation Officer)
   114, 126, 127, 169, 170,
   186, 241–2
Jobs, Steve   52
Joyce, James   152, 200–201

Kafka on the Shore   39–40
Kairos   96–7, 125
Klein, Stefan   192
Kolakowski, Leszek   87
Krakauer, Jon   1, 4, 8
Krakatoa   188, 204

labour   226, 235–6
Lafarge, Paul   194, 198, 210
Laing, R. D.   24
The Lampedusa Cross   221–2

Latin time   86
Lawrence, D. H.   235, 243
Levi, Primo   260–61
Life Speeds Up   180
LinkedIn   49
lived time   23, 40, 43–4
Lynch, Kevin, 152, 153–5

McBride, Robert   65
Macsey, Richard   164
McLuhan, Marshall   54–5, 85–6, 133
Macmillan, Harold   50
making and creating   210–13
male gaze   259
'Man is the Baby'   222
Marcuse, Herbert   210
Marcus, Greil   181
Marx, Karl   49–50
   and alienation   210
measured time 42, 182
   zero-sum nature of   62
McCandless, Christopher   1–4, 8–9, 11
media technologies   54–5
Meecham, Brian   267–8
memory   32, 37–40, 59, 87, 179
   and concentration   262–3
mémoire
   involontaire   10, 38

volontaire   10, 31–46, 89–127,
  146–56, 174–83
Microsoft   57
mid-range   179–80
mind mapping   192, 239
Minima Moralia   11
mobile phones   47
modern sport   172
morality, traditional   260
Motherwell   28
moveable type, invention of
  262
Motherwell Times   32
Muldoon, Paul 178, 179
Mulvey, Laura   259
Murakami, Haruki   39–40,
  59, 60

Neat Neat Neat   174, 176
networks
  communication   65
  of literature   120
  post-industrial   211
  time   45, 85, 87
Newton, Isaac   24
non-waiting   95

objective time   8
ocean spaces   248
Ong, Walter   262, 264
Orwell, George   32

Parker, Sean   17
patterns (in everyday life)
  163–4
peer pressure   48
photography, invention of   33
plastic pollution   248–51, 265
  and morality   260
play(time)   211
  relationship between work
  and   223–4
The Poetics of Space   39
Port Phillip Bay   67, 88, 168
post-industrial networked
  world   211
printed word brain   262
Protestant work ethic   198
Proust, Marcel   8, 23
  on memory   9, 10, 38–9,
  59, 87
  on reading   264
Proust and the Squid   261
punctuality drives   86

Raft, George
Rankin, Ian   259
reading
  brain   262–3
  printed words   262
  process of   264
  screen-based texts   263
On Reading Ruskin   264

reconstructed office chair 214, 219–224, 228–32, 235, 242

Redford, Robert 159–60

Remebrance of Things Past 38

The Right to Be Lazy 194

Rivers and Tides 213

Robbe-Grillet, Alain 135–6

CMA CGM Rossini 8, 10, 11, 38, 60, 78, 86, 98, 104–5, 138–9, 142–5, 153, 158, 162, 167–8, 177–8, 184, 190–91, 201

and flying fish 246–7

and heat 206–7

and isolation 133

and manual work (as a paying passenger) 211–15, 224–6, 229–33

and seabirds 203–4, 247

becoming someone else on 261

bubble 236, 243

captain's cabin on 253

daily physical activity on 171–2, 138, 182, 208, 244–5

departure from Melbourne 124–30

detox on 263–4

last night aboard 265

library 254–7

metalwork of 122

mind mapping on 192, 239

reading and writing rationing 136–7

sleep habits on 197–9

Rowling, J. K. 265

Savages 21–2

Schneider, Manual 97

The Secret Pulse of Time 192

Seeing Things 179

Segouin, Simone 257–9

Sekula, Allan 73, 247

Sennett, Richard 212

Sésame et les Lys 264

shipping 70–74

and piracy 83–4

Shirky, Clay 60

Shut Up 21–2

Silicon Valley 6, 19, 50–52, 61–2

Silk Factory 267–8

Singapore 237

sleep 195–7, 201

smartphones 13, 15–16, 19

Smith, Adam 226–7

Sontag, Susan 33

spatial awareness, lack of 68

The Spell of the Sensuous 216–18

splendid isolation 131–32

'The Squire's Tale' 196

Stanford Prison Experiment
   79, 87
Stossel, Max   18
subjective
   consciousness   263
   time   8, 9–10, 43–4, 64, 75,
   135
Sumatra   187–8
Sunda Strait   128, 160, 171,
   183, 186, 204
sunsets   123–5
Survival in Auschwitz   260
Swann's Way   38
Swanson Dock   70, 100–1,
   114
synaptic connections   262

technological time
   as *affect*   11
technology   56, 65–6, 219
   and cities   3
   as extensions of the body   54
   digital   4, 20
   human effects of   66
   of writing   261–2
   moveable type   262
temporal awareness, lack of
   68–9
Thatcher, Margaret   157
Thomas, Edward   199–200
Thousand Islands   204, 205
Thrift, Nigel   42–3

time   7–8, 21, 23–31, 40–41,
   201
   Ancient Greek perception
   of   96–7
   and dust   136
   and memory   39–40
   and photography   33
   and the church   42–3
   and the internet   40
   biological   23
   candles used to mark   42
   clock   23–4, 37, 40, 42–5,
   60, 85, 87, 193, 195
   elastic   8, 23
   forgetting   161
   English   86
   Latin   86
   lived   23, 40, 43–4
   mathematical   23–4, 42 *See
   also* measured time
   network   45, 85, 87
   normative understanding
   of   21
   subjective   8, 9–10, 43–4,
   64, 75, 135
   technological   11
   unoccupied   64
   virtual   55
   zero-sum   13–46
Time and Free Will   96
Time Moving (state)   95–6
time perception   192

time-theft 64
Time Well Spent 18, 19
Transmission 181
Turkle, Sherry 56, 132

ubiquity 6, 49
uncongenial labour 226
unconstrained labour 235–6
underslept state 195
Understanding Media 54
undistracted consciousness
  189
unoccupied time 64

Vipassana 189–90
Virilio, Paul 68
virtual spaces 55, 59–60
  and time 55
  colonising 55
vloggers 211–12

waiting 89–127, 153–4
  for oneself 97
  of displaced people 94
Waldorf School 52–3
Walker, Matthew 195, 197
wandering lonely 191
The Wealth of Nations 226
Web 2.0 46
Weber, Max 198
wellness 6–7
weltanschauung 85

'What can I do?' 227–28
Whatever Man Makes 235
Wikipedia 28, 29, 37, 237
Wolf, Maryanne 261, 262,
  263
Woodcock, George 44
Wordsworth, William 191
writing, technology of 261–2

YouTube 18, 21, 211
Yunus (welder) 164–7, 168,
  214

zero-sum
  equation 19, 22, 60, 195
  game 68
  time 13–46, 62
Zimbardo, Philip 79, 87

CPSIA information can be obtained
at www.ICGtesting.com
Printed in the USA
BVHW042141251119
564805BV00006B/76/P